Shepherd of
Another Flock

Shepherd of Another Flock

The charming tale of a new vicar
in a Yorkshire country town

David Wilbourne

SIDGWICK & JACKSON

First published 2017 by Sidgwick & Jackson
an imprint of Pan Macmillan
20 New Wharf Road, London N1 9RR
Associated companies throughout the world
www.panmacmillan.com

ISBN 978-0-2830-7270-3

All images courtesy of the author apart from the following:
Page 1 top © Loop Images Ltd/Alamy Stock Photo
Page 2 bottom © Joe Cornish
Page 5 bottom © The Keasbury-Gordon Photograph Archive/Alamy Stock Photo
Page 6 bottom © darryl gill/Alamy Stock Photo
Page 8 top © Richard Burdon/Alamy Stock Photo

Pan Macmillan does not have any control over, or any responsibility for,
any author or third-party websites referred to, in or on this book.

1 3 5 7 9 8 6 4 2

A CIP catalogue record for this book is available from the British Library.

Typeset by Ellipsis Digital Limited, Glasgow
Printed and bound by CPI Group (UK) Ltd, Croydon, CR0 4YY

Visit *www.panmacmillan.com* to read more about all our books
and to buy them. You will also find features, author interviews and
news of any author events, and you can sign up for e-newsletters
so that you're always first to hear about our new releases.

Shepherd of Another Flock

The charming tale of a new vicar
in a Yorkshire country town

David Wilbourne

SIDGWICK & JACKSON

First published 2017 by Sidgwick & Jackson
an imprint of Pan Macmillan
20 New Wharf Road, London N1 9RR
Associated companies throughout the world
www.panmacmillan.com

ISBN 978-0-2830-7270-3

All images courtesy of the author apart from the following:
Page 1 top © Loop Images Ltd/Alamy Stock Photo
Page 2 bottom © Joe Cornish
Page 5 bottom © The Keasbury-Gordon Photograph Archive/Alamy Stock Photo
Page 6 bottom © darryl gill/Alamy Stock Photo
Page 8 top © Richard Burdon/Alamy Stock Photo

Pan Macmillan does not have any control over, or any responsibility for,
any author or third-party websites referred to, in or on this book.

1 3 5 7 9 8 6 4 2

A CIP catalogue record for this book is available from the British Library.

Typeset by Ellipsis Digital Limited, Glasgow
Printed and bound by CPI Group (UK) Ltd, Croydon, CR0 4YY

Visit *www.panmacmillan.com* to read more about all our books
and to buy them. You will also find features, author interviews and
news of any author events, and you can sign up for e-newsletters
so that you're always first to hear about our new releases.

To mark the memory of Gordon Powell,
my father in law and captain in the
Royal Artillery, 1942–1946.
The most gracious of men.

Chapter One

Just after Easter, 1967, a door opened in my childhood and let Helmsley in. I was eleven then, the shy son of the vicar of Aughton, a forgotten corner in the Vale of York. The previous Sunday the ancient harmonium in my father's even more ancient village church had begun wailing like a dyspeptic cow. The tiny evensong congregation had tried their best to sing 'The day thou gavest, Lord, is ended', but then gave up the struggle as the organ died. The next evening my dad had scanned the adverts in the *York Evening Press* and had spotted an organ for sale in Helmlsey. So the following Saturday, Margaret, the organist, her husband, Ian, their two children, Kythe and Ronan, my parents and I crammed into Ian's Ford Cortina estate car, bound for the North York Moors, over forty miles to the north.

The first twenty-five miles passed reasonably uneventfully as the estate sped along narrow country lanes, seemingly wending its way around three sides of every field. Kythe, Ronan and I were sitting on cushions in the estate's boot, chatting happily, I-spying sundry tractors and combine harvesters working the undulating farmland, sticking out our tongues at cars behind us when they got too close for comfort. Then, after an hour, the terrain changed: our car stuttered and coughed as it climbed up Sutton Bank, a 500-foot sheer cliff with rock formations spanning all three Jurassic epochs. As the car reared up the 1:4 hairpin bends, we slid down the bare metal floor, our noses slamming into the rear window. Had we not been terrified that the estate's tailgate might spring open, launching us on the ultimate dry-ski run (or rather dry-cushion run) down Sutton Bank, we might have enjoyed the panoramic views over the vales of Mowbray and York. On a good day you can see the Pennine hills and the Lake District's mountains shimmering in the west.

No one gave much thought to child safety back then. Every day a tired old bus harvested us twenty-eight local kids to take us to the primary school three miles away. It was driven by Les, a curmudgeonly old guy with an oil-stained flat cap permanently cemented on his head. He had been badly injured when a large metal bar had fallen on him in the garage workshop, all but blinding him. In consequence, the biggest boy in the school used to sit next to him, a self-appointed co-driver, grabbing the steering wheel whenever we veered towards a ditch or hedge.

'Give me back that wheel, you little bugger!' Les would curse, a man of few words, most of them Anglo-Saxon.

The locals were very good, and obligingly moved their cars off the road at school start and end times. Any other drivers wisely pulled onto the verge as soon our ancient coach chanced upon their horizon.

Mercifully, there was no Les to hamper our crawl up Sutton Bank. As we reached the top, a dozen gliders hovered above us like eagles circling a prey. We coasted along a high plateau, the North Sea forming a blue horizon thirty miles to the east. After eight miles we sped past an ancient mile post declaring HELMSLEY ONE MILE in gothic lettering, veered to the left and descended sharply. The little town of Helmsley spread out beneath us; numerous red roofs huddled around the Norman church and ruined castle like chicks gathering around their mother hen. We swooped down into the town and through the market square – a spacious piazza flanked on all sides by shops galore, their wares liberally displayed in bright gleaming windows. We glimpsed sides of beef; mouth-watering pork pies the size of saucepans, with jelly oozing out of their crimped golden tops; enormous crusty loaves of bread; row after row of lush-looking cakes with cream cascading down their sides. We drove along narrow, winding cobbled streets whose names curiously all ended in gate; Bondgate, Ryegate, Eastgate and Pottergate all harked back to Viking times. The houses were packed closely together; tiny, terraced cottages built of cream-coloured limestone, two floors squeezed into what would serve as a single-storey bungalow elsewhere, eyebrow windows tucked beneath the eaves.

We drove up and down all these gates, eventually finding Castlegate, where our organ seller lived. As we squeezed along it, a police panda car – a blue and white Ford Anglia – pulled out ahead of us and we parked in its space. We were on the set of *Heartbeat* twenty-five years before the Yorkshire TV series took the nation by storm – except this was the real thing.

After several polite knocks, the door of number twenty-three was opened by a bleary-eyed, thickset man, dark stubble peppering his unshaven chin.

'You'll have come about t' organ I s'pose. You'll 'ave to excuse my appearance, I've been up all night wit' Fire Service.'

Still standing on the pavement, we peered through the front

door straight into his tiny living room. Over the hearth there was a large, red circular bell with Fire embossed on its centre. The rest of the room seemed to be completely filled with a huge pedal organ – its dark pine finish gave the ill-lit room an even more gloomy air.

'You can have a go, if you want,' he offered. 'It were me mother's, she had it given her as a lass when she lived in Canada. Then when she married me dad, she had it shipped o'er here. It was during t' Great War, and boat what were carrying her was chased by U-boats. But t' buggers missed – sailors always said t' organ was a lucky charm!'

Margaret squeezed into the room and sat at the keyboard, her feet pedalling the bellows. She grinned broadly as she improvised the Navy Hymn – 'Eternal Father, strong to save, whose arm doth bind the restless wave!' En route we had stopped off at Thirsk for lunch, where she and my mum had popped into a pub for a couple of gin and tonics, so she was in a mischievous mood. 'It seems to have a lovely tone,' my dad said, nodding appreciatively, as if he was Sir Adrian Boult relishing the LSO. 'How much do you want for it?'

'Well, it's a bit of a family heirloom, as well as our lucky charm. I don't think I can let it go for anything less than four t' five pounds.'

'Well, let's say four pounds and ten shillings,' my dad replied, keen to do the deal.

'Four pounds ten shillings! Four pounds ten shillings! What's thou talking about? I said forty-five pounds, and I can't take a penny less. I feel as if I'm giving me 'eritage away, even then. It's an heirloom, nothing less.'

Faced by 1000 per cent inflation, my dad decided that we all go for a walk around the town to think about the deal.

'Don't take too long, mind. I've had a lot of interest in me heirloom. If someone else should make me an offer, it'll be first come, first served, and you'll lose it!'

A charmless man, hardly a devotee of the Yorkshire saying, 'If you can't raise a smile, don't bother to open t' shop!'

We strolled up Castlegate – which was predictably over-shadowed by Helmsley's castle. The moors rose steeply ahead of us, terraced houses, art shops, cafes and bookshops lined the street on our left, and a fast-flowing beck gurgled to our right, its bank festooned with daffodils. We turned left and climbed into the castle grounds, their keep broken in two by Roundhead cannon. As we children scrambled up and down the dry moat, re-enacting the Civil War, our parents earnestly discussed whether they should haggle or accept the surly man's price.

Having exhausted the castle, we visited the church. We were always visiting churches; old ones, new ones, light ones, dark ones. As a child I found their colossal dimensions made me skittish, my head spun, the musty smell of old hymn books sickening me further: I was developing a lifetime's allergy. But the interior of Helmsley Church was different, covered in vividly coloured murals of vines and oaks and crowds of ancient Britons, anachronistically sporting Mexican mous-taches and horned helmets, grudgingly having the Gospel preached to them by a baby-faced bishop. I noticed that many of the ancient Britons looked curiously like our thickset organ seller. Above these pictures stretched another of a red-scaled dragon, twenty feet in length, with an anaemic knight on a paler horse beneath him, piercing his side with a lance. 'They were commissioned by a fiercely Victorian vicar who stayed here over forty years. I believe the artist used local models,' I heard my dad telling Ian, in hushed tones, 'It's all about Christianity versus paganism.' My vote went with the dragon; I rather took to him, with his pained eyes, fire breathing from his nostrils, blood spurting from the wound in his belly, his squamous red wings poised for flight. If only there were a few more dragons like him in church, people would come flocking back.

We wandered back down Castlegate and the adults eventually settled on forty-two pounds and ten shillings, with the amount to be paid by cheque.

'I'll trust you, since you're a vicar,' the organ seller said, defrosting a bit. 'As long as thou take it away now. You've got an estate car, we can strap it to roof!'

Ian looked wide-eyed at the prospect of his – albeit battered – estate car being used for the purpose, but cashing in his heirloom obviously energized our organ seller.

'I'll dial t' fire station and get some of the lads round to give us a hand,' he said almost cheerfully.

He ran to the red phone box on the corner and almost instantly we could hear the distant fire station's siren, and the huge bell over the man's mantelpiece started clanging. 'It'll be ringing in t' other lads' houses, they'll soon be here,' he assured us.

Within minutes, ten clones of our muscular organ seller appeared, still doing up the buttons on their firemen's black uniforms. They lifted the organ as if it were a feather, their hobnailed boots sending sparks flying as they shuffled over the stone flags, and plonked it down on the car's roof rack, which sagged under the strain.

'I've got some rope in t' shed, I'll let you have it for free,' the organ seller offered, 'and we'll tie it down.'

We crawled out of Helmsley in first gear, with the organ on top groaning discordantly as the breeze blew through its reeds. Looking out of the rear window, we children could see the organ seller and his firemen cronies standing in the road, waving off his heirloom.

'He made a hard bargain, that man,' my dad complained. 'If I never see him again, it'll be too soon.'

But I did come across him again. You see, thirty years later I buried him.

Chapter Two

I came across the organ again in 1992, when I returned to Aughton, by which time it had had a quarter of a century to settle in its new home. Yet despite nestling in a lofty Norman church rather than a cramped Victorian cottage, and despite now being looked upon by a six-foot-two man rather than a four-foot-eleven boy, it still seemed enormous. Its dark-stained pine bore a fair few scratches, revealing the lighter wood beneath; wounds from its perilous journey from the North York Moors to the Vale of York. The dark stain was also peppered with light dots, like the stars in the night sky; for twenty-five years it had been dive-bombed by Aughton Church's resident bats, whose acidic droppings had pitted its surface.

'Come, Thou Holy Spirit, Come', it droned out, joined by a few discordant voices. The music from the wheezy organ was supplemented by the haunting call of Russian geese flying overhead, their wings beating time against the night air. In the merciful silences of the service, I could hear the dark waters lapping against the churchyard's south wall. There had been heavy rainfall over Helmsley and the North York Moors for the previous few days which had swollen the River Derwent, making it burst its banks and flood the low-lying meadowland in the Vale of York.

The Derwent's wending course through Yorkshire made me think of my own circuitous route to this point. We left Aughton in 1970 when my dad was appointed to be parish priest in Scalby, Staintondale and Ravenscar, which covered the dramatic Yorkshire coastline from Scarborough to Robin Hood's Bay. So at the age of fourteen I was transplanted from sultry countryside to bracing seaside. During the summer holidays here I worked giving change in an amusement arcade on Scarborough's bustling south bay. After three years we moved again, in the middle of my A Levels, to the lively community of west Hull, with its thriving fish docks and Birds Eye factory. The smell of fish was sometimes so strong that the operating theatre in the local hospital had to be closed, on the simple principle that it was wise to avoid having consultants retch whilst carrying out complex surgical procedures!

During my first year reading Natural Sciences at Cambridge my parents moved again, when my dad was appointed vicar of Keyingham, set in the glorious countryside between Hull and the North Sea made famous by Winifred Holtby's *South Riding*. The area consists of very fecund and very flat reclaimed land, and during the long hot summers of the 1970s sported fields of golden corn as far as the eye could see. There is a string of churches between Hull and Spurn Point, mostly dedicated to St Nicholas, the patron saint of sailors, all with high towers or spires to enable the ships to navigate along the treacherous Humber. The wide river is immediately south of Keyingham, with a tiny harbour called Stoney Creek; by night you can see the twinkling lights of the ports of Grimsby and Immingham, seemingly just an arm's reach away. For six years I spent all my university vacations in Keyingham, working as a cashier in Barclays Bank in the centre of Hull before such creatures became all but extinct – our busy branch had a counter serviced by nine cashiers.

All in all, like the infant Moses, my early life had been a series of rushes. Though I attended seven different schools over my school career, I enjoyed the variety and the chance to start afresh – even to reinvent myself. I was rubbish at games at my secondary school in York, but when I moved to a new school in Scarborough I decided to go for it and be athletic. I was pretty incompetent at physics in York, but in Scarborough I decided to give Einstein a run for his money.

At Cambridge I gained a degree in Natural Sciences and Theology, and spent a further couple of years training to be a priest and working as a tutor in the New Testament and Ancient Greek. In 1981, I was appointed as an assistant priest in a large parish in the southern suburbs of Middlesbrough, with the rounded Cleveland Hills and the winding road to Helmsley on the southern horizon. In Middlesbrough I met and married Rachel, a history teacher, and in 1985, aged twenty-nine, I became the Rector of Monk Fryston and South Milford. This was a parish on the outskirts of Pontefract, home of the Yorkshire coalfield in its death throes following the 1984–85 national miners' strike. Though sited next to a very pungent pig farm, our vicarage was a lovely, new stone-built house, with a coal-fired boiler keeping us and our growing family warm 24/7 – Rachel gave birth to our daughter, Ruth, in 1985, Hannah in 1988 and Clare in 1989. In 1991 the Archbishop of York appointed me as his chaplain, and we moved to live in Bishopthorpe, three miles south of York.

Back to Aughton in 1992: the water lapping, the birds calling and the wings beating were all redolent of the Spirit of God, which had hovered over the abyss in the opening chapter of Genesis, willing order out of chaos. It formed an appropriate backdrop for tonight's service, which was a confirmation, with the Archbishop laying his holy hands on the candidates, celebrating God's Spirit being with them as cherished children of God.

'Candidates' is a bit of an exaggeration – there were only two to begin with, so hardly an evangelistic success story on the parish's part. Then one had dropped out, with no explanation, simply not turning up. The service's start had been delayed whilst we waited, with the vicar to-ing and fro-ing to the porch, willing her to come. 'She'll just be putting the children to bed, she'll be along in a minute.' And then, 'Her husband is very anti, she'll be cajoling him to come with her.' And finally, 'Oh dear, oh dear, she's not coming. We'd better start without her.' His voice was full of sadness; all the encouragement, all the patient instruction, come to nothing.

At least there was still one candidate. A little plump girl in her best pink party frock, who dangled her legs self-consciously and stared vacantly at the ancient dog-toothed chancel arch throughout the Archbishop's erudite sermon. Although the church was sadly devoid of people, for me it was full of the ghosts of people I remembered from my childhood, now no longer with us. The service over, we packed our cases, trudged back over the stony path and left the church behind, its dark limestone silhouetted against the clear starlit sky. The lapping water and beating wings waited for the next time.

There were lots and lots of next times; venues other than Aughton, with all sorts of wonderful things coming to birth. When I was offered the post of Archbishop of York's chaplain in 1991, it seemed the once-in-a-lifetime dream job, basically playing an aide-de-camp to the Archbishop's general. His chaplain accompanied him everywhere, making prior arrangements so everything went smoothly, as well as dealing with all the letters, calls and callers that came the way of such a high-profile archbishop. That was only half the job – the other half was being Director of Ordinands, taking people from their first stirrings for ministry right through to their initial post.

The Diocese of York stretches from the Tees to the Humber, from the A1 to the North Sea, and I knew it well – I had lived in eight different parts of it. I had a little bit of experience under my belt, having worked as a parish priest for ten years, and I was thrilled to say yes to the Archbishop's offer. Within eight weeks we had moved from Monk Fryston to Brew House Cottage in Bishopthorpe Palace grounds. The cottage was delightful; the former site of the kilns where beer was brewed to slake the thirst of the countless workers who tended the nine acres of palace grounds and farmed the surrounding countryside. All the farmhands had long since gone, with just a couple of gardeners remaining; their sit-on lawnmowers doing the work formerly done by fifty manual labourers. Ruth, Hannah and Clare were thrilled by their new home, and gambolled around the parkland surrounding the Archbishop's palace, their very own private garden of Eden. The palace itself was just as exciting; a vast hall and chapel built beside the River Ouse in 1215, with equally vast bits added as the years went by, reflecting the varying architectural styles of subsequent centuries. As if there weren't enough bedrooms already, one archbishop in the nineteenth century had lowered the ceiling of the thirteenth-century chapel and installed bedrooms in the roof-space to accommodate his sixteen children. Those bedrooms now served as spacious studies for the Archbishop and me, with our windows overlooking the busy Ouse; barges and noisy boat trips from York city centre distracting us from our many tasks. The larger boats had guides on board, broadcasting snippets about the palace and its archbishops to entertain their passengers. The snippets weren't always that accurate, so from time to time the exasperated archbishop would lean out of his high study window and bawl out a corrected version for the benefit of the startled trippers, who no doubt mistook these booming tones from on high for the voice of God. It must have all added to the entertainment.

The new job was highly demanding. If a problem could have been solved elsewhere, it would have been long before it got to us, so those that crossed our desk were fiendishly complex and often insoluble. Apparently, a previous archbishop had had a drawer marked 'Too difficult' where he filed the impossible stuff, and as I settled into the job I could see his point. My learning curve was very steep; I had to quickly bring myself up to speed with the complexities of a problem, make an informed decision and implement it. One new bishop, who for the previous twenty years had been vicar of a large, tough parish in Portsmouth, claimed that he had to solve more problems in his first week as a bishop than in the previous two decades.

Fortunately, John Habgood, the Archbishop of York, was immeasurably wise, and I could depend on him to guide me. He was a tall, donnish man in his mid-sixties, who had previously served as Bishop of Durham, principal and vice-principal of two theological colleges, and as a parish priest in both South Kensington and Jedburgh, in the Scottish Borders. He was the most tender of family men, with a highly talented wife who taught violin and piano, and four children. Both his father and his daughter were doctors and in many ways he approached church problems like a GP, calm and collected, desiring a cure; his nickname was The Saviour because he always kept calm and came up with a solution. Privately, however, he was a very a shy man with little time for small talk, and his great intellect gave him an intimidating air. Trying to make conversation with him at a church bunfight was painful; it was as if he had a machine in his chest which emitted invisible rays which scrambled your mind, paralysing any attempt to put two words together. Because he wasn't a chatty sort, and liked to think and write while travelling, he had an absolute rule of silence in the car. We covered about 25,000 miles per year driving to various events, which made for an awful lot of silence. I only once broke the rule, when we narrowly avoided a reckless pedestrian just before York's city walls.

'Well done, Gordon, you handled that very well,' I said to calm our rattled driver.

'Will you two be quiet? I am trying to work back here!' a voice boomed from the back.

On another occasion he broke his own rule. We were driving to a confirmation on a narrow country lane across the North York Moors, with heavy snow showers blowing in horizontally from the North Sea. As we battled against the drifts and neared our destination we saw an old lady hobbling ahead of us, making painfully slow progress with her head bowed against the wind, the snow sticking to her coat and scarf and turning them white.

'Gordon, stop a moment, we must pick her up,' the Archbishop commanded.

We stopped and the old lady bundled herself into the back of the car, and we continued our journey, though not going much faster than she had been walking.

'Let me introduce myself,' John Habgood began. 'I'm the Archbishop of York and I'm taking a confirmation at Easington.'

'Yes, I know, my grandson's being done; that's where I'm going,' the old lady replied, distinctly unimpressed.

'And this is Gordon, my driver,' the Archbishop continued.

'Oooo, very nice,' said the old lady. 'You've done well for yourself; having a chauffeur!'

The Archbishop looked distinctly miffed. 'And this is David, my chaplain,' he wearily concluded. This was a long conversation for him.

The old lady leant forward and peered at me intently, her eyelashes still covered in snow. 'Oh, I know him already. I used to sit in for his mum and dad when he was a baby.' I turned around and smiled as she continued. 'You won't remember me, luv, but I lived just up the road from your mum and dad in Lingdale – I'd keep an eye on you while they went to the pictures in Guisborough for the odd night out. You were a beautiful baby, with bright red hair. You slept like a top and never gave me any trouble.'

We continued the rest of the journey in silence.

The Archbishop had begun his professional life as a scientist in Cambridge, just after the Second World War; his first published work was entitled *The Transmission of Pain in Frogs' Legs*. He was a bit of a Heath Robinson, cobbling together scientific equipment from components he had hunted out in

Marshall's Airfield in Cambridge, which in the late 1940s was a graveyard for redundant Lancasters. Treating it like a scientists' car boot sale, he had fished out a rusty bomb sight. With the help of the odd valve, he had converted it into a cathode ray oscilloscope sensitive enough to measure electrical current along nerve canals. He held a vivisection licence, and as well as experimenting on the frogs which provided the catchy title to his first tome, he also experimented on stray cats which he and his colleagues had culled during midnight raids in Cambridge's dark backstreets. I once came across an article by the future archbishop in a learned journal of physiology, exploring the electrical conductivity of the various parts of a cat's spinal column, which contained the chilling phrase, 'If one merely cuts off the cat's head'. When measured by the sensitivities of a later age, such experimentation seems callous and barbaric. Yet as the world reeled from a war which had killed millions, with further millions injured and paralysed and aching for a cure, it is perhaps unsurprising that the suffering of the odd cat or two seemed to pale into insignificance.

Nevertheless, I side with Aloysha, the hero of Dostoevsky's novel *The Brothers Karamazov*. His brother poses the hypothetical question whether, if he could cure all the ills of the world by making just one child suffer, would that heady end justify the modest means? Aloysha, to his credit, says no: the tears of just one child are too high a price.

After a conversion experience in the early 1950s, John Habgood felt the call to ministry, and brought the same clinical precision to faith and theology that he had exercised as a scientist, although thankfully steering clear of vivisection. His talks were masterly, although he often misjudged his audience, conferring a greater intellectual calibre on them than they actually possessed. One visit in particular springs to mind, to a sixth form in Mirfield in West Yorkshire. The Archbishop was supposed to speak to the A Level science stream, but unfortunately the brighter students happened to have been withdrawn to practise for a choral performance later in the day.

'Does anyone here want to read Biology at university?' he began, in quite an upbeat way. Not a single hand was raised. 'Let me tell you what I did at university,' he continued, still upbeat. 'I read Pharmacology and Physiology; does anyone know what those two subjects involve?' Even the biology teacher looked nonplussed, let alone the class. 'Well, pharmacology is the study of how drugs affect the body . . .' he continued, oblivious to a couple of scruffy students in the back row who started to nudge each other as soon as he mentioned the word drugs. '. . . and physiology is the study of how the body works and responds. Do you know, I used to experiment on my own body,' he confided in them, relaxing as he reminisced about his Cambridge days. 'I once ate a pound of salt to see what it did to my blood pressure. Another time I ate nothing but porridge for a week, and monitored all my excreta to see what affect it had.'

They hadn't been the most engaged group to begin with, but after this revelation they had the glassy-eyed look cultivated by Tube passengers when a busker gets too close. We decided to quit while we were losing, and beat a hasty retreat.

Despite such occasional missteps, I always felt immensely proud going anywhere with him; privileged to be in the presence of a far greater and holier person than I could ever become. He was the last of the great patricians and being in his company was a real schooling, as if my faith and even my life was taken apart and re-made.

Chapter Three

Everyone I saw in my role as Director of Ordinands was disturbed. About 95 per cent were disturbed by God and the other 5 per cent by God knows what; the trick was trying to suss out what God was disturbing them into doing. In the Bible, God disturbs all sorts. He disturbs women into having babies, disturbs shepherd boys into becoming king, and disturbs prophets into taking on the king. He disturbs very few into being priests. These days virtually all disturbance is seen as a call to priesthood, which can't be right. Often I had to gently direct people to explore other equally crucial roles, like teaching or lion-taming. The role forced me to look into my own heart and try to figure out why I had become a priest.

I guess a lot of it had to do with inheriting my dad's mantle. He was born in 1929 in Chesterfield in Derbyshire, weighing in at only 3 lbs, and wasn't expected to survive. His parish priest was called out to baptize him in hospital and his mum and dad prepared themselves for the worst. But against the odds, he thrived. Sadly, his mum didn't, but died when he was just three – what started as an ear infection had spread to the brain and killed her. On the day of her funeral, a relative took my dad for a trip to the park, to keep him out of the way. But by the cruellest twist of fate, their walk coincided with the funeral cortege. 'What pretty flowers!' my dad piped up when he saw the festooned coffin passing by.

My father's father quickly remarried an eighteen-year-old girl ill-prepared for marriage, let alone caring for a grieving little boy. Soon coping with pregnancy as well, she started taking it out on my dad; beating him up, locking him in a dark cupboard. His relatives must have cottoned on to the abuse, because he was taken away for a while to stay at his Auntie Jessie's farm in Ashover – a happy summer holiday during 1934. But his stepmother decided to have a second go at caring for him, only for the beatings to return, culminating in my dad's arm being broken. The NSPCC took the case to court, with the wicked stepmother facing a long custodial sentence.

And then something unexpected happened. At a pre-trial hearing, my dad's paternal grandmother intervened and made a plea to the judge, which would avoid sending an expectant mother to jail. The deal was that my dad's father and stepmother would move out of town, and his grandmother would adopt him and bring him up as her own child.

The judge agreed to the adoption, and my dad's grandmother proved more than true to her word. She raised him and cherished him, although even their relationship clearly wasn't all sweetness and light. With several of their own children still around, my great-grandparents simply didn't have a chair at the kitchen table for my dad, so he had to stand to eat his meals, his mouth barely at table height, his chin resting on the table. He was a slow eater, so was still consuming his meal when everyone else had come and gone, and the family's fierce tomcat used to sidle up and steal the bacon off his plate.

Had the mean feline left it there, he might have got away with it. But one Sunday morning my dad returned from church to find his granddad wrestling with a sealed barrel which seemed to have a life of its own. Water was oozing from its steel hoops, the barrel was groaning and grizzling, thumping and shaking so much that his granddad could barely keep hold of it. 'What are you doing?' my dad innocently asked.

'I'm trying to drown that bloody cat!' his granddad replied. 'It stole the sausages I'd put aside in the larder for my breakfast.'

Though Dad's granddad was not religious, his grandmother was, and she regularly took my dad along to the newly built church in the heart of their council estate. The church became a second home to him; it had fired his grandmother's faith, giving her the nerve to tackle the judge and bring light to a terrible darkness. The church made a fuss of my dad, a blond-haired, blue-eyed cherub, and as time went on he joined the choir and became a server. It was a church with a strong devotion to the Virgin Mary, and in my dad's mind and life the gentle and kind mother of our Lord proved a wonderful substitute for the mother he had lost.

Though he left school at fourteen and found work in a factory office, his heart's desire was to be a priest. Unthinkable, really, for a beaten-up little lad from a council estate. For his National Service he spent two years in the RAF, serving in Northern Ireland. He was shocked by the poverty there – children walking the streets barefoot in all weathers. Then for eleven years he worked for the Church Army, the distinctly unmilitary wing of the Church of England, which trained unordained working-class lads and lasses to minister alongside clergy in parishes, specializing in outreach and work amongst the marginalized.

After two years' training, Dad was commissioned as a

Church Army Officer and spent a couple of years in Watford before he was posted to Bridlington on the Yorkshire coast. Whilst there he wed my mum, Eileen – they were sweathearts from their schooldays in Chesterfield, and had worked in the same factory – but the parish couldn't afford to pay and house a married man, so he was moved to Islington, living in a bomb-damaged flat with a leaky roof and filthy bath. My mum couldn't bear it, so moved back to live with her parents in Chesterfield, where I was born in September 1955. My dad was given the option by his dictatorial boss of having time off for either my birth or my baptism. He chose the latter, so first encountered me at my christening when I was three weeks old.

By the time I was one, my dad had been posted to the quaintly named parish of Boosbeck, near Whitby. At the other side of the North York Moors from Helmlsey, East Cleveland is rather rough and unglamorous, its landscape ravaged by the mines which were such rich sources of iron ore for the string of steel works which lit up the Tees by night. The mines had long since gone but the spoil heaps remained, casting their dark and threatening shadow over the dank villages. We lived in Lingdale, just up the hill from Boosbeck, and one such spoil heap loomed over the whole village. My dad was paid the princely sum of £5 a fortnight – when the churchwarden remembered – and we were housed in a rat-ridden hovel, with an earth closet at the bottom of the garden as our toilet. My earliest childhood memories are of deliberately opting for constipation and worrying my parents no end.

I also recall a strange incident when I was three. My dad was laid up in bed with the flu, but despite his lack of appetite my mum had cooked him a roast dinner, served on a piping-hot plate which was singeing the sheets. 'Quick, David, fetch a mat,' my mum shouted, as she and my dad held the plate in relays, passing it on before it burned their fingers. I thought it was a bit of an odd request, but I ran down into the living room and dragged the large fireside rug up the stairs. 'David, it's a table mat we needed!' my mother laughed. So began a lifetime of not quite getting it right.

The desire to be a priest was burning within my dad like that hot plate. In 1958 he went to a three-day selection conference in Sheffield with interviews and group exercises designed to test whether people felt truly called to be a priest, flushing out those who had got God wrong. My dad didn't hold out much hope; he hadn't even got a degree, let alone been to Oxford or Cambridge like most of the clergy he knew. Tongue-tied, he didn't have much to say, other than 'I feel called to be a priest.' The conference's chairman realized that beneath his distinctly un-slick performance there was a genuine, heartfelt call. So my dad was recommended, provided he pass four O Levels, which he duly did, studying by correspondence course late into the night and early in the mornings, with me playing with my tiny Matchbox fire engine by his feet. For his English O Level he wrote an essay about his wedding day which must have cheered the examiner no end – a refreshing change from the adolescent, angst-ridden outpourings of his normal clientele.

He spent two years at Lichfield Theological College, a monastic establishment like most other colleges in the 1960s, unused to having married men in its ranks. There were compulsory daily services early in the morning and late at the night; a regime not far removed from that once practised at Rievaulx Abbey just up the River Rye from Helmsley. Except the medieval monks there didn't have a warm bed and wife and son waiting for them at home – or at least they didn't let such things generally be known.

We were housed at number 66, Greencroft, a newly built but very damp council flat in the city. We were lucky – cruel colleges elsewhere wouldn't allow an ordinand's wife and family to live within a fifty-mile radius to enforce celibacy during term time. Money was very tight indeed, with just a local authority grant of £100 a year to cover everything. Meals were frugal and breakfast was regularly missed, and whilst five-year-old me didn't go to school exactly ragged, I was definitely scruffy. The elastic had long since given up the ghost on my underpants, which peeped out from the hemline of my black cotton shorts – a kind dinner lady regularly took pity on me and pulled my pants up for me. My dad supplemented the grant by delivering mail, even on Christmas Day, hopping on and off the running boards of the Royal Mail van. My mum got a temporary job, demonstrating the wonders of instant soup to sceptical shoppers in a local store. We and another college family used to pop in every lunchtime and my mum would call out to my dad as if she had never met him in her life, 'Excuse me, sir, would you like to try this soup? And would your little boy like to try some?'

Thirty years later, when I was serving as Archbishop of York's chaplain, I came across my father's file and noticed that there had been discussion about awarding him an additional £100 per annum during his training, effectively doubling his income. An archdeacon had declined the award, scrawling, 'No, a little holy poverty will do them good.' It's difficult to put into words my feelings as I read that throwaway line. I certainly felt very angry: angry at the sheer stupidity of that tight-fisted man, angry at an institution which should bring light but failed to show any compassion whatsoever. But my over-riding emotion was that I felt immensely sorry for my younger self and my parents, blighted by an unnecessary struggle.

At his ordination in York Minster in 1963, the church in the council estate in Chesterfield which had fired my dad's faith as a little boy presented him with an expensive red silk stole. Fifty years on from his ordination, though it looks a bit threadbare, I wear it with pride. It keeps me ever mindful that even a beaten-up little boy in a forgotten council estate is not beyond the reach of God.

But though my dad's vocation fired mine, at some stage you have to fashion faith and vocation to make them your own. In 1966 an event shook not just me but the whole world, and set me on my own path through my faith to vocation. It had been raining for most of the second half of October, causing a coal spoil tip above the South Wales village of Aberfan to collapse. It sped down the mountain, a veritable avalanche, and slammed into the village, engulfing farms and terraced houses and suffocating their inhabitants. Pantglas Junior School took a direct hit, with the classrooms immediately buried under ten metres of slurry. The casualty numbers were appaling; 116 children and twenty-eight adults died. Minutes before the spoil tip collapsed they had been in the assembly hall at the other side of the school, which avoided the worst of the carnage. They were singing 'All Things Bright and Beautiful'. Had the already lengthy hymn had a few more verses, they might have been spared.

There are two images from the disaster which have always stayed with me. The first is of a policeman with a taut face, barely able to control his emotions, carrying the crumpled body of a little girl he had rescued from the debris, who had miraculously survived. The second is of the mass funerals; row upon row of little white coffins lined up in their hillside grave. I was off school with a cold and watched that funeral on our black and white TV. Though eleven-year-old boys never ever cry, tears ran down my cheeks as I peered at those grainy images. And then those poor bereaved parents sang their hearts out. I had never come across the hymn before, but it seemed so beautiful, so poignant. I hummed the tune to my dad, and he found it in his hymn book, and I played and played and played it on my recorder, 'Jesu, Lover of My Soul', to the Welsh tune 'Aberystwyth'. It was the tune which caught me, not the words – after all, they had sung the hymn in Welsh, not a language in which many in Yorkshire are fluent. But the tune somehow spoke to me of God weeping with those sorry parents on that South Wales hillside, aching in agony with them.

An exploited valley in an exploited land had suddenly been robbed of its children. The children were my age, I had lived in a village over which a slag heap loomed, so it made the horrible tragedy even more personal. I guess a vocation to priesthood started swirling around that day; the idea that I wanted to spend a life convincing people who were hurting and felt abandoned, even abandoned by God, that God had not actually forgotten them but was so very close to them. God so loved the world that he impaled himself on it, although it took me twenty-five years of further study and reflection to come up with that line.

As a teenager in west Hull I'd enjoyed putting a bit of life and drama into readings from the Bible at the quite formal school assemblies and less formal church services, although I was still very shy and would usually spend an entire afternoon rehearsing a reading. One night our family was watching a rather fanciful ITV series about the Brontës. There was a vivid scene where Charlotte Brontë was kneeling at the altar rail in her father's church in Haworth, receiving Communion from the curate. Charlotte only had eyes for the impoverished curate, the curate only had eyes for her cleavage, with the backstory that they were falling in love. But it wasn't their doomed romance which caught my breath. For a fleeting moment time stood still and our dingy west Hull living room seemed bathed in light, charged with God's grandeur. The conviction suddenly hit me in the eyes that this is what I wanted to be, a priest simply feeding his people.

That conviction stayed with me through the long process of selection, culminating in an interview with the Bishop of Hull in April 1977 which did not go at all well. I was halfway through my degree at Cambridge at the time, and American Evangelist Billy Graham had just led a university mission which had painted a very black picture of humanity and a very scary view of the crucifixion, where God punished Jesus for humanity's sin. I felt in my heart it was a phoney picture, a spurious fall and an equally spurious redemption. I tended to take a kinder view of humankind, often nobly struggling with all sorts of stuff. And, post-Aberfan, I saw God more as the victim of suffering rather than the author of it, allying himself with all his aching children. I pointed all this out to the Bishop, who had just been moved to Hull from the stunning north Devon coast and was probably feeling a bit miffed as a result. Rather than agreeing with what I thought was a pretty obvious take, he actually subscribed to the view that I had labelled as phoney and sent me away with a flea in my ear. I was not to come back until I had converted all my friends at Barclays Bank, as well as persuading the manager to abolish Barclaycards, which the good Bishop saw as the greatest threat to humanity since the Black Death.

That's it then, I thought, almost relieved – I could get on with being a scientist and get a life. But the Bishop of Hull's boss, the Archbishop of York, overruled him and sent me to a selection conference. And the rest, as they say, is history.

I often thought back to that interview over my years as Director of Ordinands, when I picked up one or two tricks to check out whether people had a genuine calling or whether I needed to protect the Church and society from their delusion. Once I was interviewing a guy who was full of himself, in-forming me of the busiest of days where he led countless people to the Lord, spent hours praying, spent hours helping the needy. As he was spouting on, my secretary walked in with a tray of coffee and tripped, and the boiling coffee landed in my lap, scalding me. While I writhed in agony she tried to dab my lap with a paper handkerchief, but quickly thought better of it. All this time my interviewee was waffling on about all his good works, without noticing the crisis going on under his very nose. At the very least priests should be attentive and good listeners, so I decided he was out.

Another time I had a vicar waxing lyrical about a candidate about whom I had reservations. I asked the vicar to imagine himself very ill in a hospital bed, with his candidate visiting him as his parish priest. How did he feel? There was a long pause, 'I could only cope with him if I was well,' he admitted.

Chapter Four

In 1995, John Habgood retired and was succeeded by David Hope, who had previously served as bishop of both London and Wakefield. The son of a Wakefield builder, he was very friendly and grounded – at ease in Yorkshire. He never stood on ceremony. Essentially, he was a parish priest among parish priests; realizing the high price that priests paid as they walked with those in deep darkness and sorrow, trying to be Christ to the world and see Christ in the world. He would ring up, simply for a friendly chat, 'Hallo, it's David here, how are you doing?' He would listen and give advice, and even get angry and come out with a few choice Yorkshire phrases when he felt one of his priests was battling against intolerable situations or people. The story goes that when David Hope was a vicar in London and lustily singing a hymn during a Eucharist, a frosty server came up to him and said, 'Our tradition is that the priest doesn't sing during a service, Father.'

'I'm the vicar, it's my bloody church, and if I want to sing I'll sing, so there,' David Hope responded; argument over. He was just great. During his first two years I arranged a sort of royal tour of the Diocese of York for him. During the tour we visited the North Sea gas terminal at Spurn Point; the narrow spit that unfurls itself across the northern mouth of the Humber like a lizard's tongue.

29

'Ooooh, that's a big flame, you could light a few cigs with that,' the Archbishop quipped.

We visited the Portaloo factory in York and spent an amazing length of time there, not just admiring their loos, but also the plushest designer changing rooms and showers. We went to Aughton and peered through the windows of the little Norman church. We walked along the road to the church which had been built with the proceeds of a garden party my dad had organized in 1966. Unfortunately, the event had coincided with *that* World Cup final, but was nevertheless a fantastic success: business was brisk, and the stalls had all sold out by 3 p.m., when everyone inevitably scarpered. We visited a chicken farm near the A1, where the Archbishop retched when we stumbled into a shed containing 17,000 chickens, all high on ammonia. Distinctly green at the gills, we sailed up a very choppy Tees Estuary with the Tees Pilot, admiring the odd blast furnace still in operation beside the river before spending the rest of the day touring the high-spots of Middlesbrough, where my ministry had begun.

We descended down the Potash Mine at Boulby, with shafts and tunnels which go deep under the North Sea. It was a show-mine, and I had forgotten to tell the Archbishop that they routinely staged a mock disaster at the deepest point. There was a terrific bang as we were cast into darkness, complete with some mock dust filling the air. 'Bloody hell,' exclaimed the Archbishop. Later in the day we stopped at a church cafe on the front at Whitby, where we bought a cup of tea and an iced bun. The assistant was going to pick up the Archbishop's bun from the shelf with a pair of tongs.

'Don't bother with all that, just use your fingers, luv,' he said, reassuringly. 'They'll be fine.'

The happiest day was in Helmsley, with a tour of the surrounding moors. At the little village of Hawnby we parked on a steep hill, and I had to stand guard outside the red phone box whilst the Archbishop had a few stern words with the Bishop of Manchester. Later that day we toured the local comprehensive school, and sat at the back of class as the nervous history teacher gave a lesson on the Bayeux Tapestry. He got the Latin translation slightly wrong, and I gently corrected him.

'Don't take any notice of him,' David Hope joked to the headteacher, 'he's a right clever clogs!'

It was such a friendly school, set in the midst of the countryside with a team of teachers who were obviously contented in their skin, and pupils who were contented too. It reminded me of my happy schools in Aughton and Scarborough.

We finished off the day with an evening meeting in Helmsley Town Hall, open to anyone. David Hope gave a little talk and then took questions. We regularly did sessions like this, and I was always a little nervous, because any subject whatsoever could come up. We had made one visit to a Sixth Form in Stokesley where a girl had taken the Archbishop to task for not ordaining women, and he had got really rattled. I had tried to soothe him, even though the voice in my head was shouting, 'Go for it, girl!' Tonight the questions were edgy, making me suspect there were definite tensions within Helmsley Church itself. Part of the edginess could be explained by a new, flamboyant vicar trying to move an innately conservative place on, but there seemed to be more serious undercurrents. The new vicar himself was present at the meeting, and seemed just a tad too anxious to please. He showed great affection for a lady whom David Hope took to be his wife, but actually wasn't. It ended an otherwise wonderful day on a sour note, and as we drove home, stopping for fish and chips en route, we tried to find an explanation as to why both of us were disquieted, but couldn't.

'I've no doubt there's somert going on, but God knows what it is,' was the Archbishop's typically blunt conclusion.

The storm broke on Easter Day, 1997, when the *News of the World* featured photos of the vicar of Helmsley in bed with his mistress, and he promptly resigned. After taking the Easter Day morning services at York Minster, the Archbishop had gone away for a few days' well-earned holiday, so I rang his deputy, the Bishop of Whitby, to ask if I could help in any way with the situation.

'Yes you can. You can go there as vicar and sort them out!' the Bishop replied.

The prospect attracted me, not least because of my deep love for the countryside, which had been hardwired into my psyche during happy boyhood years in rural Aughton. Notwithstanding our infamous organ hunt in 1967, Helmsley had loomed at other times in my life, including one strange incident when I was six and both of my futures simultaneously came together. Early on Boxing Day, 1962, my parents dragged me out of bed and we caught the first train of the day from Hull to York. We were just about the only passengers – in those days everything used to shut down on the days after Christmas; there were no frantic queues for Boxing Day sales because none of the shops were open. We arrived in a deserted York, and killed time on a bright and frosty morning by walking on the ancient city walls for a while, taking in the fantastic views of the Minster as well as slightly hazy views of the North York Moors thirty miles away. With a bit of imagination, you could just about make out the chalk White Horse which Victorian school children had carved into the hillside at Kilburn. Fortunately, Terry's Restaurant, an offshoot from the famous chocolate factory, was one of the few places open, and we had a bite of lunch followed by a short bus journey to Bishopthorpe on the southern outskirts of the city. En route we went past the Terry's factory itself, and even though it too was shut down post-Christmas, we inhaled the strong aroma of its delicious chocolate in every breath. The factory, built out of red brick in 1926, was designed to look like a Georgian stately home festooned with myriad windows, each pane covered in brown chocolate dust.

'The local vicar keeps bees,' my dad informed us. 'He says they produce the only honey in the world which is chocolate-flavoured!'

The visit to Bishopthorpe was the real reason for our early morning start. Donald Coggan, the Archbishop of York, was hosting a Christmas party for clergy children. It was like a royal summons – not something you could say no to – so every clergy child from the four corners of the sprawling Diocese of York descended on Bishopthorpe that day. They were all accompanied by their very worried parents, anxious lest their offspring let some expletive slip in Bishopthorpe's hallowed confines: a mere 'blast' was enough to get you de-frocked in those days.

The Archbishop himself met us at the door and gave me a tiny piece of paper with the word 'David' written on it.

'You are David,' he informed me, in his clipped tones.

'That's right, I am,' I replied, really impressed that he should know my name.

'No, I don't think you understand,' he replied. 'This is our first game of the afternoon. I am giving all the children a name from the Bible as they arrive, and then they have to find their Biblical partner, like Adam and Eve, Samson and Delilah.' His speech was laboured, as if he suspected I was a bit backward.

'But I *am* called David,' I protested, once again not quite getting it right. Donald Coggan gave me a funny look and moved on to greet the next child in the queue. My parents twigged, and explained the game to me, and eventually I found Goliath, lurking beneath a portrait of Archbishop Michael Ramsey. At the age of six I was blissfully unaware that David, my biblical namesake, was quite a lad and that there were a fair few ladies and not a few gentlemen who could have qualified for the post of his partner: Michal, Abigail, Bathsheba, Abishag, Jonathan . . . But the Beatles and Lady Chatterley had yet to broaden Bishopthorpe's rather puritanical horizon, so Goliath was the only partner on offer.

I actually got on very well with Goliath, which is more than I can say for one well-dressed girl there who seemed to be sneering at me. Even though my parents had dressed me in my smartest clothes for the day, I think I realized I was still a bit ragged. Thinking she was mocking my humble east Hull origins, I told her to get lost. Unsurprisingly, she took exception to this and fetched her big brother. He punched me and I punched him back, all beneath the portrait of a beaming Archbishop William Temple. They weren't real punches, only taps, and my new friend Goliath pulled me away before things escalated.

'Keep clear,' he advised, 'there are three of them and they're a cut above the rest of us. They're the Vicar of Helmsley's children.'

The party ended without further incident. As our bus once

again passed Terry's, my parents started chuckling about something the Archbishop had got up to the day before. Having completed his round of Christmas Day services in York Minster, he had dragged his chauffeur and chaplain off to visit every lighthouse keeper along the Yorkshire coast. They'd spent two chilly hours driving to the first, at Spurn Point. The North Sea had broken through and flooded the final approach to the lighthouse, but, undeterred, the indefatigable Archbishop had found a convenient rowing boat and got his chaplain to row across. They then drove to Withernsea, where the lighthouse was safely on dry land, in the middle of the town. From there they drove to Flamborough Head, north of Bridlington, scrambling down the icy cliffs to the lighthouse, before travelling on to the lighthouses in the harbours at Scarborough and Whitby and finally heading home.

'The chaplain said it was nearly midnight by the time they returned. They'd covered two hundred and fifty miles in all and spent seven hours on the road. They only had a cuppa at each lighthouse,' my dad explained. 'Their wives tried to keep their Christmas dinners warm in the oven, but the gravy had dried out a bit by the time they rolled back into Bishopthorpe.'

'Why did they go around the lighthouses?' I asked. I was constantly puzzled by weird church practices, and indeed still am.

'Well,' my dad began. His speech was as laboured as the Archbishop's when he'd tried to spell out the find-your-biblical-partner game to me. 'On Christmas Day we think of baby Jesus, the Light of the World, being born. The Archbishop wanted to thank all the lighthouse keepers for the light they bring to keep ships safe, and he felt there was no better day to do that than on the Light of the World's birthday.'

Half a century on, as I recall my parents' raised eyebrows and knowing glances, I guess the long-suffering chaplain and chauffeur, and their long-suffering wives, hadn't entirely shared the Archbishop's enthusiasm. And the boozy lighthouse keepers must have been a bit puzzled by a purple-cassocked archbishop suddenly knocking on their door, bearing a box of chocolates. All because the lighthouse keeper loves Milk Tray, or perhaps Terry's All Gold.

Chapter Five

On May Day, 1997, just a few weeks after the Bishop of
Whitby had suggested I think about taking Helmsley on, I
cycled down to the polling station at Bishopthorpe Primary
School, where I voted as the bright sunshine outside caught
the air of utter optimism. I hummed 'Things Can Only Get
Better' as I pedalled north from Bishopthorpe into York along
the snaking River Ouse, past Terry's chocolate factory, recently
taken over by Kraft Foods. The chocolatey aroma didn't smell
quite as nice as when I first encountered it in 1962, though.
Perhaps memories of childhood are kind, with long hot summers and sharp delicious tastes, but somehow the aroma that
day seemed a bit bland, less appetizing. When Terry's and
Rowntree's were unashamedly York-based, rather than be-
holden to distant multi-nationals like Kraft and Nestlé, it
made for a more tasty world.

In York I dodged numerous tourists as I rode beneath the
ancient city walls, winding my way through the narrow
streets before speeding past the majestic Minster, the place
where both my dad and I had been made priests. Over-
shadowed by the Minster's west towers, I parked my bike by
the crumbling stone wall of the Purey Cust Hospital, careful
not to scratch the Mercs and Jaguars jammed into this private
hospital's car park.

The Minster's Great Peter, a bell three times the height of a man, boomed twelve noon as I walked into the hospital's office and was greeted warmly by the matron. The hospital's proximity to the Minster meant that, whenever there was a big service, clergy often used its wards to get ready. I reminded the matron how, a couple of years back, a whole gang of bishops had used the top floor to robe. They had then descended en masse in the lift in their multicoloured cope-and-mitred splendour. They emerged opposite the operating theatre only to terrify some poor soul who was just being wheeled out, who must have thought he was having the strangest glimpse of heaven. The bishops didn't help by prac-tising their rusty pastoral skills on the poor bloke – after all it was years since most of them had been parish priests, some never at all.

'Ooooh, have you had an operation, then?' one pink-coped bishop asked, somewhat stating the obvious.

'You'll be feeling a bit woozy,' said another, decked in a cope of daring yellow and purple. 'But I'm sure you'll soon improve. You're better off in here than being at the mercy of the NHS!'

'We told him it was just the after-effects of the morphine,' matron laughed. 'Now, let me take you to Lord Feversham. He's been very much looking forward to your visit,' she added, with a twinkle in her eye.

Before my all-important visit to the hospital, I had done my homework. Helmsley was a bit of a Downton Abbey of a parish, with Lord Feversham cast as their Lord Grantham. Actually, the first Lord Feversham had represented Downton and Salisbury in parliament in the seventeenth century, and was originally Baron Downton before his descendant took up the Feversham name and moved to Duncombe Park in Helmsley. Helmsley was also one of the few parishes left in Britain where the lord of the manor still appointed the vicar. As I was now up for the post, I needed to make a good impression on Lord Feversham, who was holed up in the Purey Cust with a gammy leg.

My Lord was sitting up in bed, with a linen tent over his lower half. In his early fifties, he had the look of a Tudor monarch: rotund and ruddy-faced, his bald head polished, his beard full and well-manicured.

'I'm sorry about your leg,' I began, as I took off my cycle clips, conscious that I sounded as stupid as those bishops cooing over the patient being wheeled out of the operating theatre. My pastoral concern was dismissed by a wave of a hand.

'Don't worry about that, it'll heal like it's healed before.' Even so, he grimaced with pain before continuing, 'It seems like you're the coming man! Why's that?'

So began the most surreal job interview ever. Lord Feversham punctuated each of my stuttering answers with a grimace – I was never sure whether it was his leg or my answer which pained him. We talked about Helmsley and its previous two vicars. The first went there in 1955, the year I was born, and stayed thirty-seven years unto death. He had been a shy man, deeply faithful and spiritual. Sadly, his brand of exquisite catholic worship failed to make a connection with the masses. The next vicar had then jump-started a lot of exciting initiatives, making all sorts of connections with folk who normally didn't darken the church door. He was as flamboyant as his predecessor was shy. A shade too flamboyant, as it turned out.

'He should have kept a mistress in Leeds, no one would have found him out then. Of all the stupid things, carrying on with one of your parishioners!' was Lord Feversham's brisk take on the affair, a strange view of moral correctitude. Not wishing to offend his Lordship, I said nothing out loud, but tried to adopt an expression which signalled that, as a cleric, I didn't really approve of people keeping a mistress in Helmsley or Leeds or wherever. It's often said the aristocracy have a different take on life from us lesser mortals.

We talked of Helmsley's history, and of how, in Victorian times, the parish had had a vicar who'd been a bit of an empire builder, erecting church after church in the surrounding countryside, seemingly wherever there was a huddle of farmsteads. He and a posse of assistant clergy had leisurely ridden on horseback around the moorland villages, taking services whenever a church crossed their path, building one when it didn't. One priest had even slung his hammock in the aisle of a faraway church on the top of the moors on a Saturday evening, so he could tip himself out in time for the servants' service before dawn the next morning.

'You've no horse, no assistant clergy; how are you going to cope with it all, just you and your bicycle?' Lord Feversham chuckled.

We talked of healing wounds; of harvest festivals and Remembrance Days; of being relevant whilst honouring tradition; of getting children and teenagers to come to church; of trying to lower the average age of the congregation, which as far as I could ascertain, was around seventy-five. It was all standard, boring churchy stuff to which I gave the standard, boring answers. But all the way through the interview, I was daydreaming about that dragon I had first seen daubed on

Helmsley church's wall thirty years before. Could I bring it to life, like the portraits that spring off the walls in Gilbert and Sullivan's *Ruddigore*, and bring a bit of fierce fire to Helmsley?

There was one hint in that surreal interview that traditional Helmsley was ready to change. Lord Feversham chuckled as he told me that the film *Brassed Off* had been screened the previous night at the Helmsley Arts Centre. The film celebrated a pit village's thriving brass band, set against the chill backdrop of Margaret Thatcher closing all the mines. 'My agent tells me that the whole audience cheered and clapped to a man when the plucky brass band won in the Albert Hall. If that can happen in Helmsley, believe you me, there'll be a landslide in the election today. Tony Blair and Labour will romp home.'

We chatted a bit about ourselves. He told me with tears in his eyes how his first wife had died tragically, aged thirty. He'd then married again, and he and the youthful and vivacious Lady Polly had embarked on transforming Duncombe Park. For decades it had served as a school for gals of the gentry. But with gals of the gentry nearing extinction, its time as a school had come to an end in 1980, and Lord and Lady Feversham had moved back into the place. Camping out in a couple of rooms to start with, with not much more than a primus stove and sleeping bags as home comforts, they painstakingly began to restore the house to its former glory, room by room.

We talked about my wife and the three daughters we had at primary school. 'Four women in the house, eh? You're more like a chaplain to a nunnery than chaplain to an archbishop!'

Lord Feversham jested. 'And they tell me your wife's supportive?'

'Well, she supports me as a priest, just as I support her as a history teacher,' I replied, more than a bit rattled. The days of clergy wives being unpaid curates, running around the town dispensing broth to ailing parishioners, had long since passed. 'Traidcraft's her big thing,' I informed his Lordship.

'What the hell's that?' Lord Feversham snapped.

'It's an ethical company which sells all sorts of foods and clothes and stuff from the developing world, and ploughs the profits back into workers' cooperatives and their communities,' I explained. Lord Feversham grimaced. I'd heard that his seventeenth-century ancestor, Charles Duncombe, had made his fortune anticipating Charles II suspending the Stock Exchange, compounded by some shady tax affairs. I guessed the incumbent lord wasn't the greatest fan of ethical companies. I couldn't have been more wrong.

'Well with New Labour romping home, we'll all have to be a bit more ethical in our dealings. When you've settled in, come up to the house and have lunch with Lady Polly and me, and tell your wife to bring a Traidcraft catalogue – we'll see if we can sell a few things in the visitor centre.

'Go back to your Archbishop and tell him you'll do,' Lord Feversham concluded, as I was dismissed from his court. 'You can prepare for government,' he chuckled, 'and when you get downstairs, tell Matron I'm ready for my lunch. I've already looked at the menu – I'll have the roast pheasant and game chips!'

Chapter Six

Three months later we moved to Helmsley, just as Princess Diana died and the whole nation wrung its heart out, playing out its own version of *Evita*. Thirty miles from York, Middlesbrough or Scarborough – the nearest large towns – Helmsley tends to be immune to the fads and fashions which grab the world by storm. But even so, for days afterwards people went around the town with long faces and tears in their eyes. Our arrival was cheered by a visit from Alan, my new churchwarden, who was in his mid-seventies.

'I've got a cauliflower for you, but it's not quite ready yet,' he declared on our doorstep, before making a hasty retreat. Then an hour later he returned. 'It's ready now, I'll bring it along. I just wanted to check you still were in.' As if we were going anywhere, with countless cases to unpack and a myriad DIY chores to complete. Half an hour later he was back again. 'Cook it straight away and have it for your tea.' And with that he was gone. I guessed I would be seeing more of him, if I could ever catch him for long enough. A retired GP, he clearly delivered cauliflowers like he formerly delivered babies.

I was too busy to grieve for Diana, because I had just three weeks before my official duties began in which to turn our huge and ancient vicarage into a cosy home. Early autumn gales whistled through the gaping holes in the chimney breasts where wood-burning stoves had been roughly torn out by the removal men – in a hurried departure, the previous occupants had taken all the carpets, fixtures and fittings with them. They desperately needed them for their hastily acquired new homes.

Helmlsey's vicarage, with the quaint title Canons Garth, dates from the twelfth century. When it was first built it was just a hall with a central fire; a base for the canons from Kirkham Abbey, who trudged twenty miles or so over the hills to build Helmsley's church and Rievaulx's abbey. Since then, bits and bobs had been added to make a chapel, five rooms downstairs and ten bedrooms upstairs. The parishioners were very proud of their ancient pile, stubbornly resisting pressure to sell the vicarage and buy a more modest house. But then again, they didn't have to live there, with the wind blowing through the rattling leaded windows and astronomical heating bills to run a boiler which barely kept the damp at bay. Rachel and the girls were very good about it, donning extra-thick jumpers to keep warm. Our full-of-fun Clare ingeniously organized relay races using her Sweep puppet as a baton, shooting up the narrow main staircase, clattering along the dark-beamed landing – forty feet in length – which snaked past six bedrooms, before leaping down the spiral servants' staircase and onto the home straight – another forty-foot long wending corridor with chapel, study, Tudor porch, living room and stone-flagged dining room off it – before reaching the hall and cajoling a sister or a parent to be the next Sweep-bearer. Her target was that the five of us would complete the run in five minutes; by the time we had achieved that, extra-thick jumpers were no longer necessary and Sweep sported a distinctly frayed look.

So, as the nation had a collective nervous breakdown over Diana and Elton John wailed his farewell, I worked through the night to make our house habitable; re-pointing the stonework, installing thirty-seven curtain rails and the thirty-seven pairs of curtains which Rachel ran up on her sewing machine into the early hours, fitting hundreds of square yards of carpets – bits and bobs cobbled together from previous vicarages which made a positively psychedelic mosaic beneath our feet. For most of September I was never more than a few yards away from my toolbox. Fortunately, I enjoy trying to mend things, and as I did I pondered long and hard about how to mend a broken parish.

In those early days, various people 'happened to be passing' and interrupted my labours, checking out the new vicar and his brood. They waxed lyrical about Helmlsey's faults, depressing me no end. 'People come to Helmsley to die,' the dour chair of the district council came specially to tell me. He was a thickset, elderly man, with jowly cheeks and bloodhound eyes; much like an ancient prophet imparting his message of doom. That basically was all he had to say; once he had said it, he made his excuses and left.

'The last-vicar-but-one used to come to school on a Friday morning and cane me,' another visitor, a grizzled old man, complained as he loitered on our ancient doorstep. 'I admit I used to cheek the nuns who ran school, but I was too big for them t' take on. They saved up the punishment until t' vicar came in on a Friday to take assembly. He told us Jesus loved us, then whacked us to 'ammer 'ome his message.' With that he walked away, making it clear he would never darken any church door ever again. He had my considerable sympathy.

'We used to come to this place for our inoculations. The nuns who lived here ran a primitive 'ealth service. God, those needles 'urt!' declared a bell-shaped farmer's wife over a friendly cuppa in our draughty kitchen. 'They weren't that smaller than t' hypodermics t' vet used to stick into our 'osses.

'And it was a maternity home too,' she continued. 'I had to give birth lying on a hard metal operating table. Don't let me make you blush, vicar, but my arse, sorry, my backside was freezing. It's a wonder I didn't get frostbite!'

I laughed – her straight talking was a tonic compared to all the double-speak and church politics I'd endured at Bishopthorpe.

'But I soon forgot all that when my contractions came thick and fast, blood and stuff cascading onto the floor, like I was an animal on a butcher's slab. The sister loomed over me, sneering as if I were t' worst sinner that ever graced God's earth. My Jim was pacing up and down outside, beside himself with worry. He kept sticking his 'ead round t' door, his 'air all tossled. It fair raised my spirits to see him. "Is she all right, sister? She's 'ollering somert terrible."

'"You should have thought of that nine months ago, before you did what you did to her," the sister snapped, and she pushed him straight back out into corridor. She hadn't an ounce of mercy in her. Bit ironic, when they called themselves t' Sisters of Mercy.'

Still the parishioners came. They spluttered scary tales of my immediate predecessor who, in their opinion, partied too often, drank too hard, mixed with the lowest of the low, made beautiful maidens swoon, told religious people they were hypocrites and tried to put faith back at the top of the Church's agenda. To be honest, he sounded just like Jesus. But whatever, it all seemed quite anarchic, and as I hammered and sawed and painted and cleaned, I contemplated how to restore order, as well as having to square up to those who used the anarchy as a cover to play their own little power games.

There was one visitor who was able to put me more at ease. 'It'll take you twenty years to make any impact here,' Father Bert, a retired parish priest, cheerfully advised me in his broad Geordie accent. He belonged to the High Church wing of the Church of England, hence his title. He wasn't quite as tall as me, but his back was ramrod straight, hinting at a military past. He sported a black suit and a black clerical shirt, and a good head of immaculately parted silver hair, liberally plastered down with Brylcreem. Clear blue eyes gazed intently at you through rimless glasses, giving him a bemused, prayerful, kindly air. He had popped in just after breakfast – the girls had all gone to school, Rachel had gone shopping in Thirsk, so it was good to have a voice from the world of men to banish Canons Garth ghosts.

'It's a funny old house, this,' he informed me, as if I didn't know that already. 'One of the last-vicar-but-one's daughters got in a huff, found a secret room off one of the chimneys and hid there for three days. Her parents were beside themselves. And then she just appeared, looking a bit sooty, but wouldn't let on where the room was!'

Unlike my other visitors, Father Bert was at least good enough to lend me a hand. It transpired he had been a tail-end Charlie during the Second World War, manning the rear gun turret of a Lancaster bomber. He manned the rear of my ladder now, holding it steady with his nicotine-stained fingers, the pipe dangling from his mouth emitting a plume of blue smoke like an ailing Lancaster, whilst I tried to patch up a sagging ceiling. It was all to no avail, as the ceiling came crashing down, enveloping both of us in a cloud of grey dust and revealing the wattle and daub lattice work beneath, which must have been undisturbed since medieval times.

'Ee, that took me back,' he said. 'I was always having dust like that fall about me ears, man, when those Messerschmitts used to take a pop at me!'

He shivered. It was a good ten degrees colder inside Canons Garth than it was outside that day, but it was his memories rather than my cold house that made him shake.

'It was absolutely freezing in those little bubbles,' he exclaimed. 'Even colder than this place! I suppose it stopped me dozing off, kept me alert, my eyes peeled for enemy aircraft.' He wheeled around 180 degrees, scanning my dilapidated ceiling, screwing up his eyes lest a Focke was lurking in my dangling wattle and daub. '*Heckschwein*, that's what their rear-end gunners were called – tail-end pigs. And, I'm sorry to say this, they *were* utter pigs; one slip by us and they'd show no mercy, their guns would cut us up like mincemeat.'

In cramped and freezing conditions, he had risked death and been an agent of death every day. My preparation for priesthood had been working for six years in Barclays Bank in darkest Hull; Bert had spent a similar length of time strapped into a veritable killing machine, a sitting duck for enemy fire. It's funny how life turns out.

'Let's go out for a spin while all this dust settles,' Father Bert suggested. I left Rachel a note on the kitchen table – 'Sorry about the ceiling – back later' – and off we went. I wasn't sure what sort of spin Father Bert had in mind and feared he might have a tame Spitfire parked up on Canons Garth Lane, so I was vastly reassured when he opened the doors of a rather smart red jeep. 'You need one of these for where I'm taking you,' he joked, as we roared up the 1:4 incline out of Helmsley. His jeep had all the mod cons, including an altimeter on the dashboard, and the numbers shot up like Wall Street in the throes of a bull market: 70, 80, 90, 100 metres and rising.

'That's Beckdale House, which Lord Feversham built for himself whilst the school lasses occupied Duncombe Park,' he explained, pointing to his right as the jeep veered dangerously near the verge. In a blur I saw a rather nicely proportioned mansion perched on the hilltop, south facing, with a highly desirable view over the town and the distant Wolds.

'Why on earth did he leave all that comfort to camp out in an eighteenth-century pile?' I asked.

Father Bert grinned. 'The aristocracy are not like us, bonnie lad. They stockpile millions, but are never happier than when they're roughing it in a draughty old castle, shuffling around in a pair of worn carpet slippers and stained corduroys, with nothing but a bit of mouldy cheese and stale bread for their lunch. I blame public schools, that's where the rot sets in. If they'd been educated like me in a Gateshead secondary modern, they'd look for a bit of luxury.'

The altimeter had risen to 180 metres by now, as the jeep pointed heavenwards. 'Peer over to your left and you might catch a glimpse of Rievaulx Terraces,' my clerical guide pointed out. 'They're follies originally built by another Lord Feversham with views over the valley, but the family had to sell them off when the earl was killed on the Somme, otherwise the death duties would have crippled them. Seems a bit hard that, dying for your king and country, and then being clobbered by the tax man as well as the Hun.'

It wasn't just the old Lord Feversham who had been robbed. Before retirement, Father Bert had been vicar of the moorland parishes to the north of Helmsley. He positively seethed as he told me that the glories of Rievaulx should rightfully have been in his parish and not part of Helmsley. 'What does the Vicar of Helmsley in his grand town know of rural life?' he complained, seemingly forgetting that the new vicar of Helmsley was sitting beside him, hanging on for dear life. The altimeter started soaring again, reaching the dizzy height of 300 metres before the jeep screeched to a halt as a roe deer ran across our path. 'Nearly caught our lunch there, David! Let's turn off and have a look at the view, and then we'll double back so you can taste the glories of my former kingdom!'

The forest clearing was rather aptly called Surprise View. The ground fell sharply away beneath us and revealed a gorgeous, lush green valley flanked by moorland hills, with their tops made bright purple by the heather's autumn bloom. This formed the largest continuous expanse of heather in the UK, with the UK itself containing 70 per cent of the world's heather. Bilsdale stretched for twenty miles before our gaze, with just a scattering of stone-built farmhouses clinging to the hillsides. The northern end of the valley was framed by the Cleveland Hills; of equal height to the North York Moors yet more rounded and less rugged, giving them a maternal feel. As we stood in the clearing drinking in the sight, I noticed a pine tree which had been recently felled, the sticky sap still oozing over the trunk. I counted the rings on the trunk; forty-two in total, making the tree exactly my age. Since 1955 it had

stood here through every season; from the harshest of winters in 1963 with seven-foot drifts blocking every road, to the scorching summers of the mid-1970s, when my manager at Barclays Bank in Hull bought his staff ice creams every afternoon to cool us down. Every season for forty-two years — lucky old tree!

Chapter Seven

Father Bert didn't want to linger, so we sped off back down the B road and then, after a sharp right, the jeep clung precariously to a ridge before plummeting eighty metres and crossing the River Rye into the village of Hawnby. Actually, it was two villages, due to a falling out in the eighteenth century. John Wesley had preached in the village and over fifty villagers had converted to Methodism. Hawnby's lord of the manor, the Earl of Mexborough, evicted any tenants who failed to remain loyal to the Church of England, but they managed to club together and buy land on the other side of the Rye to set-up their own farmsteads and build their own chapel. It was a sort of Methodist cooperative, and on a Sunday they'd bawl out Charles Wesley's hymns from dawn to dusk, twice as loudly whenever the earl was in residence, just to shame him. After all, there is only so much of 'Love Divine All Loves Excelling', and all the trilling connected with it, that one can take.

We climbed out of Hawnby and then turned left, descending another 1:3 hill. There was a warning sign for a ford ahead, but Father Bert sped on. 'You'll never have seen a ford like this,' he warned. Like all fords, the road dipped sharply into a stream, but this one was quite a raging torrent. The water splashed over the jeep as we dived in, but then Father

Bert made a sharp left turn, so rather than rising out of the other side, we drove along the river. I felt like a passenger in James Bond's Lotus Esprit, the submarine car in *The Spy Who Loved Me.*

'Bert, what on earth are you doing?' I shouted in panic, as a tidal surge engulfed the windscreen. 'Get onto the road!'

'This is the road, laddie, we've got another couple of hundred yards of this!'

We bounced along the river bed for the stipulated two hundred yards before making a sharp right turn onto dry land and the tarmac road that continued on the stream's other side. By night you'd have undoubtedly missed the turn – it was difficult enough to spot it by day with the windscreen wipers hardly able to cope.

'What would have happened if we'd missed it?' I asked Father Bert as we rose up the hill, whilst all the water on the hot bonnet turned to steam, plunging us into a veritable fog.

'I suppose we'd have driven down the stream for a couple of miles and ended up in the Rye!' he nonchalantly replied, shrugging his shoulders, as if driving along river beds formed a normal part of a country parson's life.

We reached Old Byland, a village perched on yet another hilltop, and pulled up beside a very smart farmhouse; an eighteenth-century stone-faced building with a stone-tiled roof, a spic and span stack yard and a highly polished Range Rover parked by the side of a barn. Father Bert got out and yelled, 'Margaret, Margaret!' After a couple of minutes a lady in her mid-sixties emerged from one of the barns, with bits of straw in her white hair.

'For goodness' sake, Father, stop bellowing, I was just

feeding the 'osses. You've fair spooked them with all that shouting.'

The normally loquacious Father Bert was silent, hunching his shoulders like a dog scolded by his mistress. Margaret bustled about in the yard; a rotund country woman, dressed in smart tweeds, with a beaming face and laughter tumbling out of her whole body.

'Now don't go into a sulk again, Father,' she said cheerfully. 'Who's this you've brought with you?'

'I'm David, the new vicar of Helmsley.' I wasn't sure what else to say, because I wasn't sure why we'd stopped by.

'Oh, how lovely.' Margaret beamed, grasping my hand with both her hands in the warmest of greetings. 'You'll stay for a bit of lunch? Father always pops in around this time of day, in fact every day for the last eighteen years, ever since he moved up here. I must be the most frequently visited woman in the diocese!' She looked at Bert fondly, gently teasing him.

'That would be lovely, but are you sure you've got enough?' I asked anxiously.

'Oh yes, don't you worry about that, I always cook a bit spare and warm it up for me tea. Come on in and sit yourselves around the table and I'll serve up.'

We were ushered into a spacious but dark kitchen, with tiny windows set in the thick stone walls looking onto the stack yard and village green. The room was full of delicious aromas. Several pans were boiling on the top of the large Aga, which as well as doing all the cooking gave the room a warm, cosy feel. We sat on Windsor chairs around a large oak table and to start with Margaret served us a thick slab of golden Yorkshire pudding, swimming in a lake of rich, brown gravy. It was the Yorkshire way; fill them up with pudding first to take the edge off their appetite for the more expensive meat served later. I'm a founding member of the Yorkshire Pudding Society, which has only one rule: no member is ever allowed to refuse a Yorkshire pudding. So I dutifully tucked in, not that I needed any encouragement – it was absolutely delicious.

'Are these made with Henrietta's eggs?' Father Bert asked.

'Yes,' Margaret replied, and then added for my benefit, 'Henrietta's my best layer, lovely brown eggs, double-yolkers, laid fresh this morning. Will you have a bit more?' she asked, noting I had wolfed the first slab down. Within seconds another slab, twice as big as the first, appeared on my plate, with another pint of gravy.

'I like to see a man enjoying his food. And you need feeding up, the pair of you are as thin as rakes!'

I thought that I wouldn't be staying as thin as a rake for long at this rate, whilst wondering how Father Bert had stayed so slim if this had been his daily fare for eighteen years. As soon as I had finished my second piece of Yorkshire pudding, Margaret put dish after dish of steaming vegetables on the table; peas, carrots, green beans, swede, a huge dish of mashed potato and roast potatoes.

'All grown by my own hand,' she reassured me. 'I've only just podded the peas. They're a bit big at this time of year, but they should be as sweet as sweet can be. Father, will you carve?'

'I always do,' Father Bert replied, as a huge leg of lamb was placed before him. 'Which one's this?'

'Oh, it's Bertha, I thought she was fattening up nicely so I took her down to Thompson's in Helmsley last week for slaughter, and picked her up yesterday. I've frozen the rest of her.'

'Ah, God bless Bertha,' Father Bert intoned, a somewhat unconventional grace. He carved four huge slices of lamb and put them on my plate, the lush juices running off and diluting the remaining gravy. Before I could help myself to modest amounts, Margaret piled on the vegetables, half a dozen roast potatoes and a mountain of mash.

'Have a bit more Yorkshire pudding to go with it,' she encouraged, as she perched a third slab on my plate. 'Father always likes a Yorkshire pudding chaser.'

It was absolutely gorgeous, but by the time I had finished it I was, to put it delicately, feeling exceedingly replete. 'Now, you'll have seconds?' Margaret asked, although it was more an order than a question.

'It was thoroughly delicious, but I don't think I could,' I replied.

A golden labrador was slumped in her basket by the Aga and hadn't taken her eyes off me since I'd entered the kitchen, her tail thumping on the basket side every time Father Bert threw her a titbit. Margaret looked at me with the same deep soulful eyes as her dog. 'Now come on, David, have a bit more, we don't want it going to waste!' Clearly saying no wasn't an option, so once again four huge slices of lamb were piled onto my plate, another half dozen roast potatoes, another mountain of mash, another lake of gravy. Complete with a fourth slab of Yorkshire. This was turning out to be a food marathon.

Miraculously I got through it all, and even enjoyed it, although I surreptitiously loosened my belt a couple of notches to ease the strain.

'Well, I suppose we'd better be getting back to base,' I

exclaimed, suppressing a belch. 'Margaret, that was scrumptious.'

'But you haven't had your pudding yet,' Margaret declared, whipping away the dinner plates and then bringing out a huge dish from the Aga's oven. It was bread and butter pudding, my favourite, cooked to golden perfection. Surely I would be able to find a little corner for the smallest of pieces? But Margaret wasn't finished. She placed a quart jug of custard on the table before disappearing into the larder.

'You just wait for her pièce de résistance,' Father Bert whispered, just as Margaret returned with a cut-glass bowl brimful with trifle.

'Now, David, which are you going to try first?' she asked.

Margaret would not take no for an answer, so bread and butter pudding was followed by trifle.

'Now, how about a bit of ice cream to finish off?'

Despite the deep soulful eyes, I shook my head, almost incapable of coherent speech. I held up my hand, 'No, no, I really couldn't, I'm fine,' I said, even though I felt far from fine. During pudding I'd surreptitiously slid my belt buckle to the last notch, yet my stomach still felt like a taut drum.

'Well, I'll put the kettle on and make a cup of tea whilst Father shows you the church and vicarage,' Margaret decreed.

Father Bert and I toddled out of the house, the golden labrador trotting beside us. Fortunately, the church was only across the green, so the walk wasn't too onerous. It was an ancient building, mostly wood, with a Saxon feel to it and a lovely musky aroma.

'It used to be a monastery,' Father Bert explained. 'But Rievaulx Abbey is just at the bottom of the cliff, and they got fed up with the monks there ringing their bells at the wrong time. They were two different orders with two different habits, in both senses of the word. They didn't take kindly to being woken by Rievaulx's bells when it was their kip time, or being summoned in from the fields only to find vespers wasn't happening for another hour. So they moved and set up another Byland ten miles away, over towards the Howardian Hills, and we became Old Byland.'

'Might have been cheaper to change the pitch of the bells – make Rievaulx C major and Byland F sharp major.'

'Do you know, I bet they never thought of that,' Father Bert chuckled. 'But I think they also got a bit fed up of being perched on this hill, too easy a target for sacking by the Scots. So they took themselves off to be nice and safe in a hidden valley. Legend has it that during one attack, the Scots tore the habits off their very backs. Those Scots have never been much good at respecting the cloth,' Father Bert joked.

Our path meandered through the vicarage garden next door to the church. The ground fell sharply away beneath it, offering breathtaking views towards Rievaulx and the River Rye. We returned to Margaret's kitchen, where there was a steaming mug of tea in each of our places, along with a thick slice of rich fruit cake and a hunk of Wensleydale cheese.

'I thought you'd need a snack after your little ramble,' Margaret chuckled.

After that feast, I felt distinctly sleepy as we shot up and down hills on our drive home, giving Rievaulx a fly-past. I always adored seeing Rievaulx Abbey, with its magnificent and haunting high stone walls, roofless church and monks' quarters. But today it went by in a blurred haze.

'When did you retire, then?' I managed to ask Father Bert.

'When I were sixty-nine, in 1991,' he replied. 'I'd just had lunch with Margaret, and I went back to my vicarage and looked at the list of visits for the day and said to myself, "I just cannot be bothered." So I resigned there and then.'

We were silent for the rest of the journey as I pondered two questions in my somnolent state. Firstly, never mind his reason for retiring, how had Bert ever summoned up the energy to visit a single parishioner after such a daily repast? And secondly, what precisely was going on between him and Margaret?

As we wended our dyspeptic way back to Helmsley, I thought about my own courtship fifteen years earlier when I was a curate in Middlesbrough. Our local bishop was a rather wonderful raconteur but as a preacher he was deadly dull – a devotee of that school of ministry where you avoided any emotion in the pulpit. In 1982, I attended a Lent course he addressed, at Swainby, another quaint village on the edge of the Cleveland Hills. At the bunfight in the church hall afterwards, I spotted this blue-eyed and fair-haired young woman; a rare beauty in a group of blue-rinsed geriatrics. 'Wasn't that bishop boring!' was my unconventional chat-up line.

Fortunately, the young woman wasn't the bishop's daughter, otherwise our relationship would have ended before it began. Instead, Rachel and I got on like a house on fire. She was a history teacher at the local comprehensive in Stokesley. Her father had been a churchwarden at a leading church in Sheffield, her mother, before her untimely death at the age of forty-six, had been the best priest the Church of England never had. After being thrown together by boredom at the Lent course, we saw each other nearly every day. On our first day out we visited Helmsley and walked around the ruins of Rievaulx Abbey. On our hundredth day out we visited

Helmsley again, I proposed, and we married at the end of July the following year, two years to the day plus one after Charles and Diana's wedding had captivated the world. Our wedding was more low key, at Rachel's home church in Sheffield. Rachel's lovely father was shaking with emotion as he led her up the aisle. The service was taken by my father, whose hands were trembling as he joined our hands together and pronounced us man and wife.

It was the best day of my life, by far. If there was anything going on between Father Bert and Margaret, then God bless them. In Tudor times, allowing its priests to marry was the best step the then fledgling Church of England ever made, enabling its clergy not to theorize about the love of God, but to root it in reality. And for the four subsequent centuries, parishes have benefitted immensely from having the Brontës and Austens and sundry other clerical families in their midst, with Mrs Vicar often proving a far more effective and matter-of-fact pastor than her ordained husband.

Chapter Eight

Fortunately, I had planned a cycle marathon for the next day, which proved a chance to burn off all the calories I'd enjoyed at Margaret's. It was also a prayer marathon – I'd spend an hour in silent prayer at each of my five churches to set my new ministry. The day was tightly timetabled so that I could cycle between each church, with people invited to join me whenever, wherever. After all the incessant DIY at Canons Garth, I was rather looking forward to a day filled with cycling and at least five hours' silence.

My first hour began at 7 a.m. in the parish church in Helmsley, a stone's throw from our home. The sun was just rising as I walked through the churchyard with its ancient tombstones, most leaning at dangerous angles with their inscriptions badly eroded. Helmsley, surrounded by hills on all sides, was in a bit of a dip, and proved a toxic sink for carbon dioxide and sulphur dioxide emitted by countless coal fires, as well as the steam engines of a former age, which eroded limestone and people's lungs. It seemed ironic that this toxic sink had not only condemned people to an early grave, but then had the audacity to erode the inscriptions on their tombstones, like a murderer trying to do away with the evidence.

This graveyard is full of indispensable men and women! I thought, as I often did whenever I wandered through a churchyard. I opened up the church and sat in the dawning light beneath the twenty-foot long dragon I had first encountered thirty years before, and tried to still myself. Three people noisily shuffled in; loudly wishing each other good morning; asking whether sundry ailing relatives had survived yet another night; checking on whether they had already eaten breakfast or whether that thrill awaited them; bemoaning the demise of the cooked breakfast in favour of the current fashion of sawdust with watered-down milk. The dragon winked at me. Eventually the silence surged softly backwards and they sort-of settled down, limiting their noise to the odd shuffle on the hard pews or the protesting rumble of an empty tummy.

The clock struck eight, the hour was up and the chit-chat immediately resumed. My three companions, faithful stalwarts who'd shown me around the parish when I was considering taking up the job, cooed over me like mother hens, questioning whether I was up to cycling twenty or so miles in such rugged terrain. I kept quiet about my secret weapon; a host of gammon sandwiches I had made the night before which I was going to use whenever my flagging energy cells needed a top-up.

My next port of call was St Chad's, Sproxton, an easy mile's climb up the A170. In the seventh century Chad was the abbot of the ancient Celtic abbey at Lastingham, nestling in the moors a dozen miles east of Helmsley. He became the second Archbishop of York, but there were mutterings about whether his appointment was valid. He demurely gave way and returned to Lastingham, but was then appointed Bishop of Lichfield as a consolation prize. The church named in his memory at Sproxton had been built during Oliver Cromwell's reign, and reflected the puritanism of a period when Christmas had been banned for being too joyous. It was just a small square meeting house with a gallery accessed by a dodgy narrow staircase. The modest altar was flanked by a set of scantily clad alabaster figures, looking more like a bunch of Grecian youths whose frolics were about to get a bit physical rather than a band of chaste disciples. I closed my eyes to stop them distracting me.

The church had originally been built two miles away, at West Newton Grange, but the village had fallen into decline and the church had degenerated into a barn, so in 1889 Lord Feversham had had it moved, stone by stone, to Sproxton; a bustling metropolis of fifty homesteads flanking the top gate into his estate. Maybe the incongruous Grecian figures had crept in then, covertly sexing up the church's Roundhead austerity. It's funny the things you think about when you are supposed to be praying.

Two women had joined me for my hour. One, a white-haired octogenarian called Lina, had been on her knees in the graveyard, weeding the steeply banked flower beds. When I arrived she followed me into church and then spent an hour on her knees inside, totally still.

'What were you praying?' I asked her later. Normally people are fazed by this question, but she answered naturally, with a timid smile, 'Oh, I just tracked through all my eighty years and thanked God for all his blessings.'

She had been born in Sproxton, and amongst other things had served as cook in various surrounding farms. She had married a farmhand and reared a family, had housed evacuees from bombed-out Middlesbrough during the war, and had torn strips off an American tank commander when the turret of his tank had dislodged the stone ball on the church gates. An unconventional but settled life, with its bitter joys and sweet sorrows, fast-forwarded through in an hour.

The other woman, Yvonne, was in her early sixties, with blazing eyes.

'What did you pray about?' I asked her.

'Actually, I was working out Pythagorean Triples.' She smiled. 'I tried to pray but I used to be a Maths teacher, and whenever I pause, it all comes flooding back.'

I came out of the church into bright sunshine, but below me in Helmsley a mist had formed, engulfing the town. I freewheeled into the mist, speeding down the steep hill, reaching nearly 40 mph. I recalled my Monk Fryston days, when I had once managed 35 mph on my bike and was ticked off by a humourless policeman with a speed camera, who didn't take kindly to my asking for the photo as a trophy. A sharp bend suddenly sprang out of the mist, forcing me back into the present as I braked hard before crossing the stone bridge into Helmsley, the fog amplifying the sound of the River Rye tumbling below me. I had a quick cup of tea and a gammon sandwich at Canons Garth, where plasterers were at work repairing our fallen ceiling. I kissed Rachel goodbye, her lips smacking of lime dust. The minor road to Carlton was a long 1:3 climb out of Helmsley which made my thigh muscles ache, although I found that thinking about Yvonne's Pythagorean Triples distracted me from the pain. Or it could be that the pain of doing Maths kicks all other pain into touch.

Carlton's church was dedicated to Aidan; another local lad and seventh-century bishop who had had the heady ambition of converting the violent north. Rather than basing himself at the intersection of the A1, M1 and M62, which would have made for speedier communications, albeit with the slight snag that it would be another sixteen centuries before they were built, he chose Lindisfarne for his HQ. An island linked to the barren and remote Northumbrian coast by a causeway, cut off twice a day by the tides, is hardly at the hub of civilization. However, it was close to Bamburgh Castle, where King Oswald of Northumbria had his palace, so Aidan was probably cannier than he seemed: get the king on side, and, surprise, surprise, all his subjects come on side too. There's a tale of Oswald and Aidan enjoying a sumptuous Easter feast, only to be disturbed by the cries of the starving poor outside the castle walls. The pair of them halted the feast, went outside and gave all their food to the poor, along with all the silver and gold plate. The poor found the roast capons, geese and sides of beef quite tasty, but broke their teeth when they bit into the silver and gold, so threw these worthless items into the sea.

Carlton Church hadn't been used for worship for decades, but a kind shepherd's wife had been in the day before to clear away all the massive cobwebs and dust the pews. Carlton was tiny, with just a few ancient farms straddling its one street. The tiny church was rather sweet; it had been built in Victorian times but had the air of a traditional Norman church with its nave, chancel and tower. Before moving to Helmsley, I had written to every parishioner advertising my day of prayer. Obviously the word had got around, and folk who had been baptized or married in Carlton Church ages back, before being scattered to the four corners of Yorkshire, all returned to base. The little church was packed with about thirty folk, who chatted to each other as I sat in silence in their midst. Looking at the state of some of them, never mind being baptised or married there, I wondered whether they hadn't been buried there too, and had come back to haunt me. I closed my eyes but could still hear them.

'I met Colin at a dance in t' village hall. He took me home on his motorbike, but he was too busy fondling me legs rather than steering the thing. We skidded on some gravel, I came off and I grazed my hands somert terrible.'

'Eee, Eva, poor old you,' her audience chimed, oblivious to me.

'I managed to get back on t' bike, wrapped me hands around him and we went and knocked up the doctor's. She wasn't best pleased, but then when she saw Colin, with his white shirt absolutely saturated in blood where I had clung on to him for dear life, she went into doctor-mode. "You need the hospital, not me, young man," she said.

'"No, I'm fine, doctor, it's me girl, she's badly grazed her hands, can you sort her out?"'

It transpired that the good doctor didn't just patch her up. She was so taken with Eva's sunny personality, as well as noticing that her grazed hands were the hands of a hard-working young woman, that she engaged her on the spot to be her housekeeper.

'She wasn't an easy woman, mind, but she twisted the old earl's arm to let me and Colin have cottage opposite t' church when we eventually got married. One of his hounds had got a bit carried away and had taken a chunk out of his leg, and so he'd come to the doctor for a tetanus jab. I think she was holding a huge hypodermic above his quivering backside when she asked him about giving Colin and me a house, so he didn't have much option but to agree!'

Her audience guffawed. 'Are you sure it was his arm she twisted, Eva, or his arse?' someone jested.

'Shh, new vicar might be listening,' Eva replied. Actually, the new vicar was trying to pray. 'It was a grand little cottage,' Eva continued. 'Luxury, with an outside cold tap. It was a bit of a temperamental old thing, but it saved me having to fetch all our water from the village pump like rest o' t' folk in Carlton.'

It was all fascinating stuff, akin to listening to a radio broadcast, so I gave in and let it fill my allotted hour. I duly learnt that Eva had only ever had one holiday; her honeymoon in an overcast Morecambe, which had proved more than enough for a lifetime. More guffaws from her audience. She was a true country woman; tattie-picking, pea and bean harvesting, drawing and dressing pheasants, gutting pigs, giving tips along the way on where to gather the best blackberries, bilberries, wild raspberries, strawberries and apples. Even where to find lost rings. It seemed that years back, the good Eva had lost her engagement ring, and though she searched the highways and byways she failed to find it, and finally Colin bought her a replacement. Even so, she still grieved for the original. Then one day she chanced upon it in a box of rags she used for making clippy mats, whatever they might be. It seems that her joy knew no bounds, spurring her on to gather her friends and host a party of Gospel proportions: 'Rejoice with me for I have found the ring I have lost . . .'

My hour had come, I had to move on, but clearly Eva had only just got started. As I left I saw her face for the first time – settled in its skin, beatific, radiating joy.

Eva's tenacity took me back to my teenage years in west Hull, which was as urban as Helmsley was rural; a vibrant place with an open-all-hours shop on every corner, their lights blazing out and cheering the dark streets. It was a friendly, close and caring community, united by a common bond of grief when any Hull trawler failed to return from fierce and freezing Icelandic waters. When the trawler *Gaul* sank in 1974, with the loss of all thirty-six hands, a fisherman's wife called Lil Bilocca took on the authorities, demanding an inquiry. The official explanation was that a thirty-foot freak wave had sunk the trawler in the Barents Sea north of Norway. But there were rumours that a Russian submarine had either caught in the *Gaul*'s nets and dragged her down, or had deliberately fired on her and sunk her. Big Lil wouldn't take no for an answer; she had been a doughty defender of fishermen's rights and their right to basic safety ever since January 1968, when three trawlers had sunk within weeks of each other. To be honest, had she taken on a Russian sub, I wouldn't have rated its chances very highly! West Hull was full of women like her; no-nonsense, fiercely loyal people who told it straight, no matter how important and powerful their audience. Eva struck me as another Mrs Bilocca, not afraid to bring down the mighty from their seat and exalt the humble and meek, singing a latter-day Magnificat with their lives.

Chapter Nine

It was a long pull out of Carlton further up into the moors, but then all of a sudden I reached the top, Cow House Bank, and beheld a similar glorious view to that of the day before, only shifted a couple of miles to the right, with the North Sea a hazy blue line on the eastern horizon. The road dropped down the cliff through a forest of pine trees and as I sped down on my bike I took in great gulps of clean and ice-fresh pine vapour; not so much a cycle-ride as aromatherapy. By the bottom of the cliff I must have been doing about 30 mph before I realized there was a deep ford ahead. It was too late to brake, so I scissored my legs as my bike divided the water. Fortunately, there were no rocks on the river bed to catapult me over the handlebars and I passed through the waters unscathed. Indeed, I had enough momentum to get halfway up the hill at the other side, before my aching legs had to take over.

When it wasn't pine forest, the terrain flanking the road was bracken; lush and green and very tall. I wasn't entirely sure where my next port of call was – my only direction was to look for a church by a tilting red phone box in the middle of nowhere. In the midst of the green, I suddenly saw post-office red to my right, but where was the church? Leaving my bike propped up against the phone box, I walked down a sheep track, the grass cropped close like velvet. To my left was not so much a rhododendron bush as a rhododendron forest, and, peering through the thicket, I spied a tiny church with a tiny spire. I opened the stiff oak doors and found myself in a magical interior; a simple building with whitewashed walls but a kaleidoscope of a roof, the rafters painted the brightest red, blue and green, with the interior doors and surrounding mouldings the same hue. There was a tiny nave and even a tiny south aisle, with coloured shutters to isolate it and turn it into a schoolroom.

John Betjeman, the poet laureate, had written a poem celebrating East Moors – 'Perp. Revival i' the North' – after he had chanced upon it while visiting Lord Feversham. He described seeing 'something in the painted roof / and the mouldings round the door'.* The line had to end with 'door' to enable the next stanza to rhyme with the name of the architect, Temple Moor.

I sat on one of the bench pews, alone and silent for a couple of minutes before the doors burst open and an old man and a younger woman came in, complete with four springer spaniels straining at the leash. I smiled, re-closed my eyes and returned to silence. Or rather, I didn't.

'When's t' service going to start?'

'I've told you, Dad, it's not a service, it's an hour of silent prayer with new vicar.'

'Where is he, then?'

'He's over there, Dad.'

* From 'Perp. Revival i' the North' in *Collected Poems* by John Betjeman; 'Summoned by Bells,' from *Collected Poems* by John Betjeman © 1955, 1958, 1962, 1964, 1968, 1970, 1979, 1981, 1982, 2001. Reproduced by permission of John Murray, an imprint of Hodder and Stoughton Ltd. Reproduced by John Murray Press, a division of Hodder and Stoughton Limited.

'When is he going to start t' service?'

Suddenly the sound of hounds baying filled the church, which set the four spaniels off howling.

'Quieten down, you little buggers, behave yourselves in church,' the old man shouted, sending a kick or two in their direction. 'Where's the new vicar going to live, then?' he asked his daughter.

'In Canons Garth, Dad.

'How do you know that?'

'Because I drove past when the removal van was there and I saw him lending a hand.'

'When am I getting my car back?'

'When the garage has fitted a new battery, Dad.'

'What was wrong with the old one? I know these roads around here like the back of my hand – I hardly ever switch the headlamps on. And once I've climbed Cow House Bank I always turn ignition off and freewheel down to Helmsley.'

'I've told you to stop doing that, Dad. These modern cars aren't like the old Humber you used to drive, you need to keep t'engine on for t' power steering and servo brakes!'

'Pah, rubbish! When is t' service going to start?'

'It's an hour of silent prayer, Dad – I've told you already.'

'Are we going to the doctor's when t' service has ended?'

'Yes, Dad.'

'I'm not seeing that woman doctor.'

'She's better than the men, Dad.'

'I don't care, I'm not seeing a woman. It's not right.'

'But she's lovely, Dad.'

'I'm not seeing her, and that's that. I've got my dignity. There are parts of me that only my mother and your mother have seen, and I want to keep it that way. I'm not showing myself to a woman doctor.'

'For goodness' sake, Dad, give it a rest. All we want her to do is to sign your repeat prescription. She'll let you keep your trousers on!'

And so they prattled on, father competing with daughter, baying hounds competing with howling spaniels as the hour ticked by. To distract myself I gazed at the church's east window, depicting Mary Magdalene, its patron saint. The Gospel's ultimate shady lady, sporting a revealing bright-red dress, was stooping beneath Christ's cross and holding up a chalice to catch his blood. *Indiana Jones and the Last Crusade* and *The Da Vinci Code* all combined in this one stained-glass window at the end of the earth. It set me thinking, why dedicate the place to Mary Magdalene when the other churches preferred more local saints? This church was set in a garden, just like Mary Magdalene's chief work was set in a garden where she met the risen Christ on the first Easter Day. But was that all, or was the long sought-after Holy Grail buried beneath it? Or was Mary Magdalene herself buried here, making her a wee bit more local than I first thought?

'He seems a nice enough fellow. I'm sure he'll be all right once he starts a service,' the old guy blurted out, jolting me back from fantasy to an albeit strange reality.

My hour up, I had a word or two with the father and his long-suffering daughter. 'Nice weather for September,' I said, stating the obvious.

'Yes,' she replied, 'it'll make for a good harvest.'

'Why didn't you have a service, young man?' her father blurted out. I just smiled; his daughter smiled back with a twinkle in her eye.

After they had departed, I walked around the outside of the church as I munched a couple of gammon sandwiches. At the church's east end was a tiny school house, with kennels in the garden housing about thirty hounds, all of them pushing at the wire netting, snarling and barking at me – the mystery of the baying was solved, at least. In my mind I went back half a century, and where the hounds now bayed, I imagined the shrill voices of children at play, ducking in and out of the rhododendron forest.

My mind also went back thirty years to my boyhood days in Aughton, which, like East Moors, had seemed like the end of the earth. We moved into Aughton's elegant Georgian vicarage during a torrential downpour at the end of September, 1965. The removal van sank down to its axles on our waterlogged drive and the removal men had to use four sacks of our precious coal to give the wheels purchase. The wheels spun and the men dived for cover as our coal shot everywhere, peppering our new home's white facade with black specks.

The next day dawned bright and clear, and I remember a glorious sense of freedom as I ran across soggy field after soggy field with Susie, my Welsh collie. The River Derwent, into which Helmsley's River Rye flows, had burst its banks yet again, and the flood water lapped against the ancient church walls, the autumn sun reflecting on the shimmering water, turning it into a field of gold. At the bunfight following his official licensing as vicar, my dad had joked about needing a motor boat rather than his Vespa 90 to get around his new parish.

Moving to be a vicar was a promotion for my dad, with his salary increased to £1000 per year. But when his first monthly pay cheque arrived from the Church Commissioners, it amounted to the princely sum of £29.

'Surely there has been some mistake,' my dad complained to the Commissioners. 'It should be eighty-four pounds rather than twenty-nine pounds.'

'No,' they replied, 'twenty-nine pounds is our contribution. The rest is paid from glebe rent, which you have to gather from your tenant farmers.'

For our five years in Aughton, my dad had to employ an agent to collect the rent, paid six months in arrears, sometimes gladly, mostly grudgingly, often only in part or not at all. Some farmers paid in kind; a sack of blighted potatoes, the odd brace of pheasants riddled with shot, a rooster or two which had died of old age.

A gazetteer described Aughton as 'forlorn and faraway', and in many ways it was still 1865 rather than the swinging sixties. Never mind Harold Wilson's white heat of technology – some farms had resisted the advent of electricity, which had reached the village in 1947: 'We're not having them cables near our cattle, they'll sour t' milk.' Instead they milked by hand in shady barns lit by oil-light, more likely to fry the cattle than any electric cable. My dad visited one un-electrified farm where the old grandma sat by the Yorkshire range, (a fire, cooker, warming cupboard and hob, all contained in a black-leaded cast-iron case) stirring a stew on its red-hot top. In one hand she held a spoon and in the other a thick candle, which dripped globs of wax into the gravy below.

It was all more than a bit crazy. My dad was quite go-ahead and installed a phone in the vicarage; prior to that I think the vicar had been summoned by carrier pigeon when auntie took a turn for the worse. Our number was Bubwith 243. The churchwarden, who had a party-line with us, was Bubwith 242, the other churchwarden was Bubwith 241 and the vicar of Bubwith was Bubwith 240. There was an ancient phone box in our tiny village, much like the tilting phone box at East Moors; it served as the only place of entertainment other than the ill-attended, freezing church. I think its number was Bubwith 239 – a wild departure from the 240s. The problem was that every phone line went through the phone box, so by picking up the receiver you could listen in on any conversation going on. Many village folk whiled away the long, cold wintry nights by cramming into the dimly lit phone box to eavesdrop on vicar talking to vicar, warden talking to warden, or warden talking to vicar.

One warden, Norman, was a farmer who mostly grew sugar beet and potatoes – just one harvest a year followed by liming the furrows with thick white dust. After a hard day of such liming he went wearily to bed. He got up the next morning and drew his curtains, 'Ee heck, Olive!' he exclaimed to his wife as he surveyed his fields, 'There's been one hell of a heavy frost.'

The once-a-day bus service to York used exactly the same timetable deployed in 1865, even though a motor coach had long since replaced coach and horses. The bus, straight out of *The Titchfield Thunderbolt*, inched along the country lanes, growling in second gear. Few people had cars in those days, so the slow bus was the only form of transport, making York seem far more than fifteen miles away and the rest of the world positively light years away. Though my parents hated the isolation, I absolutely adored it; playing with the local urchins on the farms and in the fields, re-enacting ancient battles as we scaled the mount on which the Norman keep had been sited, using stout branches freshly torn from trees to put the keep's infant defenders to rout.

I regularly walked through the fields with my collie, and watched her chase hare after hare. In our five years there she never actually caught a single one, even though she was fast enough to keep pace with the hare's top speed of 35 mph. They were always more nimble than Susie; changing direction and even doing u-turns in an instant to outflank her. I adored Susie and I adored the hares: both wonderfully made. Though the hounds billeted at East Moors' old school house were wonderfully made too, I hoped they had no better luck than my faithful pet, and that all the beautiful hares and foxes they chased managed to outrun them.

Chapter Ten

Bidding East Moors and all my Aughton memories goodbye, I scissored my legs once again as I cycled through the ford, and then zigzagged from left verge to right verge as I lumbered up the punishing hill. At the peak I turned right onto a track that followed the ridge, with Bransdale and then Bilsdale a glorious panorama spread out to my right. The track rose out of the forest onto the open grouse moor, with the birds taking flight as I approached, shrieking their protest with their distinctive rattling cry. I had to resist looking at the view and instead held onto the handlebars for dear life as I pedalled through pool after pool of standing black water, deep and peaty. It was slow progress, and several times I was forced to put my foot down in the middle of a pool to steady myself, drenching my socks and trouser turn-ups.

I blame my tiny school at Bubwith (village of the infamous telephone exchange, three miles from Aughton) for sowing deep within me a lifetime's obsession with lonely, cold and wet journeys through wild places. We had the most fantastic, inspiring head teacher – a guy called Roy Nixon. He was a polymath who seemed to have all the time in the world to explain stuff to you and stretch your infant knowledge. He was particularly kind to me; I was a painfully shy child who could hardly string two words together, and he really drew me out of my shell and taught me to speak in sentences.

One assembly he staged a real coup. Even though we were only ninety-six strong, and Bubwith was miles away from anywhere, our innovative head managed to host a visit from a man called Green – the last surviving member of Shackleton's Antarctic Expedition of 1914–17. This Ancient of Days, well into his eighties, decked in a moth-eaten woolly jumper which smelt strongly of fish, showed us his glass slides on his magic lantern: their ship the *Endurance* crushed by pack ice and sinking; the bleak Polar landscape where they sheltered beneath upturned lifeboats for five months, surviving on a diet of penguin and seaweed; the inhospitable cliffs of South Georgia, which Shackleton and five others had to scale before they could summon rescue. But more than those pictures, I recall his haunting tale of how every time they did a head count, they always felt there was one more member in addition to their crew of twenty-nine. I guess it primed me for a lifetime feeling there was an extra person walking beside me.

After Mr Green had gone, Mr Nixon seemed more concerned about his journey to us rather than his epic crossing of the Antarctic fifty years previously.

'He absolutely insisted on coming all the way from Hull on public transport, struggling with his magic lantern and heavy glass slides,' he confided to me afterwards. 'I'd offered to pick him up, but he'd have none of it. Absolutely incredible!'

Although I said nothing at the time, I did wonder that if someone had rowed 800 miles across the frozen Southern Ocean, then perhaps even a thirty-mile bus journey from darkest Hull would hold no fears.

After thirty gruelling minutes chancing it as an amphibian

vehicle – Shackleton would have been proud of me – I reached the Surprise View I'd visited with Father Bert the day before. I then sped southwards down the welcome tarmac of the B road for a couple of miles before taking a sharp right to shoot down Rievaulx Bank. Clinging to the side of the dark wooded hill was my final destination of the day; a tiny little church which in medieval times had served as a slipper chapel for Rievaulx Abbey – the place where pilgrims would remove their shoes before walking the final hundred yards barefoot.

The church had a steep, stone-tiled roof. As I walked towards the door, there was a loud rumbling as one large tile noisily slid off and impaled itself into the ground, just feet away from me. I felt a bit queasy as I realized that this instant gravestone could have been mine.

'They're always doing that!' an old chap, who had followed me up the path with his wife, calmly explained, as if it were nothing more lethal than a falling conker, rather than ten kilos of sharpened stone. 'When they restored the place in 1907, they attached the tiles to the rafters with oak pegs, which have rotted long since. It's only moss and friction which keeps 'em in place now.'

Frank chatted on for the entire hour – I had long since abandoned hope of any silence. He had a large grey and chrome-yellow moustache, and a set of false teeth which seemed to have a life of their own, moving on a horizontal plane whilst his lips moved on a vertical one. His lean frame was covered by a thin gabardine coat, the colour long since faded, with a piece of twine serving as a belt. His wife, whom he strangely addressed throughout as 'mother', was portly and flushed-face, and was heavily cardiganed – a wise precaution in this chilly church on a chilly autumn afternoon. They lived in an old cottage in the abbey's shadow, and all his life Frank had worked as a shepherd. When the monks arrived in the twelfth century, they'd used sheep to civilize the wilderness and the subsequent wool trade made the abbey prosperous. The monks had long since gone, but the sheep and shepherds remained.

Frank walked the hills in his thin gabardine in all seasons, literally watching his flocks by night.

'Ee, Vicar, spring is the sharpest time – those east winds blowing in from t' North Sea cut through you like ice. You have to be out and about though, cos it's lambing time, and there's always some ewe who'll bed down on top o' moors, but then can't get her lamb out. Then's when I have to spring into action.'

Frank must have been knocking eighty, so the prospect of him springing into action seemed quite something. 'Most of the time, I'm just walking the hills, watching and waiting, singing the psalms the nuns taught us at school.'

He immediately piped up with the Twenty-third Psalm, 'The Lord is My Shepherd', occasionally hitting the right note in the midst of a fair few sharps and flats. I wondered if David, the shepherd boy who became king, ever imagined his psalms being sung in these far-away hills three thousand years on.

Frank's other big thing was a prisoner of war from Bavaria named Max. Like many POWs, Max had opted to work on the land, and had helped Frank with his shepherding. For three years of his life Frank had not walked the hills alone, but had had a companion by his side, learning each other's language, singing each other's songs. Frank suddenly launched into song again, a famous German tongue-twister:

Heut kommt der Hans zu mir,
Freut sich die Lies.
Ob er aber über Oberammergau,
Oder aber über Unterammergau,
Oder aber überhaupt nicht kommt,
Ist nicht ge wiss.

Again, his elderly voice strained to reach the right notes. There were tears in his eyes.

'He was a fine fellow, very artistic, such delicate hands. He was brilliant with the difficult births; gentle, able to get in to places I couldn't reach with my clumsy hands, ease the lamb out. I've lost a fair few lambs since.'

'Don't take on, dad,' his wife chimed in, putting her arm around him. 'They were so close, Vicar, him and Max, but they've kept in touch. We holiday every year on his farm in Bavaria, then he returns t' compliment and stays with us. You must visit us and have a look at all the delicate tapestries he's done for us; the Alps, Bavarian villages, Oberammergau . . .'

Frank sang the refrain again and then broke off. 'Max took us to the Passion plays there one year, the day they staged the crucifixion. It was done very simply, with no fuss. The cross was lying flat out on t' stage and the villager playing Jesus just laid down on top of it. Then you heard the sound of nails being hammered in. Imagine hearing that sound ringing out from every speaker. There was absolute silence in the auditorium except for some of the women sobbing. Ee, the men weren't far off crying either.'

I cycled back up Rievaulx Bank, so steep that I had to breathe in frantic gulp after frantic gulp of air to provide enough oxygen for my pounding heart. The day hadn't quite gone to plan, with silent cycle rides rather than silent churches; even so, there was a definite holiness in chatter such as Frank's, a David making lonely hills alive with the sound of his psalms, and finding his Jonathan.

After a rapid and bracing descent into Helmsley, I parked my bike outside Canons Garth, popping in to church to end the day, as I ended every day, with Evening Prayer, before locking the place up for the night, just in case those buried in its vaults made a bid for freedom. Just one person joined me, Derek, who was profoundly deaf. He was clearly a jack-of-all-trades, preparing the place for worship, clearing up afterwards; a care-taker-cum-odd-job-man who made sure things were decent and spic and span. Well into his sixties, he had a muscular build, yet his movements were graceful, his voice soft, asking me about my day, gazing at me intently and carefully reading my lips as I made reply, quite a normal conversation. He laughed when I told him about Eva's grandstand performance at Carlton.

'Before the deafness set in, I was the local postie, walking just about the same route you've cycled today. In those days Eva had the farm close to East Moors Church – there was always a kettle singing on the range, a cuppa and a piece of cake to set me on my way. There was this one time when I was shadowed on my route by a time-and-motion wallah from York. He raised his eyebrows at stopping for a cuppa. But after another six miles tramping the moors from Bransdale to Bilsdale, he'd changed his tune. I reckon he wished he'd lingered for a second cup!'

Derek was a mine of information. Eva had been educated at the little school house at East Moors; a bright pupil at a bright school. With only a handful of pupils drawn from the dwindling population of the moors, its roll was boosted in wartime by a couple of dozen evacuees from Middlesbrough, initially billeted in the church. But the children's new surroundings didn't quite give them the peace they'd hoped for, as Derek explained: 'The Luftwaffe had been bombing the yards and steelworks on the Tees every night, so the children came to escape it, but the very day they arrived, the RAF had had target practice on the moor and had set the heather alight. That night the Luftwaffe mistook the heather fires for the Middlesbrough furnaces, and dropped their bombs over East Moors. No one was hurt, just the odd sheep was fried, but the Middlesbrough kids were in a right state, with Eva and the other older girls doing their best to calm them.'

The evacuees didn't stay long after that inauspicious start. Without them the little school was unsustainable and closed in 1944, so Eva moved for her final school year to Lady Feversham's School in Helmsley. It seems they didn't know what to do with her – she was brighter than the teachers, let alone the pupils – so she spent that year outside, trimming the huge beech hedge which encircled the school, cementing the deep love of the outdoors which had been fostered at East Moors and which never left her.

I bade Derek a carefully annunciated farewell and returned home to admire the freshly plastered ceiling. Our youngest daughter, Clare, was missing her friends from Bishopthorpe, so Rachel had cooked her favourite tea – sausage, baked beans and chips – to cheer her up. It cheered me up too, after my twenty or so miles, rising and falling some 3000 feet. The girls chattered on, as was their wont, and I simply listened to them fondly. 'Poor Dad,' Hannah piped up, 'we must be a bit of a shock after all those hours of silence!'

If only . . .

Chapter Eleven

I'd decided to take time out from ancient vicarages and equally ancient churches and visit Ryedale School, the local comprehensive which I'd first encountered en tour with the Archbishop the previous summer. It drew most of its pupils from Helmsley and Kirkbymoorside (another moorside market town seven miles to the east of Helmsley) and had been built in 1952 adjacent to a railway station on the edge of a tiny village, which was a mid-point between the two towns. The cunning plan that most of the children would be able to travel there by rail was thwarted by the closure of the branch line just a year after the school was built.

I'd booked myself in to take assembly. Our eldest daughter, Ruth, had just started at the school, but was amazingly relaxed about her street-cred being undermined by her dad making a fool of himself before all her new friends. With my legs still aching after the cyclothon the day before, I set off just before Ruth caught the school bus, cycling along the undulating A road that skirted the foot of the moors. The land rose sharply to my left, where combine harvester after combine harvester struggled with an almost vertical ascent up the steep moorside, gathering the golden corn. Ancient school buses inched past me, belching out blue palls of diesel exhaust, and a series of HGVs, hurtling towards Helmsley, rocked my bike as they sped past.

The heavy traffic made me a bit nervous and caused flashbacks to an incident in 1970, shortly after my father had moved from Aughton to his new post in Scarborough. Running across the road to catch the school bus, I was hit by a motorbike and took two days to come round in Scarborough Hospital. By then it was a Sunday and the Salvation Army were going around the wards loudly playing hymns for the patients – *Brassed Off* meets Kings College Choir on a bad hair day. Disorientated young me woke up to the discordant strains of 'How Great Thou Art'. I didn't feel that great with a fractured skull and broken pelvis. If this is heaven, I thought, count me out.

Shivering at the memory, I turned right off the trunk road as soon as I could and rode over an old railway crossing, with the gate and signal box still intact, up a steep hill and then through a thick forest, where the sharp smell of pine was so strong that it cleared my lungs and made my eyes smart.

Suddenly, the forest cleared and beneath me sprawled the school, there in the middle of nowhere. The red-roofed, two-storey building spread out for 200 yards; a sea of glass facing south and catching the sun, set in acres of playing fields. As I cycled up, I realized the view was an education in itself, with the fierce moors sharply rising to the north and the gentler wolds to the south.

I walked through the main entrance at five to nine as the pupils were streaming into the school hall. At the entrance to the hall a small man with blond hair, blond bushy eyebrows and piercing blue eyes hovered in the alcove, his face taut with tension. 'Tuck that shirt in, do that tie up,' he barked.

Sleepy-eyed, thickset lads went through the motions, notion-ally tightening their ties only to loosen them again as soon as they were out of the tense man's gaze. Something stirred in the back of my mind from our previous visit; the fierce little man was the head teacher.

'Hallo, I'm David,' I said to the Head, self-consciously checking my own black shirt was tucked in as I did so. 'Thanks for letting me take assembly. I so enjoyed my visit with the Archbishop last year.'

'Take that earring out!' he shouted, over my shoulder. The effect was so terrifying that I felt my ear lobes for any offend-ing jewellery. He looked me up and down, as if checking out my uniform. No problems with the tie, since I was sporting a dog collar. 'We'll make sure we translate the Latin correctly this time,' he quipped, before barking at a surly youth for having his shoelaces untied.

All this fierce discipline made me zone out, and I travelled back in time to my first ever assembly as a visiting curate, barely days after starting in my first post in Middlesbrough. I had moved into a furnished bungalow, owned by a certain Miss Dobson, who – as well as being a leading light in my new church – was the headmistress of a primary school in the roughest part of town. In lieu of rent, she insisted that I lead an assembly. To be honest, I was hoping to leave it a bit before shy old me first ventured into schools, but Miss Dobson was the sort of headmistress who brooked no refusal. So against my better judgement I found myself sitting at the front of the hall, shaking. They all marched in under Miss Dobson's eagle eye, backs ramrod straight, arms swinging by their sides – and that was just the teachers!

My assembly was quite simple, as assemblies go. Just a bag

of crisps, which I invited some of the 250 children to sample and guess the flavour. *Salt and vinegar?* No. *Cheese and onion?* No. *Plain?* No. They all looked puzzled, because there weren't really any other flavours around in those benighted days before Gary Lineker had taken the crisp world by storm. 'The flavour is fish and bread,' I boldly proclaimed. My infant audience looked even more perplexed. My point, of course, was simple. Jesus had fed an audience twenty times as big as mine with the equivalent of my bag of crisps. To hammer home my point, I taught the children a Victorian hymn, which in my nervousness I crooned (or rather croaked) like Elvis Presley:

With two little fishes and five loaves of bread,
five thousand people by Jesus were fed.
All of this happened because one little lad,
gladly gave Jesus all that he had.
All that I have, all that I have, I will give Jesus all
that I have.

I then bade them all a hurried farewell and got out while the going was good, speeding away in my Simca 1100; a miracle in itself, since the words 'speeding' and 'Simca 1100' didn't usually occur in the same sentence.

'Stop running, Debbie!' the Head screamed at a late-comer, forcing me to return to the present. A scruffy, bearded man sauntered through the main door, hair ruffled, wearing a baggy woollen jumper and muddy corduroy trousers. 'Morning, chaps,' he said, before shuffling down the corridor, walking against the flow of pupils funnelling into the hall.

'Who's that?' I asked, thinking it was perhaps the

groundsman – someone less likely to be on message with the Head's high standard of dress code and behaviour.

'Oh, that's Fraser,' the Head replied. 'He's a geography teacher and Head of Humanities, we'll catch up with him later.' The flow of pupils subsided to a trickle and we walked into the hall.

'Please stand!' the Head boomed. You could hear a pin drop as we marched down the central aisle, the eyes of 350 teenagers staring to the front. As the Head and I mounted the stage, I got that familiar feeling in the pit of my stomach; not the odd flutter, but as if the whole of the Natural History Museum's Butterfly House had been re-sited in my lower abdomen. I had been doing this sort of thing for fifteen years, but every time, without fail, I found taking an assembly in a secondary school a near-death experience.

The Head briefly introduced me and then I was on, face-forward, with 700 teenage eyes boring into me.

'Good morning,' I squawked in a voice an octave above its normal pitch. 'I know you've probably never done this before, but I've brought along a banana and I want you to insult it.'

I took a banana out of my case and held it up high, noticing out of the corner of my eye that the Head was giving me a pitying look. I decided to bring him on board, so got him to hold up the banana whilst I continued. 'I realize you might be a bit shy, or not able to come up with the right words, so I've brought a few suggestions and I want you to shout them out,' I explained. One by one I fished a series of cards out of my case, on which I'd felt-tipped things like 'You're yellow', 'You're spotty' and 'You're bent'. The tightly disciplined pupils took a fair bit of encouragement before they yelled them out, but they got there eventually.

The original idea for this assembly wasn't mine – I'd heard second-hand how an elderly woman priest had tried it at a secondary school in a rough part of Middlesbrough. When she'd invited the unruly mob before her to fling insults at the banana she quiveringly held in front of her, oblivious to the phallic symbolism, she'd got considerably more than she bargained for. I'd honed the assembly, warding off the four-letter expletives that had assailed her by inscribing insults on cards beforehand.

I carefully examined the banana, which the Head was still holding. 'Well, you've hurled all those insults at it, but it doesn't seem to have affected it much. Mr Jenkinson, would you like to peel it, just to check?'

By this time Mr Jenkinson was getting jumpy about being my stooge, so decided to take a different tack.

'I think it would be a good idea to be a bit more interactive, so let's get a volunteer from Year Eleven. Anyone like to help the Vicar?' he asked, peering at the audience. No one so much as blinked, let alone moved. 'Tracy,' the Head called to a blonde-haired girl skulking on the back row, 'come up here and help the Vicar!'

A sixteen-year-old girl sauntered down the aisle, her hips swaying. 'Tuck that blouse in!' the Head roared as she climbed the steps onto the stage. I felt sorry for the girl, forced to adjust her dress before 349 pairs of staring adolescent eyes. 'Tracy, peel this banana to check it's OK,' the Head commanded, taking over my lines.

He realized his mistake as soon as he handed over the banana. Tracy, none too pleased at being hauled out of her seat and doubly miffed at having to adjust her blouse, decided to wreak her revenge. Giving a dark smile, and flashing her eyelids demurely, she held the banana firmly in her left hand and with her right hand slowly and tantalizingly drew the skin down, a millimetre at a time. Several Year 11 boys on the back row – and quite a few Year 10, Year 9 and even Year 8 boys – looked highly flushed and stared blankly ahead, or closed their eyes, or suddenly started studying their footwear. Her staged performance somewhat stole my show, because when she finally peeled the thing, half of the audience were oblivious to the big reveal: rather than staying intact, the inside of the banana all fell out onto the floor, in pre-cut slices.

'Did you see that,' I shouted, all too aware that by this stage half the audience weren't seeing anything, 'After all our insults, the banana looked fine on the outside, but inside it was all cut up. Next time you insult someone, remember that. They might look fine outside, but inside they are all cut up.'

Despite the unexpected turn, my assembly had been short and sweet.

The Head then waffled on about the results of a rugby match with some neighbouring school, followed by his deputy confusing us all about which bus to catch where in order to get home. We marched out and stood by the hall door. A young woman teacher gave me a broad smile, 'You're different, not like all the other clerics we've had in, who've bored us stiff!' she said with typical Yorkshire directness, oblivious to the Head's eyes boring into her. 'Tell me, how did you do it?'

I took her aside and whispered my secret to her, 'I got a needle, pierced the skin at several different points and then moved the needle around to slice through the inside. It's a bit like keyhole surgery.'

'Brilliant, utterly brilliant,' she laughed. 'But thank God

you didn't get Tracy to do the piercing – we'd have had to carry out several lads on a stretcher!'

Whilst the Head continued his survey of errant ties and shirt tails, I moved over to the reception desk and chatted to the secretary. I'd noticed her before the assembly, and the motherly way she had been dealing with all the children who had wandered over – returning their lost property, lending them a tie because, when rushing to get dressed at some unearthly hour, they had absent-mindedly forgotten to put one on. I recalled the school secretaries from my youth, who would have put the fear of God into God, and simply thanked her for not being like them.

'You've obviously got a mother's touch,' I said. 'How many children do you have?'

'Just one boy,' she replied, her eyes filling with tears.

I realized I'd put my foot in it as she told me how her other son had suddenly died just after Christmas – massive heart-failure whilst playing football. We were separated by a glass screen and the whole school was parading just a few feet away from us; not the best conditions for a highly sensitive pastoral encounter. I simply said how very sorry I was for her, let her tell me about her son – an old boy of the school – and his final, fatal day on 28 December. It was a terrible, terrible loss at any time of the year, let alone at Christmas.

The secretary's grief reminded me of sharp losses in my own life and ministry. Rachel and I had been married for just over a year when she fell pregnant. We were both so thrilled that we shouted the news from the roof tops, and our family and the whole parish rejoiced with us. Rachel's father, step-mother and two brothers were coming to stay with us for Christmas, with Miss Dobson, now retired, joining us on

Christmas Day to keep us all in order. With Rachel blooming in the first trimester of pregnancy, it was set to be the most joyous of times.

Then, just before Christmas, twelve weeks in, she had a miscarriage. It happens a lot at that stage, apparently, with one in four pregnancies miscarrying in the first three months. We didn't know that then, and whenever life turns to death it still hurts, whether it happens to billions or just dozens. Thirty years on, the images are still sharp. Waiting for the ambulance, Rachel so brave, blood everywhere, her school's deputy head ringing up to ask if she had a lesson plan for the day. Then, before she was rushed into theatre, praying with her the loveliest prayer from the Book of Common Prayer:

> *Unto God's gracious mercy and protection*
> *we commit thee. The Lord bless thee, and*
> *keep thee.*
> *The Lord make his face to shine upon thee,*
> *and be gracious unto thee.*
> *The Lord lift up his countenance upon thee,*
> *and give thee peace, both now and*
> *evermore. Amen.*

In any situation, I can never pray that prayer without tears coming into my eyes. Miss Dobson had joined us in the hospital, just to keep us steady, as well as regimenting all the staff, who clearly didn't meet her highest of standards. Rachel came home the next day. Though I felt utterly useless, I put vases of her favourite freesias in every room.

It was to prove the strangest Christmas, celebrating the ultimate birth when we no longer had a birth to look forward to. A few people called around; most didn't. Most of the clergy who called were hopeless; of the 'better luck next time' school. My elderly Lay Reader brought a lovely bunch of flowers, but was hardly able to say anything, his eyes full of tears. A very tough lad in the top class at primary school, who invariably talked to me after I'd taken an assembly and who had started coming to church, stood on our doorstep hopping from one leg to the other, with a bunch of carnations in his hand. 'My mum sent these for your wife, and hopes she soon gets over her troubles,' he managed to blurt out, before making a hasty retreat. He was called Peter Kermode, but not a single pupil or teacher ever once mocked his surname, because he was such a toughie.

Sometimes, though, the Lord gives rather than takes away. Our GP in Monk Fryston once tipped me off about an expectant mother who lived near the church, who was very ill with pneumonia. Because of her pregnancy, he couldn't prescribe the strong antibiotics necessary, so he had to let the illness take its course, fearing that both mother and child wouldn't survive the night. I called around just before 11 p.m. The door to the house wasn't locked, so I walked in, and was accosted by an au pair who had little English. I guess she originated from a Catholic country, because when she saw my dog collar her eyes lit up. 'You want my mistress? I will take you to her.'

She led me up the stairs and there, in a large and draughty bedroom, lay her mistress, sweating profusely despite the cold night, writhing in her bed, rambling and delirious. I simply sat by the bedside, held on to her hand whilst she tossed and turned, and prayed for her and her unborn child. Realizing there was little else I could do, I stayed for a few minutes longer and left. I bumped into the GP the next day. 'The fever broke early this morning, she'll be fine,' he told me, smiling from ear to ear.

I suddenly came to, realizing I had shared too long a silence with the grieving secretary. 'Did you know your son died on Holy Innocents' Day?' I blurted out, as if she was an expert on the intricacies of the Church calendar. I was clutching at straws, desperate to say something, when actually my sympathetic silence had been more appropriate.

'No, I didn't know that,' the secretary softly replied. 'What's special about the day?'

'It's when we remember all the innocent children Herod massacred when he tried to do away with Jesus. I always celebrate Communion on that day, so will always remember your son from now on.'

It was well-meant, but I am aware I always come out with such trivia in the face of utter grief – when you can do nothing to bring back the love of someone's life. God bless her: she smiled and looked grateful. And I suddenly realized she wasn't wasting the love she could no longer give her son, or letting it eat her away; she was pouring it out here, soothing kids that missed Mum.

The Head and I popped into one or two lessons. The first was a German lesson led by the young teacher who had complimented me on my assembly, who seemed a bit nervy after the Head and I invaded her class. I had done German O Level, so could just about remember how to pronounce things. I mentioned the Oberammergau tongue-twister Frank had sung to me the day before; the class knew it, and sang it to me, a sea of treble voices more in tune than Frank's. Then on to a geography lesson led by Fraser, who wasn't in the least fazed by our presence. He was talking to the class about the flock of sheep he kept in his spare time, getting up early in the morning to feed them before he sauntered into school.

'You see, they don't take much looking after, cos they're 'efted, 'efted to local hills.'

'What does hefted mean, sir?' a pupil asked, less Yorkshire than his teacher.

'Well, they're 'ardwired with knowledge of t' local terrain. It passes through the genes, from ewe to lamb. Intuitively, they know every nook and cranny, good pasture and barren ground, safe shelter and treacherous spots. It only works in a small area, take 'em to another hill, another valley, and they're totally lost. But keep them in t' place they're 'efted to, and they virtually look after themselves. Frees me to come teach you lot!'

The class was focused and attentive; not a single child was playing up. Most of the kids' families would be involved with work on the land in one way or another, and clearly Fraser addressed their condition, deep speaking unto deep. A hefted teacher. As I cycled back home I wondered how long it would take for me to become a hefted vicar.

Chapter Twelve

Though Helmsley had been on my horizon for pretty well all of my life, and was gorgeous in every compass direction, such faraway places can take a bit of settling into. The ancient vicarage needed a lot of sorting, and though I enjoyed practical jobs, I was primarily a priest rather than a builder or a carpenter. And most of the folk were so old – certainly old enough to be my parents, if not my grandparents – and were pretty set in their tried and tested ways. I could see from the look in their eyes they were thinking, 'Who does this youngster think he is?'. When Goliath saw David, the ruddy-faced young shepherd, running towards him whirling his sling, the First Book of Samuel tells us that Goliath despised him for he was but a youth. Call me paranoid, but I feared Helmsley's Goliaths despised me, another youthful David, for similar reasons. I took comfort that one day my stone would come . . .

In theory, cycling back to Helmsley along the former railway line should have made me feel a bit hefted, tracing the path of ancient steam trains that had daily supplied this part of the world before the advent of motor transport. In the event, I didn't do much cycling, because the line was blocked with farm gates and fences and overgrown with briars and thickets which tore my skin as I battled through, my heavy bike across my shoulder. The line was laid on the bed of an ice-age lake; Lake Pickering. In prehistoric times it would have been Yorkshire's own Lake Windermere; its waters lapping against the moors to the north and the wolds to the south, with an ice sheet to the east neatly delaying the waters' escape to the North Sea. Lake Pickering had long since dried up, but it formed a flat respite for settlements like Pickering, Kirkbymoorside, Helmsley and numerous villages to flourish without having to cling to too many hillsides. When I wasn't wrestling with thorns, the views to the right and left were fantastic. The railway bridges over the River Riccall and beneath various country lanes were fantastic too; beautifully fashioned arches of stone waiting for the moment the odd vicar passed by, now the trains were long since gone.

The former track led into the eastern side of Helmsley, which boasted a newly built development of affordable and luxury housing. Local stalwarts, whose pinnacle of daily pleasure amounted to watching *Countdown*, fantasized that east Helmsley was a den of vice, pedalling prostitution and drugs. Actually, it looked quite smart, and it was me who lowered the tone; muddy and scratched and with more than the odd bit of bramble hanging in my hair and clothing.

But I suppose dens of vice don't really get going until later in the day, and often retain a respectable front. I recalled my one and only visit to a brothel, in the early days of my ministry in Middlesbrough. I was visiting families who'd put in a request to have their baby christened, with one visit in an overspill estate. The inhabitants of downtown Middlesbrough had been transported out there in the 1970s when their homes were demolished to make way for a shopping centre. They were none too thrilled to be uprooted from what had been a very close and thriving community and their understandable ire fuelled the estate's already very rough reputation. I knocked on the door of an ordinary-looking house, which was answered by an elegant young girl in a dressing gown who giggled when she saw my clerical collar.

'I've come to see Maria about her baby's baptism,' I stuttered, and was shown into a very exotic lounge; the walls festooned with some very strange pictures. I waited and waited and waited for the mother, whom I realize now was otherwise engaged (at the time, as a naive young curate I hadn't a clue what was going on there). Eventually, Maria appeared, looking very flushed, and we talked about the baptism, the water symbolizing that God is for life and that God loves her baby from day one.

We used to have baptisms during the parish Eucharist, and she came along with her baby and the other scantily clad girls and cheerily filled a pew. The rest of the rather posh congregation looked down their noses at them, not used to young women entering their hallowed confines and liberally displaying their charms. I did the usual follow-up visit, taking a baptism card and a bible as a gift from the church, but for obvious reasons didn't visit the address again. As I cycled around the estate in the months to come, I used to see her pushing her baby in a pram and the other girls pushing other things, and there would be a friendly wave, a friendly conversation. Given the congregation's distinctly cool reception, I felt they deserved a medal for having anything whatsoever to do with us.

Cycling down Bondgate, I was jolted out of my latest wander down memory lane by a stocky old chap, with a full head of greying hair, standing smack in the middle of the busy road, tottering from side to side as he waved his stick at passing vehicles. He spat out expletives in what I guessed was some Eastern European language – either that, or I really had had a very sheltered upbringing. I veered towards him, got off my bike and walked him to the kerb, the traffic hooting at us impatiently. He waved his stick at them again, 'You are vorse than the Nazis, trying to run Tadeusz Dzierzek down!'

'Where do you live, sir?' I gently asked, trying to calm him down.

'Elmslac Road, number forty-two,' he replied.

I roughly knew where it was; a post-war estate of nicely built houses to the north of Helmlsey, about half a mile away. 'I was going that way myself,' I lied. 'Let me walk with you.'

We walked up Black Swan Lane, a narrow street squeezed between the Black Swan and Crown hotels. As we walked, boy did Ted talk. 'I realize from your accent that, like me, you don't come from round here,' was my conversation starter, which opened the floodgates, as he poured out his life story. He was very fluent and his words had a well-rehearsed air; I guess this was by no means the first time he had told his story, and that I was the latest victim of this moorland Ancient Mariner's tale. He had grown up somewhere in Poland – I'd asked him to repeat the name three times, but I couldn't get my tongue around it. I didn't risk asking him a fourth time – his eyes had blazed with fire at my interrupting his monologue at all, and the stout stick he had waved so threateningly at passing motorists was a bit too close for comfort. At the tender age of fifteen he'd joined the Free Polish Army, trained as a cook, been captured by the Nazis and had been harshly treated along with other Slavs, imprisoned deep in the heart of Germany. Eventually they were liberated when American bombs breached the prison walls, enabling Ted and his Polish comrades to swim across the Rhine to freedom.

'Ve ver down to skin and bone, nearly done for,' he said. 'Ve slept for two whole days in an American field hospital, where they nursed us back to health, inch by inch. I picked up the lingo pretty quick, so the Americans appointed me shop steward of my fellow Poles; a kind ov between-go.'

'Go-between,' I corrected.

'Yes, that's vot I said,' he snapped.

'The Ruskies had taken over my country by then, so I had no vish to return.' He stopped and spat as he said the word Ruskies. In fact, he was doing a lot of stopping as he told his tale. I realized this was going to be a very long walk. 'The Americans liked me,' he continued, 'gave me the option of repatriation either in the USA or the UK. I opted for the UK, because it vos a lot nearer my homeland, and also because you had stood vith us vhen the rest of the vorld turned a blind eye.'

He had found work on the Isle of Skye, of all places, working in forestry, as well as keeping his hand in as a chef. Work brought him south to Helmsley, where there were saw mills galore. Here he'd found Annie, driving tractors around Duncombe Park's Waterloo Forestry Plantation. 'She started doing that in the Var, and carried on. It vas love at first sight, but I never thought I'd end up marrying a tractor driver!' Ted informed me, with a merry twinkle in his eye. They'd settled down, initially living on her parents' farm by the very same ford at East Moors I had splashed the day before.

'Vhen the children came along I gathered rushes by the ford and made them hats, the Polish way. Then ve moved to

Helmsley, but we kept returning, for picnics and rush hats too!' He smiled.

He was very proud that he'd worked as chef at the prestigious Black Swan for thirty-three years. His culinary skills were ahead of his time, 'My smoked garlic sausage vos legendary,' he proclaimed. Apparently he had smoked it in his back garden, oblivious to his neighbours' complaints about the continuous blue plume of smoke which hovered over their gardens and soaked into the walls of their homes. His life's high point had clearly been when Prince Stash Radziwiłł – 'the best king Poland never had' – had stayed at the Black Swan and had come to Elmslac Road to have tea with his compatriot, his chauffeur-driven Rolls turning every head in Helmsley. Walking with a bramble-scarred vicar pushing his bike, albeit at a stately pace, didn't have quite the same effect.

His wife, Annie, spotted us approaching their home and rushed out to check all was well. She looked a bit like Beatrix Potter's Mrs Tiggy-Winkle, without the prickles. Though she was bell-shaped and carrying a bit of weight, her quick movements exuded a sense of busy-ness. She was wearing the loveliest cotton summer dress, with a large floral print that blended nicely with the Michaelmas daisies that festooned their immaculate little garden. Her face was round and full; flushed cheeks, a broad, friendly welcoming smile. But there were worry-lines around her eyes, betraying her relief that soldier Ted had returned home safely from his wanderings.

'Don't fuss, voman,' Ted teased, warmly embracing her. 'I just thought I'd bring Father David home and treat him to the same tea I gave Prince Stash!'

I sat in Annie and Ted's kitchen and drank a glass of weak black tea, to which Ted had added a generous slug of vodka.

Annie had already started rustling up some lunch, and Ted the chef took over. Annie told me how, when he was working, Ted raced between The Black Swan and home, cooking at both places every day, even on Christmas Day. 'None of this convenience muck, mind,' she added. 'He can make the most delicious stew with the broken pheasants the shooters don't want to take home to their fine ladies.'

Incredibly, they had raised eight children in this small house, never resorting to 'convenience muck', with fish fingers and even Heinz tomato ketchup strictly forbidden.

As I left I admired an ancient bull-nosed Morris Oxford parked up in the drive. 'That's served us vell,' Ted said, stroking the bonnet. He told me of a trip to Poland in 1963, crossing the Iron Curtain, with tins of food and tin-openers and LPs and stuff hidden in the boot beneath blankets. Essentials to us; luxuries for his deprived countrymen.

'Ve came back with gorgeous glassware, and goose feathers so Annie could make eiderdowns to keep us varm in your terrible vinters, like the von ve had in '63.' Ted showed me the passenger door, badly pock-marked. 'Look at that, they shot at us, my own countrymen, as ve vere crossing the border, they couldn't even bear goose feathers being smuggled out to the West. Pah!' He spat on the ground, showing his utter contempt for those who had become communist lackeys.

'Ah, ve had such sad times, such happy times vith this car,' he continued, his mood brightening. 'Vhen the kids had their summer holidays, we used to rise at four a.m. and Annie and our eight children sqveezed into this little car. Ve reached Scarborough by dawn, with the red sun rising over the sea ahead of us. Ve had our pick of the freshest seafood from the fish market by the harbour. So much more succulent than fish fingers! Mark my words, David, keep clear of all this processed food – absolute muck and so very bad for you.'

Chapter Thirteen

Rachel had cooked fish fingers, oven chips and frozen peas for lunch. As I munched my meal rather shamefacedly, I told Rachel Ted's story. By coincidence, that morning she'd had a 'welcome to your new home' card from Pessy, her former neighbour in Sheffield who now lived in Israel. Pessy's story was as remarkable as Ted's.

'So remind me, where was she living to start with?' I asked Rachel, as I dipped my third fish finger in a pool of Heinz tomato ketchup, trying not to think about what Ted would say.

'They lived in Leipzig, but they got out sharpish when Nazi stormtroopers started rampaging through the town on Kristallnacht in 1938,' Rachel replied, with all the precision of a history teacher. 'Pessy must have been only two or three at the time, but she has very strong memories of hiding with her mother and father in a neighbour's cupboard, with the stormtroopers banging on the door, wanting to know where the Markiewiczes were. The neighbour risked her own life sheltering them, and then bravely squared up to the stormtroopers: "Oh, the Markiewiczes left here ages ago. *Gute Nacht, meine Herren.*" I think the neighbour couldn't bear the thought of the little girl being taken. Whilst all this was going on, Pessy remembers her mother quietening her and whispering in her ear, "*Shh, shh, mein Liebling!*"'

It sounded like something from *The Sound of Music*, with Maria shushing little Martha when they were playing hide and seek with the Nazis in the nunnery. 'So how did they get out?' I asked, crunching my fourth fish finger.

'Pessy's mother wrapped her in a shawl, sat on the front of a hay wagon, and they pretended they were the waggoner's wife and daughter. The waggoner had been well-paid by Pessy's father, and he took them all the way across Germany and they even managed to fool the border guards and crossed over into Belgium. They lived in Antwerp for a while – Pessy's dad was an international fur trader, so easily found work. But then, when invasion threatened, they had to flee again.'

Rachel told me how Pessy had been set on her dad's shoulders, walking tall, remembering for the rest of her life the sorry stream of refugees. They slept where they could. One night they were sleeping in a barn by an airfield, when her father woke up his wife and daughter. 'We must go,' he had ordered.

'Not so fast, not so fast, the child is sleeping,' Pessy's mother had protested.

'No, we have to go now,' her father had insisted.

'I think he'd had some sort of premonition, maybe a dream from God,' Rachel explained. 'As they looked back to the barn they'd left only minutes before, they saw it blown to smithereens by Nazi Stukas.'

The next part of their story revealed how their flight continued, following the direction of the arrows in the opening sequence of *Dad's Army*. They ended up stranded on the Dunkirk beaches, where the British Expeditionary Force was making a hasty retreat. Pessy's mother approached a British captain. 'Take us with you,' she had begged.

'Madam, it is simply not possible,' he had replied, 'we have to give priority to our British soldiers.'

The troops were already packed like sardines onto the boats; there was hardly any room for them, let alone civilians. But quick as a flash Pessy's mother had snatched the gun from his belt and held it desperately to her little girl's head.

'If you don't take us, I'll shoot my daughter, my husband and myself. We'd be better off dead than butchered by the Nazis.'

The captain had taken fright and said, 'Come on then, madam, come quickly,' pushing the three of them into a tiny boat. Pessy and her parents had squeezed into the boat's engine room, where Pessy was fascinated by the short, blond-haired mechanic; with bright blue eyes and weather-beaten skin, his face smeared with machine oil as he desperately tried to keep the engine ticking over.

Their troubles were far from over when they landed in England. German-speaking with no papers, they were classed as enemy aliens and interned in a camp on the Isle of Man. But somehow Pessy's uncle, who'd escaped to the USA, was contacted. He vouched for them and they were released. The family eventually ended up in Bletchley in Buckinghamshire, where they trudged around, knocking on door after door looking for lodgings, only to be turned away time after time: 'No Jews here.' And then one Gentile family took them in, renting them an attic room. Amazingly Pessy's father found work, dealing in furs in London. With his first wage he bought a pair of candlesticks so that his little family, with nothing except their precious freedom, could keep their Sabbath in the presence of the Holy One of Israel.

Having polished off the fish fingers, I tucked into a generous slice of moist chocolate cake that Rachel had baked freshly that morning. 'You've got Pessy to thank for this recipe,' she reminded me. Rachel's mother had died when she was just sixteen, her brothers fifteen and eleven, with the whole family cast into utter grief. The first to visit them was Pessy, their Jewish neighbour, bringing the most delicious chocolate cake: 'A little something to sweeten your terrible bitterness.'

The card Rachel had received from Pessy that morning hadn't just prompted memories of chocolate cake recipes, but also contained an intriguing postscript to her Exodus story, a flashback clearly prompted by our own, albeit more modest, exodus from Bishopthorpe to Helmsley. Pessy had written paragraph upon paragraph in her tiny, spidery handwriting, absent-mindedly peppered with the odd Hebrew letter. Still savouring Pessy's chocolate cake, I read how, in the early 1970s, she and her family had holidayed in the Scottish Highlands, where they caught a tiny ferry across to Iona. The particular smell of the diesel fuel triggered sharp memories from Pessy's childhood, and she asked the fresh-faced young captain if the boat had ever been further afield than the waters around Mull.

'Aye, but only once, long before my time. In 1940 it crisscrossed the English Channel to bring our lads back from Dunkirk,' he answered.

He showed Pessy a plaque beneath the mast, simply stating that the boat had seen valiant service at Dunkirk and, along with a flotilla of boats of all shapes and sizes, had plucked the British Expeditionary Force from certain death.

'Any of that original crew still around?' Pessy asked.

'Just Paddy in the engine room,' the captain replied. Pessy ventured down below and recognized a shortish man, whose skin was deeply tanned, his eyes bright blue, his hair no longer blond but white. She spontaneously threw her arms around him, profusely thanking the man who'd saved her and her family and numerous others. Not surprisingly, given all the people they'd rescued, he only had a vague memory of Pessy.

'I spent most of the time down below, nursing the engine,' he'd explained. 'I just went up on deck once at Dunkirk, our very last trip. The German army were closing in and all hell was let loose. I peered through a pair of binoculars at the Nazis on the shore. I cannae forget the look of utter black fury on their faces because we were thwarting them. Just as well that I hadn't seen that look before we embarked, or I'd have never set sail.'

I put down the letter in awe. 'And if he'd never set sail, you'd never have got the recipe for that wonderful chocolate cake! Do you think I could have another piece?' I asked, cheekily holding out my plate for more.

Rachel ruffled my hair, 'Trust you to reduce the epic of a lifetime to a piece of chocolate cake,' she laughed.

Chapter Fourteen

The sun was low in the sky as I walked down Castlegate, the beck which bisects Helmsley bubbling by my side. It was a beautiful autumn evening, the air very crisp, and the town seemed very still now that the numerous day-trippers had deserted her. I stopped by a terraced stone-built house, whose front door opened straight onto the pavement, and I was suddenly transported back thirty years to my first visit to Helmsley when we came organ-hunting. This house was a few doors down from our organ seller's, but the line of cottages, originally built by Lord Feversham in the nineteenth century to house his estate workers, all had a very similar look to them. In fact, if it wasn't for the different coloured front doors, I thought, they'd be indistinguishable.

That took me back to my Middlesbrough days, when my boss was making an urgent call by night to minister to a dying man who lived on an estate of very similar-looking bungalows. My boss, bearing a passing resemblance to Darth Vader in his black cassock and cloak, perfunctorily knocked on the back door. He then breezed straight in, as was his habit, only to surprise a young woman in a revealing negligee who had popped into her kitchen for a glass of water and got more than she bargained for. She screamed loudly. 'Sorry, luv, wrong house,' my boss shouted, as he made a hasty retreat.

You live and learn. As a parish priest I tried to visit at least twenty homes a week, but I always knocked on the door and waited respectfully on the step. Over time, as you hop up and down before front door after front door with neighbours' curtains twitching, you develop an intuition for whether someone is at home or not; telltale signs, stealthy footsteps and creaks often reveal that someone is in but avoiding you. There's a French proverb, 'God called but you were out!', which I often reflect on when people play evasion games. In Middlesbrough there was a woman I used to visit regularly, who was in the final stages of MS. There was a sign beneath her doorbell that read PLEASE RING AND BE PATIENT. She was a lovely soul who was at ease with herself, despite her failing body; definitely worth waiting for.

No need for patience on Castlegate. As soon as I knocked on the door, there was a loud barking, sounds of a scuffle and shouts of 'Down, Gus!' The door was opened by Joan, a smartly dressed lady in her seventies, sporting a crisply pleated skirt and a high-necked, starched cream blouse, with perfectly coiffured white hair. I only had a glimpse of her before she lurched to the right and disappeared inside the house.

I followed her in and realized she was trying to restrain a boisterous boxer dog, who singularly refused to be controlled as it dragged her around the room. 'Heel, Gus, heel,' Joan shrieked, tugging at his lead to no avail, as the dog pulled her through into the kitchen, leaving a sulphurous odour in his wake. Stooping to avoid banging my head on the low beams, I followed Joan, who was trying to tie the dog to a thick stainless steel rail which bordered the hob of a shiny red Aga.

After several failed attempts, she finally found a slip knot which did the trick.

'Alan's just in the garden, I'll go and fetch him,' Joan said, leaving me at Gus's mercy. Fortunately, the leather lead was thick and strong and the Aga firmly fixed, so I was safe. Even so, there was a look in Gus's eye and I made a mental note that if I was ever walking down Castlegate and saw a huge boxer bounding towards me, with an Aga bouncing behind him, then I should run for my life.

For the rest of my visit Gus tugged violently at the leash and panted more and more because of the unbearable heat of the oven, despite noisily lapping up the multiple bowls of water that Joan supplied him with. Alan came in from the garden and washed the earth off his hands in the kitchen sink, with Joan bustling around him. He was the churchwarden who had visited us on our first day, eventually leaving us with one of his prize cauliflowers as a welcome, if rather strange, house-warming present. A retired GP, as churchwarden he fulfilled an ancient office which made sure the church building and its life, worship and ministry were ordered decently. Churchwardens are canny folk, and as well as keeping the vicar up to speed with all the local gossip, they try to save the parish from the vicar's good and not-so-good intentions.

'Just wait a minute, Alan, let me move the bowl of washing-up out of the way, we don't want soil getting into the pots.'

'Stop fussing, woman,' Alan snapped. Though wearing his gardening clothes – an old shirt and a pair of worn corduroy trousers – Alan was as smart as his wife. His bearing was erect, his full head of grey curly hair immaculately groomed, his eyes steel blue, with his rimless spectacles perched on the end of his nose giving him a studious look.

There was a pot of beef shin bubbling on the hob. The smell was absolutely delicious, and between bowls of water Gus perched his front paws on the rail and tried to reach the pot. He shot back and howled as the red-hot hob scorched his nose, reverting to pulling at his lead once more. 'Ee, you're a comical dog, Gus,' Alan laughed.

The kitchen, like the front room I had briefly passed through, was cluttered with Mouseman furniture; English oak crafted with medieval tools in Mousey Thompson's workshops at nearby Kilburn, a trademark tiny mouse carved on every piece. Despite being contemporary in one sense, in that it had all been made in Joan and Alan's lifetime, every piece of furniture looked as if it had been carved in Tudor times. Alan pulled out one of the stout chairs arrayed around the equally stout table and invited me to sit down. Alan and Joan sat on two arm chairs on either side of the Aga, with Joan gazing at me intently throughout, fluttering her eyelids demurely. I looked down, shy as ever, ostensibly examining the table top. Actually it was quite interesting, not flat at all, but undulating, with ridges and furrows of oak. Mousey Thompson never used a plane but an adze, a medieval chisel, which gave any top this effect.

I had called around to get to know them a bit better, and didn't have to do much prompting before their story poured out; Alan did the talking and hardly paused to take a breath. In his time he had clearly been the GP of which dreams are made, running his surgery from their home in the centre of Leicester along with Joan, who was a practice sister and midwife, and furnishing it with the same Mousey Thompson oak, transported by open truck in all weathers from Kilburn. He had trained at Leeds University and the General Infirmary, a student doctor in the casualty department, yet the rush and tumble of the longest hours and the hardest work never blunted his compassion. Though he seemed somewhat reticent about sharing his experiences (that is to say he paused in his monologue for about two seconds) he recalled a mining accident, all-too common in the 1940s. The injured miner's colleagues, faces and hands jet-black with coal, carefully carried in their twisted brother, handling him with more tenderness than any nurse or orderly.

'I can still hear their quiet whispered voices; voices of direction and of reassurance for their wounded friend,' he said.

Alan told me his habit as a GP had been to do home visits at 7 a.m. before his surgery – 'If they needed me, they welcomed me, whatever the time.' He was clearly shocked that sometimes people cared less than he expected them to.

'Do you know,' Alan recalled, 'one Christmas Day I had had a busy morning doing house calls, and had just returned home and was making a start on our Christmas dinner when the phone rang. It was a patient from another practice, but they didn't want to disturb their own doctor, who was a grumpy old so-and-so. They didn't seem to worry about disturbing me! But they were concerned about their baby, and wanted me to call around straight away. I rushed over, only to find them tucking into their Christmas dinner, with not a poorly baby to be seen. "Our Lee's in his cot in the bedroom at the top of the landing," the father informed me, nodding in the direction of the stairs. "He's snuffling a fair bit." Then he went back to cutting himself a thick slice of turkey breast and putting it on his already piled-up plate.'

Alan shook his head as he told me how neither the man nor his wife went up with him to the little lad's room: 'I found Lee lying on his back in his cot. He was snuffling, but he soon stopped when I picked him up. I took his temperature and did all the other checks, but it was just a cold. His nappy hadn't been changed for hours, so, holding him at arm's length, I carried him downstairs and plonked him in his father's lap. The father looked none too pleased – by then he was savouring a huge portion of Christmas pud. "This is very serious indeed," I said, putting on my sternest face. "It's not a doctor this child needs, he needs you two to get off your backsides and take turns to cuddle him. If you leave him in his cot, the cold will go to his lungs and we'll be looking at a case of double pneumonia before we know it. And for goodness' sake, change his nappy, and make sure it's changed at least every two hours. I'll give your own doctor a ring and ask him to call around tomorrow to check you've been doing what I told you."

'Then Lee's mother chimed in, looking terrified. "Oh, there's no need to trouble him," she says, "if it's just a cold."

'I looked her in the eye. "No, I'm duty-bound to pass on the details of my visit, and the remedy I've prescribed. Make sure you do it, otherwise you'll have hell to pay on Boxing Day!" That fixed them!'

I told Alan how I'd been similarly called out one Sunday lunch by a baby's mother, who insisted that her child needed baptizing without delay: 'I thought the little one was at the point of death, so I cycled around straight away. The chubby baby was in its play pen, bouncing around, clearly in the rudest of health. "Why the rush?" I asked.

"'Oh, she's putting on weight ever so fast," the mother explains. "Another week and she won't be able to fit into her christening gown. It's a family heirloom, and I won't have her baptised in anything else.'"

Alan chuckled, 'Ee, what people interrupt us for!'

We talked some more about local events and the news, particularly about Princess Diana's recent funeral. I mentioned, when I managed to get a word in edgeways, that I admired the Queen for remaining composed throughout, despite the intense complexities. But Alan chuckled, and recalled the Queen's visit to Selby Abbey to distribute the Royal Maundy in 1969 – the Abbey's ninth centenary. Alan had been brought up in the area, and Her Majesty had arrived the evening before on the Royal Train, which had holed up for the night in the sidings at Barlow – Alan's home village in the distinctly unglamorous region between Selby and Goole. When the Queen drew back the curtains of her royal carriage the next morning, she had been faced by scores of loyal villagers lining the tracks, who had twigged that the Royal Personage was in their midst and were eager for a glimpse of Her Majesty in her night attire. 'Three cheers for Her Majesty,' they had cried. Apparently Queen Elizabeth had given them the iciest of stares as she had wrapped her dressing gown around her, looking as if she would have preferred a more gentle and private awakening.

We laughed about Yorkshire folks' very quaint and queer ways. 'I would have thought you'd have been glad to escape to Leicestershire – they're relatively normal there. What made you return?' I asked.

'Leicester was OK,' Alan replied, 'but away from York-shire I felt as if my very soul was slowly drying out. It's like anaemic patients needing a top up of iron now and again; I needed a top up of Yorkshire. So whenever we could, we came for a few days' break at the Black Swan. Helmsley is Yorkshire at its best; the hills, the straight-talking folk, the shops – they weren't that fancy when we started coming here, but the stuff they sold was real.'

He recalled how in the 1950s their slumbers in their five-star hotel room had been disturbed by the milk churns being delivered at 4 a.m. by horse and cart. Alan clearly loved his food – simple Yorkshire cooking, with treacle sponge his favourite pudding: 'None of that French muck these posh hotels insist on serving up these days.'

'Mind you, we made an exception for Ted Dzierzek's smoked garlic sausage,' Joan interrupted. 'It was absolutely scrummy. Have you met Ted?' I admitted I had, and told them a bit of my encounter with him earlier that day.

Though Joan hardly took her eyes off me, Alan hardly took his eyes off her, and he clearly cherished his wife. They'd met when he was a trainee doctor and she a trainee midwife, and they had both been doused when a pregnant woman's waters broke as they inspected her 'down below'. After that joint baptism they'd formed a team for life, for better and for worse, for richer and for poorer, in sickness and in health. And in a GP's life there'd been a heck of a lot of sickness, and a heck of a lot of health.

I realized they had had no children, which seemed more than a bit cruel, given how many babies they had brought into the world. I guess their patients served as their children, not to mention a succession of boxers, of which Gus was the latest lively incarnation. And though there was enough doctoring to fill a life, and compensate for their lack of children, there was clearly much, much more to Alan. Since retirement his medical skills had been transferred to nurturing the church as well as nurturing the soil. His allotment was of legendary quality. I had noticed this small strip of land squeezed between the castle and the church whenever we had visited Helmsley on our days off from Bishopthorpe. Usually there was a small crowd of tourists, who had ignored the castle and stopped to pay homage to Alan's garden instead; the lines of onions and cabbages and cauliflowers, regimented in rows like perfect soldiers standing to attention. Alan told me how he often feigned deafness when he was working on it, otherwise he would have spent all his time being complimented and questioned about his produce.

During a brief interlude when Alan nipped to the loo, Joan told me how – on top of all her other duties – she had cared for Alan's mother, who had suffered a severe stroke which had left her body badly twisted. Each and every night in their flat above the surgery she had tenderly washed and dressed her. Then, until sleep overtook her, she had read to her from St Luke's Gospel – her all-time favourite book. One Thursday in May 1973, as the old lady lay dying, a GP from another practice had visited and asked her if she knew the day of the week, just to check how compos mentis she was. 'Why, it's Ascension Day!' the old lady chirped, putting the GP to shame, who had somehow overlooked the festival which is the crescendo of Luke's Gospel. The legend is that Luke was a doctor before he took to Gospel-writing, although doctoring clearly never left him – Luke's Jesus is like a tender, merciful GP; at it 24/7, always desiring his patient's healing.

It was well after 9 p.m. by the time I left Alan and Joan's and stepped out into the dark autumn night, having listened to their tales non-stop for over two hours. As I plodded my weary way home, I had the strangest feeling that St Luke was still alive and well, living in Castlegate smack in the middle of my new parish, having picked up the odd cauliflower and sulphurous, hyperactive boxer along the way.

Chapter Fifteen

On the last Friday in September I sat on the damp pavement opposite Claridge's, begging, for eight long hours! I ought to explain it was Claridge's of Helmsley that I had pitched outside; more modest than its counterpart in Mayfair, it's just a rather lovely book and gift shop. Whenever you wandered in to find a gift for a birthday or anniversary, Ken Claridge, the owner, would hover over your shoulder, asking who you were buying for, what you had in mind, what your budget was, and then suggest a rare book or gift which you would never have dreamt of without his help; your own personal shopper. Over the years I was able to go in and ask, 'What card did I buy my wife for her birthday last year?' and he would remember and make sure I didn't buy the same one again.

This Friday was the church's Gift Day, and it was customary for the vicar to hover all day by the lychgate and receive everyone's gifts in support of the work of the church. The lychgate proved a handy umbrella or sunshade to offset too much rain or shine, but afforded little protection against the equinoxal gales which whistled down the high street on this particular morning. The custom of having a Gift Day wasn't unique to Helmsley; the Church of England, through its parish system, is there for everyone 24/7, irrespective of their faith. A Gift Day gives the parishioners a chance to say a little or a big tangible thank-you, and really helps with keeping the church roof on and paying for the colossal heating bills. I had written to over 1500 homes to introduce myself and invite people to bring their gift and have a chat.

Friday was always market day in Helmsley. Traders had set off by night from far-flung corners of Yorkshire and had parked their vans and trucks by the lychgate, flanking me with a wall of metal. I felt under siege, invisible to the very passers-by I wanted to notice me. So I despatched Alan, my gentle churchwarden who had helped me to set up, to find the offending stallholders and persuade them to move their trucks on. They were not best pleased about this to say the least, and I was treated to some surly looks and choice language as I began my stint. 'Bloody vicars!' one said, as he climbed into his cab, only to reverse into the van behind with a sickening crunch. A more fundamentalist cleric might have seen it as divine justice.

They weren't all surly. The man who ran the flower and plant stall stayed to chat when he came to move his lorry. His was clearly cold work, as he wore woollen mittens on his fingers, a balaclava on his head and a thick woollen cardigan over another thick woollen cardigan; dress more suitable for the trenches on the Western Front rather than autumnal Helmsley. He worked the longest of days, getting up while it was yet night at 4 a.m. to carefully pack his lorry with the latest blooms from his nursery at Flamborough Head before driving fifty miles over the top of the Yorkshire Wolds. Yet rather than having a weary air, he was immensely cheery. His description of his journey was lyrical; the sun rising behind him over the North Sea, highlighting the contours of the rolling chalk hills with their patchwork quilt of fields and forests.

He had passed through village after waking village, the red-bricked houses clustered around their ancient stone church, their fires freshly lit for the day, aromatic wood-smoke spiralling up from each chimney. He left me with a bunch of yellow freesias for my good lady, and £5 towards church funds – my first donation of the day.

Father Bert rolled up, puffing at his pipe, and stood to attention by my side; a cross between a sentry and Santa's little helper. He lined people up along the pavement to have their allotted time with me, then gave me a whispered commentary about them after they had departed, which the waiting queue eagerly strained to overhear. Choice comments such as 'Did he only give you a pound? Mean so-and-so, he owns three farms and has a fleet of Range Rovers!' and 'She'd talk the hind legs off a donkey, that one – make sure you've got nothing on for the rest of the day when you visit her home!'

Mind you, they all talked. Life after life was unfolded before me as they handed over their donation. Committed to the lychgate for the day, I was a bit of a captive audience – I could hardly make my excuses and rush off to my next appointment. I have to admit my mind wandered more than once when they were telling me about Auntie Doris' second cousin's stepson's sister. Had it been put to the test, my recall for the numerous genealogies that were unfolded before me that day might not be up to University Challenge standards. Father Bert gave me a useful summary.

'David, everybody in these parts is related to everyone else,' he said. 'But just because they're related doesn't mean they get on – most of the time they're at daggers drawn. Until, that is, you insult one of their relations, then they'll launch themselves at you like a bitch deprived of one of her pups.'

Minnie in particular stuck in my mind, because of the distinct and rooted life story which she shared with me that day. I saw her coming a long way off; her approach painful, step by step, Zimmer-frame inching before her. When she eventually reached me, she plonked herself down on the stone steps by the gate, clearly here for the duration as she let the tape run, regaling me with details of her school days and adult life. The youngest and brightest of fourteen children, she'd gained a scholarship to Lady Lumley's Grammar School in Pickering, travelling along the picturesque line that I'd battled with a couple of days before.

'The school train was known as "the monkey train" because of all the tricks we got up to,' Minnie the Minx informed me, with a glint in her eye. 'It would be a rare trip when someone's school cap or boater wasn't thrown out of t' window – their dad would have to drive them back on his tractor and tramp the muddy fields to find it. I'd once cooked a gooseberry fool in the home economics lesson and was bringing it home on the train. Because it looked right yucky, another girl threw it out of the window and it shot down the whole length of the moving train, smearing every window. People thought it was sick!'

There were separate compartments for boys and girls, strictly enforced by the guards, with budding Romeos risking decapitation to lean out of the window and shout sweet nothings at their Juliets in the adjacent carriage.

'Ee, one lad wasn't backwards about coming forwards when it came to that kind of thing, so me and my three friends stole into his carriage when the train was stopped at Sinnington. We held him down, tied him to the luggage rack and then left him there when we got off at Helmsley. The carriage was shunted into the sidings at Ampleforth, and a cleaner found him later that night; Mr Casanova had cooled down somewhat by then!'

Minnie was so taken with the railway that on leaving school she became a Goods Clerk at Helmsley station, before she was quickly promoted to Goods and Passenger Clerk at nearby Nawton.

'It was only a railway in the back of beyond, but it employed a heck of a lot of people. There were men walking t' line every day to check for wear and tear, wheel-tappers to check the bogies, signalmen, level-crossing men . . . Then there were goods galore for us girls to weigh and charge before we could release them. The station yard was full of carts, and their massive cart-horses, champing at the bit, waiting to take the stuff to local shops or farms. They were twice as high as me and more – I was absolutely terrified of them.'

Minnie's hard work had been intensified by the war. 'When all the lads at RAF Wombleton had been demobbed at a stroke, me and my friend had to issue them all with the appropriate railway ticket – the total cost was £2000. That was a fantastic sum when not many fares were much over half a crown. By the end of that day we were proper done in, but when we balanced up we were only sixpence out – the brute of a stationmaster still kept us back until we'd found it.'

Minnie told me how even her back-of-beyond railway had its fair share of tragedy. 'There was a summer excursion coming back from Scarborough, packed to the rafters, and a stray Messerschmitt strafed it. All the passengers threw themselves onto the carriage floor, and thought they'd been spared.

But when they stopped in Helmsley, no guard got out to wave the train on; they found him lying dead in his guard's van, riddled with bullets, blood everywhere.'

Minnie had had a near miss herself during the war whilst travelling on the train to York for her day release class. The night before, a German bomb had dropped in between the sleepers on an embankment and blown the earth beneath the line away. So when Minnie's early-bird train passed over it, the rails snapped and sent it hurtling down the bankside.

'Ee, Vicar, the wagon next to ours was smashed to smithereens, but we crawled out of t' wreckage and walked the line back to Coxwold, then made our way to York via the East Coast Main Line. Keep calm and carry on was the order of the day!'

With that she rose painfully to her feet, pressed a ten-pound note into my hand and made a departure as slow and stately as the steam engines whose life she'd ordered.

Whilst Minnie had been chattering on, Father Bert had dealt with the ever-lengthening queue of folk; taking their donations and listening sympathetically for a couple of minutes before dismissing them with his, 'Youse can see our Vicar's a bit busy now. Youse better get back to the market before the fish stall runs out.'

Once Minnie had departed, Father Bert filled me in with further details. 'She's a grand lass to be sure, coping with all that stuff that the war threw at her. Mind you, she'd been well trained for war by having to deal with the Ampleforth College train.'

'What was that then?' I asked. I knew that Ampleforth College, a prestigious public school, was just over the hill from Helmlsey, and that it was run by the Benedictine monks at Ampleforth Abbey, but I'd never heard about a train.

'Oh, it was a special from King's Cross that ran at the beginning and end of term, bringing all the posh pupils from down south and picking up lads from Donnie, Selby and York en route. It never appeared on any timetable, but it took a heck of a lot of organization. It had a goods van at the back packed with the boys' trunks, which was shunted down a track that led right down into the abbey for the college porters to unload. The line to the abbey wasn't much more than a tramway, really. When the school needed a second cricket pitch, the monks themselves, helped by a few prefects, re-laid the track, shifting it a couple of hundred yards. It certainly wasn't safe enough for human traffic, so the boys got off at Gilling and marched up to the school – it was a crocodile to behold, believe you me.'

There were a lot of images there to take in. The one that gnawed at my mind most was the King's Cross Express gingerly inching its way around the Second XI cricket field, hoping against hope that the monks had tightened all the bolts and hadn't been distracted by vespers. 'So how was Minnie involved – I thought she worked at Nawton station?' I asked, forcing myself back to some sort of reality.

'I think they commandeered the staff from all the nearby stations, just to control things. God knows how many adolescent boys had been cooped up together for over five hours in cramped carriages, so getting them off the train onto the short platforms and through a small country station was quite a challenge. Several monks travelled on the train and acted as honorary guards to help keep order, but even then you needed nerves of steel to sort it all out. The war was nothing compared to that.'

Over the summer our daughter Ruth had been reading *Harry Potter and the Philosopher's Stone* by J. K. Rowling, a first-time author, which had been published in June. Ruth's eyes had been as wide as saucers as she read about the Hogwarts Express, staffed by wizards, leaving Platform 9 ¾ at King's Cross. As Father Bert regaled me with tales of the Ampleforth special, I began to wonder if this was where J. K. Rowling had got the idea from. As he was talking, Father Bert frequently checked his watch, as if he were an honorary guard waiting to see off a train.

'If you can cope without me for an hour or so, I'd better be on my way,' he declared. 'Margaret will be expecting me for my lunch. If there's any to spare, I'll get her to plate something up and bring it back for you.'

So off he toddled to catch the Helmsley–Old Byland special, complete with a turn-around stop at a dining car par excellence.

Chapter Sixteen

No sooner had Father Bert departed than Lord Feversham roared up in his Range Rover, hobbled out and pressed four crisp twenty-pound notes into my hand. He winced as he sat down on the steps 'My gammy leg's giving me gyp again!' Then he assumed the role of showman.

'Roll up, here's your chance, vicar in the stocks, one day only, throw what you like at him!' he chuckled. 'Have you had any difficult customers?' he asked *sotto voce*. 'Anybody you want me to sort out?' His eyes narrowed, giving him that mean Henry Tudor look that had sent shivers down my spine back in May. I guess he'd be a handy guy to know if I wanted anyone hung, drawn and quartered.

'No, they've all been quite sweet,' I replied. 'The stall holders from the market weren't best pleased, having to move the vans they'd parked in front of me, but that's about all.'

'We didn't have all that coming and going when I was a lad, it was a very local affair,' Lord Feversham recalled, peering over towards the market square with a faraway look in his eyes. 'The Friday market consisted of delicious produce grown in our walled garden or by our tenants in their little cottage gardens, along with a wild venison stall.' He paused as he smacked his lips. 'The deer were originally farmed, but the soldiers billeted at Duncombe Park during the war had broken through the deer park fences with their tank manoeuvres – careless buggers – and the roe deer have roamed wild ever since.'

Lord Feversham told me with relish how the stallholder operated a strict pecking order as to who could buy his venison. Lord Feversham, his household and his estate workers had first pick, then Helmsley's other inhabitants, then anyone else who'd made the long journey from high over the moors – incomers from Bilsdale or Bransdale or Fadmoor who were rewarded with the gristliest cuts for their trouble. 'No more than they deserved!' Lord Feversham chuckled. 'But I'm glad no one has had a pop at you, Had you been Vicar Gray, mind you, you wouldn't have had such an easy time!'

My ears pricked up. Quite a few people I'd encountered in my first weeks had described my indefatigable Victorian predecessor in reverential tones. Back in May, Lord Feversham had mentioned this veritable saint during my interview for the post, describing how he had built churches galore in local hamlets, including East Moors, Carlton, Sproxton, Rievaulx and Pockley. He'd then organized a posse of clergy to take seventeen services each Sunday, with one having to ride up to East Moors on Saturday night. Gray was no respecter of bad weather: one cleric had been nearly sucked into a bog when his horse had sunk up to his girths; another had got lost above Rievaulx in a snow storm and lost two toes to frostbite; a third had had to be rescued from a flooded River Rye at 1.30 a.m.

He was no respecter of authority either. He'd installed a black marble altar in Helmsley Church in memory of his father, who'd been a fiercely orthodox Bishop of Cape Town. The Archdeacon of Cleveland, who was in charge of church fixtures and fittings, objected to the installation, but drew this curt response from Gray: 'I spent six yoke of oxen ferrying the stone from Helmsley station. If you wish to remove it, you can provide the oxen.' The good archdeacon wisely decided to let sleeping dogs, and more importantly sleeping oxen, lie.

Gray was a social reformer too, railing against the demon drink, founding a temperance society, night classes, a library and a debating society (where women were to remain silent). When we moved into Canons Garth the girls helped me clear towers of dusty magazines from my study. Clare knocked over one tower, taller than her, and as we gathered up the scattered magazines, I came across a few ancient copies of Gray's parish magazine from the 1870s and 1880s, with some handy if confusing hints for rearing potatoes, poultry and children, including the insistence that 'tea, beer, whiskey and other stimulants should never be given'. Obviously Helmsley's chickens were something else until Gray took them in hand! In another magazine, Gray, a celibate bachelor, warned women against the perils of lacing up their corsetry too tightly and offered this touching encouragement for the hardpressed housewife: 'No house need to be dirty: soap and hot water with a little hard work can do wonders. A woman is worth nothing if she cannot keep her house clean.'

He fought for time off for apprentices and better conditions for workhouse children, made his clergy walk the muddy furrows beside ploughboys to give them their confirmation lessons, improved the post office and built an open air swimming pool, ran a soup kitchen when unemployment hit the town hard in 1886, and dispensed an endless supply of beef tea from his vicarage for those laid low with influenza.

'I thought Gray had had forty-three golden years,' I said to

Lord Feversham, feeling exhausted just thinking about all this hyperactivity.

'Far from it. Forty-three years at war, more like. That chap could have picked a fight in an empty room. The first thing he did when he arrived in 1870 was to ostracize single mothers – something like one in six births was illegitimate in those days. The mother of one of the poor girls threatened to pour a bucket of boiling water over his head if he dared to show his face on market day. As I said, the Friday market is not a patch on what it used to be! Apparently he used to fight local pugilists with one hand tied behind his back; mind you, he'd only take them on when they had drunk their fill and were worse for wear, just to show the benefits that being a teetotaller in tip-top condition brings.'

Lord Feversham was in his stride now. 'He took against my great-great-great uncle, the first earl. Always on at him about the state of the town drains, how unhealthy it was to drink from the same beck you did your washing in – as if a bit o' dirt ever harmed anyone. Accused him of single-handedly causing a typhoid epidemic, killing four people a year, would you believe! The old earl was no stick-in-the-mud. He was ahead of his time, very ecumenical. Gave the monks at Ampleforth land in Helmsley to build their chapel on. Gray was furious, accusing him of selling the Established Church down the river for the sake of a few votes.'

'But surely Gray wasn't all bad – what about the children's pageants in the castle he organized in the 1890s, watched by thousands? They had to lay on special trains from York.' Earlier, Minnie had gone on about those excursions, part of the local railway folklore.

'What, you mean when he got all the local urchins to sing

the 'Magnificat' in Latin and all that bollocks? Fat lot of good the 'Magnificat' in Latin would do you when you ended up black-leading a fireplace, cleansing a cow or felling a tree. Just brainwashing, if you ask me. And Gray could be a brute with children. One little lad failed to doff his cap to him as Gray passed him on horseback – Gray horsewhipped him all the way home, and then insisted his father give him a good beating too. So don't you ever feel inferior to the likes of Gray. You modern clergy may be a bit wet, but at least you're kind.' He raised himself up from the steps and shuffled over to his Range Rover.

'All right for some, able to park their posh cars here,' a man mouthed, presumably one of the stallholders we had moved on.

'Just bugger off!' his Lordship replied, before turning back to me. 'Oh, I nearly forgot, Lady Polly wondered whether you and Rachel were free for a spot of lunch tomorrow. Shall we say one for one-thirty?'

I promised to get back to him once I'd checked with Rachel. His eyes narrowed, his brow furrowed – clearly this wasn't so much an invitation as a summons.

'But I'm sure she'll be free,' I stuttered.

He roared off in his Range Rover, and I passed the rest of the lunch hour talking to two pleasant young women with pushchairs. In one pushchair sat a little girl with blonde ringlets, ruddy cheeks and piercing blue eyes, in stark contrast to her mother, whose hair was black and skin ivory.

'She takes after her dad,' she explained, when she saw my puzzled look. 'He's a monk, or at least he used to be!'

As first lines go, this took some beating. It transpired that her husband had been a monk, but had found even what was quite an ascetic monastery too worldly. On the principle of 'if you can't beat them join them,' he decided to work his deeply held faith out in the world. Something quite a lot of religious people do these days – the churchy term for it is 'new monasticism.' Working as a lab technician at Ampleforth Abbey School, where an older colleague had introduced him to her daughter – she instantly became the love of his life, and in the course of time they married and set up home in Helmsley. Whilst mum was telling me all this, the little girl chuckled and giggled with sheer delight.

Another little girl, dark-haired and olive-skinned, sobbed uncontrollably whilst her equally dark-haired and olive-skinned mother chatted to me.

'Don't worry, she's just been to playgroup,' her mother explained in a thick French accent.

'Oh, I'm sorry,' I replied. 'Are there problems with the group?'

'Oh no, it's run by two lovely farmer's wives who are so kind to Teresa when she misses me – they're always giving you big cuddles, aren't they Teresa?' she said, stroking the little girl's head before turning her attention back to me. 'It's just that we're French, so we speak French all the time at home – when they speak to her in your Yorkshire dialect, she doesn't recognize the tenderness.'

She pressed a fiver into my hand before breezing on her way with her wailing child, leaving me with a lot to think about. How often did *I* get the inflection and nuance wrong, and people craving affection heard only harshness?

My musing was interrupted by Father Bert coming around the corner, bearing an enormous plate covered by a polished silver cloche. 'Margaret's sent you a bit of her fish pie, it being

Friday,' he explained. He delved into his jacket pocket and handed me his pipe before thinking better of it, 'No, you don't want that.' He delved again and produced a fork. 'That's better!'

I sat on the steps and consumed the generous portion of creamy mashed potato saturated with salmon, shrimps, cod and smoked haddock; the North Sea concentrated in one dish. Fortified by a lunch that was completed by the friendly staff from Claridge's bringing me and Father Bert a steaming cuppa, the rest of the afternoon whizzed by. The number of people tailed off as the market began to pack up. Alan took our takings for the day, with Gus acting as fierce guard dog and tugging at his lead. After about half an hour Alan returned, beaming from ear to ear.

'We're well up on last year, so well done!'

The success was absolutely nothing to do with me, since I'd only just arrived in the place. Next year though, would be the test of my mettle. I packed away, happy with the day and moved by all the conversations, but simultaneously wondering how to break his Lordship's invitation to my Rachel, who took after her mum in being a fierce socialist, so tended to be resistant to summons by imperious aristocrats.

Chapter Seventeen

Expecting a lunch of medieval proportions, Rachel and I cycled to Lord and Lady Feversham's in order to work up an appetite. A little chap in a wooden kiosk saluted us as we breezed through the main gates of Duncombe Park. We veered off the drive and took a sharp left to take a more scenic route through the 300 acres of parkland, although all the routes in and around Helmsley are pretty scenic. We bumped up and down over two meadows and hauled our bikes over a couple of stiles, before following the River Rye on its meander through the estate. We stopped by the Cascades, where the torrent plunges over a spectacular six-foot waterfall. Alan had told me that in very dry summers he and Gus had gingerly walked across the Cascades, but if I'd tried to do so now I'd have been swiftly swept downstream to Malton.

Alan had also tipped me off that many parishioners sneak into the park when his Lordship isn't looking and throw the ashes of their nearest and dearest into these waters, a Yorkshire Ganges. I was rather taken with this modern-day Viking funeral, where the deceased's voyage bisects Yorkshire; they would join the Derwent above Kirkham Priory, the home of the Augustinian monks who had founded Helmsley Church and built our vicarage, before their ashes would wend their way through the fecund meadowlands of the Vale of York, briefly flirting with the Ouse before being swept out to the North Sea by the Humber at Spurn Point.

Above the Cascades, the path rises steeply onto an old concrete tank road laid in the war, when the 22nd Dragoons had occupied the expansive grounds, enabling them to practise manoeuvres prior to the D-Day landings. Our problem was that the roads had been built for tanks and not for bicycles. Each concrete slab was about thirty feet in length and joined to the next slab with cement. This had been repeatedly patched in the decades since the war, only to be quickly eroded by the fierce moors weather. The uneven joins and the massive potholes made it a boneshaker of a ride. Rachel and I jolted our way up the 1:3 climb, our calves screaming in pain, any progress hindered further by sharp hairpin bends. Our reward for this strenuous climb was that as we cleared the forest, the big house was open to our gaze like a scene from *Brideshead Revisited*.

We continued towards it, and, as we sheepishly wheeled our cycles through the iron gates that guarded the circular drive, left a furrow in the deep gravel. The huge, eighteenth-century neo-classical house, complete with side bays and detached wings, sprawled before us. I don't think we were actually open-mouthed in awe, but it felt like that. We parked our bikes to the side of the sweeping stone staircase leading to the grand entrance, and knocked on a modest little door at ground level – the entrance reserved for tradesmen and vicars. Whilst we were waiting, Rachel straightened her posh dress and attempted to comb her curly fair hair, windswept after the climb. A woman-what-does eventually opened the door and invited us to follow her as she limped along the dark passageway, dragging her left leg. The passage opened into what must have been the servants' basement kitchen in a bygone age, but now served as a snug-cum-kitchen for the family. His Lordship rose from a large oak chair, the back and seat lined with cracked and faded red leather embossed with the family crest.

'Welcome, Vicar, but more importantly, welcome the good Vicar's lady, to my humble abode!' he intoned, in a voice which had more than a passing resemblance to Laurence Olivier's *Now-is-the-winter-of-our-discontent* speech. He bowed his domed head before Rachel and gallantly kissed her hand, giving her a lupine smile. 'Welcome, my dear. Polly, come and meet the Wilbournes.'

Lady Polly had her back to us, busily stirring a large cauldron of soup bubbling on a black-leaded Yorkshire Range. She turned and gave us a radiant smile which lit up the dark kitchen. In contrast to his Lordship's bulk, she was petite. Though she had an apron wrapped around her, and her face had a ruddy sheen from working over a hot stove, she carried it off well; an aristocratic beauty with eyes that twinkled mischievously.

'Oh Peter,' she said, her accent cut-glass with an Irish lilt, 'do stop trying to ape Henry VIII! Rachel and David, thank you so much for coming. Don't take any notice of him, he will play his tricks!'

'You know I like to have my fun, my dear!' Lord Feversham chuckled fondly.

Once Polly had stopped Peter having his fun, lunch was just fine. It wasn't exactly lavish; homemade bread buns and a particularly strong Cheddar washed down with a thick potato and leek soup made by Polly's fair hand. The conversation was easy: talk about how our girls were settling into school;

Polly glowing with pride about her son's prowess at Latin and Greek and showing informed concern as to how Rachel was coping with moving into an ancient pile. Whilst we were chatting, Hoover, one of their pet Sussex spaniels, sprang onto the table and stole the afore-mentioned strong cheddar. The woman-what-does was summoned and began to chase after, or rather limp after, the dog as it disappeared down the dark corridor.

'Don't worry,' Lady Polly shouted, 'just bring another piece.'

After a considerable time the woman-what-does returned, bearing a smaller piece of cheese on a plate. It looked more like Emmental than Cheddar, perforated with holes that looked suspiciously like teeth marks. Nevertheless, following his Lordship's example, we each cut a piece of cheddar, savouring the unique combination of flavours – cheese seasoned with dog saliva. Hoover eventually returned, his tail between his legs, his soulful eyes full of remorse for his misdeed.

'Hoover, do that again and I'll give you a good thrashing,' his Lordship shouted, the sense of threat being undermined by a loud chuckle. 'Remember how I sorted out Molesworth, Polly?'

Polly gave a girlish giggle. 'It was just after we had re-taken possession of Duncombe Park,' she explained, making it sound like an invasion. 'Molesworth was Peter's pet Sussex spaniel. Anyway, a couple of visitors had sneaked in and were walking past the house when along came Peter with Molesworth, who had a live rabbit in his jaws. The visitors were horrified, and even threatened to report him to the RSPCA. "You're quite right, I'll deal with the blighter straight away," Peter said, and he dragged Molesworth round the corner into the courtyard, out of sight. The next thing they heard was a shotgun going off, followed by the howls of a dog in its death throes. The visitors rushed away, grateful to have escaped with their lives. They must have been thinking they'd met the maddest peer of the realm. Little did they know that Peter's impression of a dying dog was his legendary party piece!'

Lord Feversham duly obliged us with said party piece; plaintive, ear-splitting howls which reached a crescendo before tailing off and ending abruptly with a tremendous thud as Peter kicked the table to complete his dance of the dying spaniel. We all duly laughed, but Hoover howled in sympathy.

After lunch, Lord Feversham proudly showed us the palatial rooms whose design was influenced by Sir John Vanbrugh, the architect of Castle Howard, where *Brideshead Revisited* was filmed. Duncombe Park was originally completed in 1713 before being extended in the 1840s by Charles Barry, who took time off from rebuilding the Houses of Parliament for a North York Moors' sojourn. Much of the main house then had to be rebuilt at the end of the nineteenth century after a disastrous fire. The whole place was not static, but organic; evolving even now as Lord and Lady Feversham restored the cornices, coving, wallpaper, drapes and windows to their Georgian glory, and added modern touches of their own.

We ended up in the chapel-cum-mausoleum – so chilly you could have freeze-dried blackberries in it. Pride of place on one ledge was a soldier's helmet perforated by a huge bullet hole.

'That belonged to my ancestor Charles, Second Earl of Feversham,' the present Earl explained, a wobble afflicting his normally stentorian tones. 'He was a bright spark – went to

Eton and Christchurch at Oxford, and became a Conservative MP. He took the nom de plume Viscount Helmsley to try and disguise his aristocratic origins,' he chuckled, 'merely reducing his rank one level! He ended up commanding the King's Royal Rifle Corps, which he formed at Helmsley in 1915. All the tenants and estate workers enlisted with him, of course. But he caught a packet the next year at the Battle of Flers-Courcelette. Saddest thing is that he took his deerhound to the front – she took a packet too and was buried along with him.'

We stood in respectful silence, looking at the bullet hole which broke the family's fortune and thinking of the other bullets which decimated the flower of Helmsley's youth. Mercifully, we were spared his Lordship doing an impression of a dying deerhound.

We walked around to the back of the house; the side normally hidden from the public. There the most gorgeous scene unfolded, nothing less than a Garden of Eden; the wooded ground fell away to reveal the velvet-green fields surrounding the River Rye, a silver ribbon bubbling through the undulating meadows. I thought of Viscount Helmsley adoring the same scene daily; striding out with his faithful deerhound, fully expecting that one day he would die here, a heaven on earth, only to be killed in the darkest and bloodiest jaws of hell.

Chapter Eighteen

I never sleep well on Saturday night, anticipating the Sunday ahead. I have terrible nightmares where I am leading services in my pyjamas, failing to get my tongue around the Tudor English used at the early Communion, fumbling around in the Prayer Book, persistently turning up the Burial of the Dead rather than the Gospel for the twenty-second Sunday after Trinity. On the Sunday after our visit to Duncome Park, I woke just after six and tiptoed down the dark stairs, not wanting to disturb the girls. I dressed in my study, where I had laid out my clothes the night before, but realized I had stupidly left my only pair of shoes in the bedroom. To return up the creaky stairs and even more creaky landing would have risked waking the whole house, so instead I donned my muddy wellingtons and hoped that my bleary-eyed parishioners wouldn't notice them beneath my robes.

I squelched into church, which was still in darkness. I couldn't find the light switches, so instead I gingerly felt my way along the altar rail and choir stalls. I swore as I jarred my ankle on a step I didn't know was there, felt bad about cursing in such a hallowed spot, and eventually plonked myself down on a pew beneath my friend, the twenty-foot long dragon. For an hour I drank from the still silence and the darkness and greeted the dawn, which slowly turned the dragon's dull grey to fierce red.

Just before 7.30 there was a great clattering as the deputy warden made his loud entry and put on all the lights, burning my eyes accustomed only to darkness. 'Morning, Vicar,' he shouted across to me, as candles were lit, books were piled up by the door (in case there was a surprising surge of worshippers) and loud greetings were exchanged with the dozen or so who had come early to be sure of a seat. Abandoning any hope of further silence, I put on my robes and stood outside the church door, watching the waking town. A sleek tabby cat stole behind a gravestone, stalking a blackbird, busy foraging for insects in the golden carpet of leaves, oblivious to the approaching huntress. Shopkeepers swilled down the stone flags outside their cafes, with the flotsam and jetsam from the previous night's revelry in the town's numerous pubs swirling into the beck. Saturday night is party night in Helmsley; the estate workers descend from the moors, drink their fill and then noisily wander around the town to 'sober up' before driving home.

'I see you've got your wellies on, Vicar,' one eagle-eyed man shouted, sloshing his mop. 'Perhaps you can give us a hand!'

A heavily bearded tramp, who'd been sleeping rough by the beck, walked stiffly and slowly down Castlegate and came to a halt outside Rivis' cafe. It was as if a rendezvous was pre-arranged, because no sooner had he arrived than a slim young woman brought him out a mug of tea and a bacon buttie and gave him a hug. A weary-looking young guy with bags under his eyes passed by, pushing a screaming toddler in a pushchair. 'Little bugger's kept us up all night teething,' he said, shrugging. A young man emerged from a house in Castlegate, tucking his shirt into his trousers and tightening his tie with an illicit look about him; he turned and passionately kissed a young woman in a skimpy nightdress standing just inside the red door. Chefs in attire as white as mine loitered outside the kitchens of the Black Swan and the Feathers, which both front the market square, having a crafty fag whilst their bacon crozzled. An immaculately made-up lady in a mink coat stared into the middle distance as her cocker spaniel did its steaming business by the church wall. There were constant comings and goings at the newsagent's opposite the lychgate, stocky farmers with weather-worn faces hauled themselves into mud-splattered Land Rovers, staggering under the weight of their Sunday papers with supplements galore, as if they were heaving bales of hay. They slid open their windows and talked loudly with other farmers arriving in Land Rovers about the terrible price of sheep and the need for rain, their breath condensing in great white clouds in the frosty air. The church clock chimed eight and I started my first service of the day: Almighty God, unto whom all hearts be open, all desires known and from whom no secrets are hid . . .

It was all over in half an hour. My taciturn and arthritic congregation suddenly put on a surprising spurt as they headed home for a late breakfast, wishing me a curt good morning as they sped off. I sped off too, and snatched a bowl of Shreddies with my chattering daughters before returning for the big event. Father Bert was already in the vestry, fretting. Like me he hadn't slept at all well, but his nightmares are different from mine; bombers being shot from the skies rather than prayer books with pages perversely sticking together.

'I've never slept well before celebrating Mass,' he confided.

'Well, Father, if you think of what we're doing, who could sleep?'

Tomes have been written about what goes on or doesn't go on at Communion; people have gone to the stake denying it all or believing it all. I believe it all, because otherwise ministry is utterly pointless, but I don't make a song and dance of it. I like to go for simple sentences, like 'We leave Holy Communion with the taste of Christ on our lips to give people a taste of Christ in their lives.'

Derek was there too, firing up a sort of portable stove called a censer – basically two metal hemispheres dangling from a chain. The lower hemisphere contains self-igniting charcoal tablets which Derek had lit and were now fizzing nicely; dull red if not quite red-hot yet. The upper hemisphere acts as a perforated lid and when you swing the whole thing on its chain, the incoming air acts as a bellows, making the charcoal tablets white hot. If you put three or four grains of incense on the charcoal then clouds of incense emerge – acrid smoke to some, a fragrant offering to others. To get the thing going nicely, Derek swung the censer through a few complete revolutions, narrowly missing Father Bert and me in the process but unfortunately clonking it against a cupboard, which sent a shower of sparks onto the carpet. Father Bert and I gamely stamped out the embers before they melted too much of the soft furnishings, and then we were ready to start the service. The general public haven't got a clue that preparing for worship is so complicated.

And that's only for starters. Using incense involves a series of dance steps which would bring the most experienced competitor in *Strictly Come Dancing* out in a cold sweat. Whilst swinging the censer, bow twice, take four steps sideways, three steps backwards, four steps sideways, bow twice again, take four steps sideways, three steps backwards, then finally four steps sideways. Remember that you're doing this with a white-hot portable oven emitting clouds of noxious vapour while negotiating a series of stone stairs. Then later in the service, repeat the action, but swing the censer over the bread and wine, completing two circles anti-clockwise and one circle clockwise followed by three signs of the cross.

The wine is contained in a chalice, a silver bowl set on the thinnest of stems standing on a starched white cloth. Call me over-cautious, but swinging a portable white-hot stove not once but six times over a top-heavy, unstable vessel brimful with red wine perched on a bleached-white altar cloth strikes me as a rail crash waiting to happen. Back when I trained for the priesthood in Cambridge, we were told that if you ever spilt consecrated wine on an altar cloth, sanctuary carpet or stone, you could summon a team of nuns who would devotedly wash the cloth, lick the stones clean or even consume the carpet. Apparently this top-secret order continuously travelled up and down the A1 in a Mini, and could be contacted on a radio whose exclusive frequency would be revealed to you at your ordination. I think our tutor was having us on.

Roman Catholic churches wisely avoid this pantomime and just have a fixed censer, either set on the floor or suspended from a beam. Legend has it that in the seventeenth century the scientist Galileo watched such a giant censer swinging from a beam in Pisa Cathedral and calculated the earth's gravitational constant. That constant equals the length of the chain divided by the square of the time it took the censer to complete a full swing, with the whole lot then multiplied by $4\pi^2$.

Apparently, he estimated the length of the chain and timed the swing with his pulse, since watches had yet to be invented. Assuming that he didn't hit on the correct form for the equation first time around, it must have been a very long and exceedingly boring service. I've tried it myself in very boring services with dangling lights swinging in a draught and it does work – if you measure the length in metres and time in seconds, the answer should be around 10.

Dance moves notwithstanding, the service went fine, with Father Bert following me around throughout like a faithful sheepdog – or perhaps my rear-end gunner. We were through within the hour, which is always my aim, keeping things nice and tight on the 'if you don't strike oil in ten minutes, stop boring!' principle. You pack a lot of things into that hour; singing, reading, preaching, praying, sharing bread and wine. The service in church is a springboard for service in the community. At least in theory.

'What are you doing for the rest of the day?' I asked one old dear, shaking her hand as she was leaving.

'Ee, luv,' she replied, 'I'm going home to recover. All that singing, smoke and stuff has fair taken it out of me. I'll make meself a cup of coffee, cut a slice of sponge cake and have a nice lie down on my settee!'

Out of a congregation of about forty, Lord Feversham had been the last to receive the bread and wine, moving stiffly as he knelt at the ancient altar rail, the latest in a line of Fevershams who had knelt there over the centuries. 'Are you free this afternoon?' he asked as he was leaving. 'I thought I could take you for a spin in the Land Rover and show you those water races I was going on about yesterday. You can come too, Bert, if you want.'

'I wouldn't be free until about three, my Lord. I have a luncheon engagement,' Father Bert explained.

'Well, let's make it three then, if that's all right with you, David,' Lord Feversham replied, with a definite glint in his eye and a dark smile which revealed he knew all about Father Bert's luncheon engagements. I left the two of them, put my robes in my rucksack and pedalled up the hill to catch my final service of the morning at Rievaulx. As I laboured up the steep slope, motorbikes galore soared past in the opposite direction. Helmsley market place is a Mecca for motorcyclists on a Sunday. They race from Middlesbrough; roaring over the Cleveland Hills then through Bilsdale, rising again over the moors before dropping down the final strait to congregate in Helmsley. Apparently it's akin to the Isle of Man TT races, with thirteen minutes for the twenty miles from Stokesley to Helmsley the record to beat. Never mind Stokesley, it takes me twenty minutes to reach Rievaulx just one mile into the hills, but then again, I only have two legpower compared to their hundreds of horsepower.

A nice chap who is restoring the old mill turned up and played his cornet to keep our hymns reasonably in tune. He tended to run out of puff by the second verse, however, so then our singing had to keep him in tune. Frank the shepherd, who had kept me company on the day of prayer, arrived in the same shabby gabardine with a piece of twine for a belt and took the collection; not too onerous a task given that there were barely half a dozen other worshippers. As he did so he sang what could politely be termed a howling descant to the hymn, nicely blending with the off-key notes of the struggling cornet player. I was barely able to keep laughter at bay. When I'd trained for the ministry, my tutor had advised me that when I felt a fit of giggles coming on during a church service, I should think of the saddest thing that had ever happened to me. Similarly, when you feel on the brink of tears, think of the funniest thing. It just about works, although contorting your face with conflicting emotions makes for a painful time.

There was a distinguished-looking guy there who lived in a cottage opposite the church. I later learned he was a renowned musicologist; he had lectured at Oxford and had regularly written the blurb on the cover of classical CDs. He had the bewildered look that Persephone must have sported when she was wrenched from the Elysian Fields and found herself wintering in Hades. I knew how he felt.

Chapter Nineteen

I had to lean over the handle-bars pedalling up the heavily wooded Rievaulx Bank, otherwise I would have fallen off the bicycle backwards. Once again, on the basis that maths kicks all other pains into touch, I derived the formula for quadratic equations from first principles in my head. In an instant I found myself magically transported to the top of the bank, the pain in my thigh muscles banished by algebra. And it was a magical sight; the Rievaulx Temples rising to my right arching protectively over the Abbey, and to my left the purple-topped moors, climbing to their peak at Surprise View. The descent into Helmsley was a sharp one, topping 40 mph on my cycle's speedometer. I overtook a Reliant Robin trundling down the hill at a steady twenty-five, the driver and his good lady with mouths agape at being passed by a vicar on a bike. I pulled in sharpish, narrowly avoiding a little red jeep speeding up the hill, Father Bert at the wheel, licking his lips at the feast which awaited him in Old Byland.

The road takes a tight right before entering Helmsley. I had to brake hard to avoid landing in the beck and catapulting into the prettiest cottage garden, the flowerbeds a firework display of autumn colours. I'd landed in a fair few gardens when I'd first learnt to cycle as a curate in Middlesbrough – a novel if painful method of evangelism. Somehow, presenting yourself as the immaculately dressed expert puts folk off. Hobbling up to their back door with grazed hands and muddy knees, apologizing because your bike has cut a swathe through their carnations, alters the dynamic and enables real if colourful conversation.

To revive me after a long morning of cycling and Communions, a sort of churchy version of an Iron Man triathalon, Rachel had served up a delicious chicken roast with all the trimmings.

'Will you play cricket with us this afternoon, Dad?' Ruth asked, as I slumped down on a kitchen chair. At the tender age of eleven she was one of the meanest bowlers I had ever encountered, and never missed an opportunity to drag me out onto wherever we improvised a pitch.

'We'll be all right until three-ish,' I replied, helping myself to a mountain of mashed potato to fortify myself for the innings ahead. 'But after that, Lord Feversham is showing me and Father Bert his water races.'

'Is it like a duck race?' Hannah asked, intrigued. Just before we left Bishopthorpe, her school had organized one on the River Ouse, which proved thrilling primarily because it hadn't quite gone according to plan. The Ouse was in flood at the time, and all the plastic ducks had swum downstream at break-beak pace, defied the deputy head's brave attempts to net them at the finishing line, and instead made a bid for freedom as they hurtled towards the Humber and the North Sea. No doubt some beachcomber in Denmark was at that moment scratching his head as to why 202 identical yellow ducks had been washed up on his shore.

'No, it's not quite as exciting as that,' I replied. 'The water races are channels that bring water from the north side of the moors to the south side.'

Hannah's eyes glazed over. It isn't easy to compete with the mass migration of 202 plastic ducks, but I persevered. After all, as a vicar I was an expert at injecting excitement even into the dullest stuff.

'Imagine this is the north side of the moors and this the south,' I said, moulding my mashed potato into two parallel mountain ranges with a valley in between, as you do. 'The main gradients follow a north–south line, but there is also a very gentle slope west–east towards the North Sea.' With my knife I managed to give my twin mountain range a tilt towards the oven. 'Now, imagine there's a spring on the north side. If you cut a channel westwards down the north–south slope, and then bring it back eastwards along the gentle west–east slope, you should get water to the southern peaks.' I carefully cut a channel with my knife and poured a trickle of gravy onto the north side of my mashed potato mountains. For a moment my gravy race worked, before the whole lot dissolved into a soggy brown mass.

'Just eat your lunch before it goes cold,' Rachel sighed. Kitchen-science isn't really her thing.

But it is my thing. Deeply sad though I was to leave Aughton in 1970, one compensation was that my new school in Scarborough instilled in me a fascination for maths and physics which has lasted a lifetime. I suddenly started mucking about with machinery, trying to repair broken lawnmowers and washing machines, occasionally with some success. Inspired by the experiments we did in the chemistry and physics labs at school, I repeated simple experiments in our home. For instance, I used the transformer from my old railway set, set up a cathode and anode by wiring it to a couple of graphite leads from my propelling pencil, and by the principle of electrolysis, turned a jug of saltwater into a jug of Domestos. The kitchen smelt very strongly of chlorine for a few days – more Western Front than Scarborough – and though I didn't exactly turn water into wine, I found the spirit of experiment and discovery very thrilling. I used bits and bobs from around the home and in the back of drawers to calculate immense invisible entities, like the speed of light and force of gravity.

Years later, when I was selecting and training people for ordination, one of my killer questions was, 'What in your heart of hearts do you feel you were born to do? What activity makes you think, "I was made for this?"' Quite a lot told me that they had been born to conduct evensong, an answer which always made me rather sad – far too narrow and churchy when there was a whole world out there to enjoy. A dental technician told me that he had been born to make people smile, which seemed a priestly vocation if ever there was one. But not a single ordinand ever told me they had been born to mend things, an activity which for me was like coming home.

'Dad, stop daydreaming and eat up your lunch,' my daughter Ruth commanded. 'We'll never get this cricket match started at this rate!'

I duly obeyed and, following a hurried treacle sponge washed down with a scalding cup of tea, I was bowled out no less than twenty-four times, caught eleven times, and scored a measly thirty-seven runs for all my efforts, with two balls lost for all eternity in the graveyard thicket.

Talking of eternity, as so often happened when I played with the girls, I replayed in my mind their birth and early life.

One Sunday in the middle of October 1985, in my first year as Vicar of Monk Fryston and South Milford, I had rushed around taking five services, and on top of that we had all the churchwardens to lunch and the church treasurer to supper. We retired just before midnight.

'We'll have to get some sleep before our baby is born,' I said to Rachel, who was by then eight months pregnant, before turning off the light. Just one hour later I was turning it on again because clearly the new baby was on its way. I drove Rachel to the famous St James's Hospital in Leeds at breakneck pace, but for the next twelve hours not much happened, until the midwife decided the baby was highly distressed and Rachel was rushed off to theatre for an emergency caesarean. For an hour I wandered around the hospital, feeling totally lost, realizing that life hung in the balance. I came back to the maternity ward and someone came out of theatre and dumped a set of notes on the nurses' station, which I read upside down. 'Live baby, mother in recovery.' Within minutes the live baby was brought to me; a tiny little girl with wisps of blonde hair and eyes tightly shut. Then Rachel was wheeled in and held her in her arms, with her smile positively radiant and beatific. Time stood still.

After a few minutes I realized I had better call Rachel's dad, and found a nearby payphone. 'Rachel's had a baby girl and they're both fine,' I began. 'We're going to call her Ruth, after Rachel's mum.'

That was it, just eighteen words, my heart was too full with joy to say anything else; Rachel's dad's heart too full to reply.

I brought Rachel and Ruth home a week later. Freesias, Rachel's favourite flowers, were in every room once again, along with mountains of baby clothes and toys and cards –

gifts from family and friends and a host of parishioners. Given the trauma she had been through, Ruth didn't sleep that well for the first three months, and I used to take my turn in the night, soothing her cries with John Betjeman's poetry, which I was keen on at the time. Before Christmas we had a carol service in Monk Fryston Church, accompanied by the slowest brass band in creation. Rachel brought baby Ruth along, and we suddenly noticed that whenever the brass band played, Ruth stopped crying. So that Christmas Rachel's brothers and I kept doing trombone impersonations, no doubt aided by eating copious amounts of brussel sprouts, to placate Ruth's cries. There's always a trick to calm every child.

We felt very fortunate, realizing that prem babies don't always make it. A couple of years later one of the many parish mums gave birth at twenty-five weeks to a baby boy, who died in her arms as her husband looked helplessly on, just minutes before medical help arrived. I had come across the couple before – I'd baptized their first child, they were very pleasant, very civil, but I didn't feel I'd made much connection with them.

But even so, when I heard about their loss I felt compelled to go and see them, simply because I was so utterly sorry for them. The searing grief of bereavement is compounded by people giving you a wide berth because they don't know what to say, especially when you lose a child.

I didn't know what to say either, but I knew I had to be there. So after evensong one September Sunday night I detoured via their home, sat with them, listened to them, held them in their grief.

In due course we had the little boy's funeral. I dug the grave myself to keep the costs at zero. The father carried his son into church in a little white coffin which he placed on the altar, his wife and their two-year-old daughter by his side. And that was the congregation. It proved too much for the hardened undertaker, who had to leave us to our own devices. I can't believe it now, but we had a hymn, 'All Things Bright and Beautiful'. God knows how we sang it. Ray, the boy's father, had played rugby for Castleford so was used to bellowing out rugby songs. Like Eric Morecombe he could manage the right notes, but not necessarily in the right order.

Yet we managed the hymn, we managed the sorriest of funerals, and we shook hands at the church gates and they walked away. Or rather, they didn't. I saw a lot of them in the next few weeks, as I was always popping in. And as weeks turned to months, Ray and his wife, Sue, got confirmed. Six months later Ray became my churchwarden, and this hard-talking Yorkshire businessman woke up our sleepy parish and proved my right-hand man.

By Christmas 1987, Rachel was once again great with child, as the Authorized Version of the Bible so quaintly puts it. By then Ruth was two, and on 6 January – the Feast of the Epiphany celebrating the Magi bringing their gifts to the infant Christ – Ruth brought her yellow blanket to her mum, saying, 'This is to keep the new baby warm.' That blanket was her favourite possession, in fact we had to resort to subterfuge to clean the thing, waiting until she had fallen asleep before we sneaked it away, quickly washing it, tumble drying it, and returning it to her bed before she awoke. Yet at Epiphany she gladly offered it for the new baby.

The new baby arrived nineteen days early on 10 January, a normal birth this time, another little girl whom we named Hannah. She was a very placid baby, and indeed became quite a wondrous child. Once I lost my cool at tea time, when food was flying all over the place. Hannah, still less than two, looked into my eyes and simply said, 'Be happy, Daddy.' The first night we moved her out of her cot and let her sleep in a normal bed, I was awoken by a loud but muffled wailing. I traced the sound to Hannah's bedroom, and it was coming from a lump at the bottom of her bed. 'Help, I'm a bit stuck,' the lump wailed. In her sleep she must have burrowed down the bedclothes, only to awaken trapped in her dark cocoon. Hannah joined about a dozen church babies and for years I didn't need to write more than the first line of my sermon, because I could guarantee the rest of it would be cried out. So I made the first line a very good one.

Our own set of babies was completed with Clare Iona in November 1989, a child who chuckled almost from her very birth; always seeking fun, a great joker, never happier than when she was given games for her birthday or Christmas which would draw all the family in. The countryside around Monk Fryston was a bit flat and boring, so for my days off we used to drive into the hills, walking above Helmlsey or in Swaledale or Wensleydale. We often called in at Harrogate en route, so the children could browse the toys in the Early Learning Centre and we could buy a treat from Betty's iconic bakers. Two weeks after Clare was born we took her to Swaledale, walking on a deserted road high above the Swale at Muker, a favourite spot. The north wind was like ice and cut through layers of clothing and flesh to the bone. Poor Clare howled and howled and would not be quietened. With hindsight it seems cruel exposing a newborn baby to the wildest Yorkshire weather. Except Clare grew up to adore exploring the moors and hills in even the fiercest conditions, almost as if we inoculated her at just two weeks old against the worst the elements could throw at you. Just like mending things was like coming home for me, moving to Helmsley was a coming home for Clare.

Chapter Twenty

At 3 p.m. precisely I climbed into the passenger seat of Lord Feversham's Defender, grateful for a sit down following my Helmsley cricket debut. We climbed up the B road, a stream of motorbikes overtaking us on their way home to Middlesbrough, having had their fill of Helmsley. Father Bert was installed on the bench seat at the very back, scanning the road behind with eagle eyes and acting as Lord Feversham's rearview mirror.

'Six motorbikes approaching at ten o'clock, my Lord, estimated speed eighty-four mph, followed by a Harley Davidson with a girl pillion, estimated speed seventy-two mph. By the way, you're pothering blue smoke.'

'Don't worry, Bert, all Defenders do that. Their differential always whines, so you can hear 'em coming, and they always burn a hell of a lot of oil, so you can smell 'em when they've been. Like most of my tenants, they whine on approach then leave a stench behind!' Lord Feversham chuckled at his own joke as we reached Surprise View then dropped down into Bilsdale, the road falling away so steeply that you simply couldn't see it over the Defender's bonnet. Father Bert went pale.

'I never like nose-dives – too many of my friends never

came out of them,' he said, his face so, so sad it wrenched my stomach.

So many parishioners talked to me about the war. I realized that Helmsley had a high concentration of over-seventies, for whom war had loomed. The aftermath of the First World War would have dominated their childhood; absent fathers and uncles lost in the trenches, wounded veterans, blinded by mustard gas or with lost limbs, an all too visible reminder of the conflict. Then came their own service in the Second World War, taking on a ruthless killing machine. I guess it wasn't just Pessy's Paddy who was terrified of the utter black fury on the faces of the enemy. I listened respectfully to all their many tales, realizing the time for telling them was rapidly running out. It was my privilege to listen beside them for what remained of their day.

The beauty of Bilsdale's green fields, bounded by dry-stone walls criss-crossing the valley with a handful of farmsteads perched on the sheer hillside, restored my cheer. In the middle of nowhere we drove past the Sun Inn, with a sandwich board announcing QUIZ NIGHT EVERY WEDNESDAY 7 P.M. MADGE'S HOMEMADE PIES SERVED FROM 8 P.M. FIRST-COME, FIRST-SERVED! Clearly Wednesday night was party night.

'But where the heck do they get any customers from?' I asked, looking at the swathes of green for miles around, inhabited only by sheep.

'Oh, they walk down from their farms in Bilsdale, Brans-dale, Beckdale, East Moors or wherever,' Father Bert explained. 'Madge has a powerful outside light which attracts moths and farmers from miles around!' He chuckled to himself as he continued, 'It's finding their way home after closing time which is the problem – they tend to lose their bearings when they've had a skinful. It was better in the old days when they rode over on their farm horses. Then when they staggered out of the pub they could just slump into the saddle and the horse would know its way home.'

'Yes, I rue the day we saw the last of our farm horses,' Lord Feversham interrupted. 'They were truly hefted to the hills; however many new-fangled gadgets, no tractor can match them.'

'Many a night I was called out when I was vicar to find the lost shepherd,' Father Bert continued, with a wistful look in his eye. 'Locating them wasn't very difficult – they were singing so loudly I could hear them even over the revs of my jeep. I used to bundle them in and drive them home into the tender arms of their good lady wife, who gave them a reet ear-bashing for troubling the vicar.'

Lord Feversham suddenly pulled off the road and we bounced along a rough track; one of the many green lanes with a surface of closely cropped grass. 'We're too early in the day to be chasing Madge's lost shepherds, Bert. I thought I'd show David the source of the Carlton Water Race.' He spoke in hallowed tones, as if we were Livingstone and Stanley, tracing the source of the Nile.

We trundled up a hill for about a mile, heading towards the Bilsdale TV mast. 'It's over a thousand feet high, you know,' Father Bert informed us. 'And that's on top of a moor twelve hundred feet high. I used to gaze at it when I drove down the A1 from County Durham. I never dreamt that I'd end up as vicar of it!'

Lord Feversham pulled up sharply, 'There she blows,' he shouted, hobbling over to a spring gushing gallons upon gallons of crystal clear water. He cupped his hands and slurped noisily, 'Absolutely beautiful, not a hint of chemicals,' he said, beaming.

My eye was caught by a darting movement to the side of his feet, as a yellow adder with characteristic black zigzags slithered away, deciding it was no match for Lord Feversham when it came to a drinking competition. Riding on the adder's back was a miniature version of itself; I blinked a couple of times, wondering if being bounced around in the Land Rover had given me double vision.

Father Bert allayed my fears. 'You were lucky that adder didn't nip you, my Lord. They get very protective when they're carrying their autumn babies,' he wryly commented.

'Pah, no snake is going to take me on,' Lord Feversham laughed. 'My leg is so full of antibiotics that I would poison it rather than it me!' He looked reflective for a moment. 'Mind you, thinking about adders slithering all over the moors, I wonder if that's where Joseph Foord got his idea from?'

During yesterday's visit to Duncombe Park, Lord Feversham had waxed lyrical about this guy, who had served as land agent to his ancestor Thomas Duncombe in the eighteenth century. He was a local boy made good, who knew the area like the back of his hand. The problem was that whilst there was a plentiful supply of springs in the valleys, any water on the uplands quickly drained away through the pervious limestone.

'Things came to a head in the long hot summer of 1762,' Lord Feversham informed Father Bert and me. 'Every single cow grazing at Old Byland died in the drought. The knock-on effect was that our tenant farmers had no income to pay their Michaelmas rents, so the whole economy of our estate was grinding to a halt.'

'Ee, just imagine, no roast beef on Margaret's table. I don't know how I would have survived, man,' Father Bert joked.

'Well, there would be hell of a lot of scrawny beef to consume to start with,' Lord Feversham pointed out. 'But then nothing but famine for months afterwards. Clearly something had to be done.'

They had tried to sink wells, but digging through the limestone to a sufficient depth below the water table was impossibly hard manual labour. Bringing water from the valleys by ox cart, though a slightly easier option, was slow and cumbersome. Joseph Foord had come up with the ingenious solution which I had ably demonstrated to the girls over lunch, until my scale mash-model of the North York Moors had dissolved in a mush.

'He must have been quite something striding the hills with his telescope, spirit level and surveying poles,' Lord Feversham pondered. 'It was all very minimalist, creating his own relief maps, employing just a handful of men to dig shallow water channels which snaked over the hills, using hollowed-out tree trunks as makeshift aqueducts, taking advantage of the west–east decline.'

'How did they seal the water in?' I asked.

'That's the beauty of it, they didn't. Using puddling clay or cement or whatever would have taken ages and cost the earth. All they did was line the channels with gravel and sand, and let the rushing water and gravity do the rest. They leaked something terrible, but there was so much water gushing from the springs it didn't matter. And it was uphill-downhill sort of stuff.'

'How do you mean?'

'Jump in the Land Rover and I'll show you.'

We bumped back down the track and drove back up Helmsley Bank, our engine roaring on the steep incline. Just at the base of Surprise View we turned left onto a forest track, lined with a thick carpet of pine needles which nicely cushioned our boneshaker of a journey. Father Bert had retaken his seat as tail-end Charlie. 'Barn owl at ten o'clock, David,' he informed me. The owl, with its characteristic white face and light beige wings, glided behind us, tempted by the fading autumn light, its head slowly scanning the undergrowth. 'He's a canny lad, following us. He's hunting any mice or voles disturbed by his Lordship's chariot! They're nature's ultimate killing machines, you know.'

It took me back to when I was a teenager in west Hull, and we had a barn owl who regularly perched in a recess in the chimney stack in our Edwardian vicarage, scanning our lawns and the adjacent park for its supper. My parents had bought my brother a border terrier puppy, and one twilight I was exercising the almost full-grown dog in our garden when I realized the owl was swooping down on it for a kill, mistaking its light-brown colouring for a rabbit's. The dog turned, snarled and gave one sharp bark. The owl suddenly realized its mistake, that this was a rabbit with a definite attitude, not to be messed with. It aborted its mission in the nick of time, scraping the lawn with its talons as it desperately flapped its wings to achieve the lift it needed.

My mind jerked back to the present as Lord Feversham suddenly turned off the ignition and made the engine stall. It was uncanny: climbing up the track, surely we needed a lift like that owl's to stop us grinding to a halt. But instead we actually picked up speed.

'It's what I said, uphill–downhill. We're quite close to the route of Foord's Carlton Water Race here,' he said. 'You think you're climbing, but that's an optical illusion, because the hills are actually falling towards the North Sea.'

We coasted up and down for a couple of miles before reaching Cow House Bank, the steep hill between Carlton and East Moors which I had cycled up and down when I'd toured all the churches earlier in the month. Lord Feversham pulled up and scanned the hillside. 'We cleared away the bracken a couple of years back and uncovered the race, which was still trickling with water despite it not being used for forty years. Let's have a rummage and see if we can find it.'

Lord Feversham, Father Bert and I scoured the hillside like detectives doing a fingertip search, until Father Bert suddenly dropped down two feet.

'I think I've found it, my Lord,' he shouted. 'Give me a hand, David, and pull me out!' He laughed as I nearly toppled in with him. 'That's reminded me of a funeral I took in Cold Kirkby. We got to the grave, but one of the sides had fallen in overnight, so the undertaker leapt in with his shovel and cleared the bottom, sending a shower of soil over me and the chief mourners.' Father Bert covered his head with his hands, acting out the charade. 'When he'd finished I leant over and took hold of his hand to pull him out, but the gravesides were so slippery, I fell down on top of him. Ee, it was an absolute shambles trying to scramble out!'

Father Bert explained that the old lady they happened to be burying had become more than a bit cantankerous in her declining years, so her relatives and friends weren't too upset at losing her. 'But they all wept at that graveside, tears running down their cheeks with helpless laughter, flowing like one of Foord's water races! I could hardly keep a straight face

as I intoned, "Earth to earth, ashes to ashes, dust to dust",
because I was absolutely covered with earth, ashes, dust and
God knows what else. Margaret was by my side, tittering
throughout. She wasn't tittering when she had to wash my
white surplice not once but five times to get all the mud out,
though.'

The three of us scrambled up and down the hillside, kicking the bracken out the way for about ten feet to reveal the
watercourse, a trickle surreally running uphill.

'See what I mean, uphill-downhill,' Lord Feversham lectured, pointing out the obvious. 'By the laws of gravity the
water should be going down, but instead it's going up!'

Our water-race seminar was suddenly interrupted. 'What
the 'eck are you three getting up to?' a grey-haired and somewhat bedraggled woman shouted across to us as she emerged
from the bracken at the other side of the road, carrying two
bulging carrier bags.

'We were just showing David the water race, Eva,' Father
Bert replied, quickly climbing out of the stream, where a
moment before he had been merrily splashing, as thrilled as
a toddler in a paddling pool. 'What are you up to, then?'

'I've been gathering blackberries – they're never lusher
than by the old water races. I wanted to catch them before the
Devil pissed on them!' she informed us.

'Don't worry, David,' Father Bert responded, noticing my
frown. 'It's just a country expression, isn't it, Eva?'

'Oh yes,' she explained. 'There's one day in October when
t' blackberries turn. The day before they will have been
plump and sweet, but then overnight they wither and taste as
sour as vinegar. We call it the Devil pissing on them!'

'My Lord, can I ask a favour?' she continued. 'I've walked

out 'ere from Helmsley and I'm fair jiggered. Any chance of a lift back?'

'Of course, Eva, be my guest,' the genial Lord Feversham replied. We all climbed into the Land Rover – Eva, Lord Feversham and I huddled together on the front bench seat, Father Bert once again at the back. I realized this was the same Eva who had held court in Carlton Church for my so-called hour of silence. It was her smile that jogged my memory; she smiled broadly at the prospect of a ride home, the same smile that had lit up her heavily lined face in Carlton Church. She was lean, like many who had worked hard on the land for a lifetime; a wiry frame, muscles taut with energy. She was sitting very close to me and I could feel her warmth positively radiating through her thick clothes and stout coat.

'Tell us what you know about the water race then, Eva,' his Lordship asked as we roared up the bank and headed home.

'They were still using it when we moved into Carlton as newlyweds in the 1950s,' Eva began, moving animatedly as she spoke (movement compounded by the bouncing Land Rover). She hardly took a breath before continuing, 'We had an outside tap, so I was spared the trek to t' pump. The pump was at a trough, which was topped up by t' reservoir, which itself was fed by the race. My, it were a bit complicated. But the reservoir was ten-foot deep and eight-foot wide so there were always enough water for whole village. It were a foul colour, though, with little creatures swimming in it. The 'ealth officer condemned it time and time again as unfit for human consumption, even though we always boiled it.' As she recalled the taste of the polluted water, Eva pulled a sucking-on-a-lemon face. 'I wasn't surprised it was so filthy. As kids we used to walk along the race as a short-cut to school, splish-splashing in our muddy wellies, and there'd be bird muck and sheep muck and leaves and God knows what else on them. Over t' years people were fined for softening their sheep skins in the race, or steeping thatch or watering their horses. It should have been called a sewer race rather than a water race!'

'So how did they keep it flowing?' Lord Feversham asked, crashing into second gear as we pulled into Carlton.

'If you rummage through your records at Duncombe Park you'll find the estate employed a waterman, my Lord. If we had any trouble, we used to send him a postcard and he'd eventually come out and unblock it or fix any leaks with puddling clay. And boy, did we have trouble!' Eva paused for dramatic effect before reeling off a list. 'Moles and rats would burrow into the race and suddenly find they had an ocean flushing through their tunnels, children would be little beggars and kick t' sides of the race in just for fun, carts and cattle crushed the race sides in when they tried to cross it, not to mention snow and leaves and dead sheep bunging it up. There were one farmer who kept diverting it to irrigate his land. He may have irrigated his land, but it didn't half irritate us.' Eva broke off, chuckling at her clever play on words. 'We never had it blocked by a dead shepherd though, although it's a wonder, considering the state some of 'em used to come wandering home in after an evening at Madge's Sun Inn. You deserve a medal, Father Bert, for saving them from a watery grave.'

Father Bert beamed serenely, puffing at his pipe.

'The whole race was always leaking,' Eva went on. 'There were one stretch where we were threatened wit' strap as kids if we even ventured anywhere near it. Ground was so sodden beneath it, it were an absolute quagmire which would have sucked you down, never to be seen again. Mind you, the leaky races came to our rescue when we had those terrible moorland fires in t'summer of 1960. By then we'd been put on to mains water, but t' local firemen opened up the races again and let them douse t'smouldering hillsides. If it wasn't for those races, everything would have been ash!'

'Perhaps we ought to make Joseph Foord a local saint,' I joked.

'He were clever, but he were no saint,' Eva continued, as if she had gone to school with a man who had died over two hundred years ago. 'I bought a book on history of Helmsley from Claridge's years back, and I read it from cover to cover – it weren't half a gripping read!' she joked, a twinkle in her eyes. 'But it had pages galore on Joseph Foord. He took the old earl to court for not paying him his dues as his agent, and won. Nobody dared to do that in those days. Lord Feversham walked these hills like a god, and God help anybody who crossed him!'

'What's changed?' Lord Feversham interrupted. 'I may not be God, but as far as you're concerned, I'm the next best thing!'

'And then he got a girl in the family way, but refused to admit that he was t' father and do the decent thing and marry her,' Eva continued, blithely ignoring Lord Feversham's chilly tone.

'Given his skill for transporting liquid up and down hill and dale for miles, perhaps he merely ejaculated at East Moors and she conceived in Bridlington!' Lord Feversham guffawed.

Eva blushed. 'Ee, God-like or not, you gentry are mucky beggars. And in front of our new vicar and Father Bert to boot. You ought to be ashamed of yourself, my Lord! Foord refused to wed her anyhow, even took the girl, whose child he'd fathered, t' court for defamation. He were drummed out of the Quakers for failing to repent and joined the Church of England. Mind you, thinking about it, even if he had wed her, he'd have been drummed out of the Quakers. She was his second cousin, and they were very particular about that sort of thing.'

'Good old Church of England, we'll let anybody in!' Lord Feversham said, still chuckling away as we turned the corner and all Helmsley was set before us: the church with its tall Victorian tower, the ruined castle, the red-roofed town with the beck tumbling down Castlegate, no doubt drawing its water from one or two of Foord's races somewhere or other. All blazing in glorious autumn sunshine, looking picture perfect.

'I don't care what you say, Eva, he was a saint,' Lord Feversham said. 'He built seventy miles of water races to all these moor-top villages, quenching their thirst for almost two hundred years. You can allow a man who does that a bit of latitude with the odd foolish night of passion! And as for taking on my ancestor, well, he was a queer old stick who deserved taking down a peg or two.'

He dropped Eva off at a small terraced bungalow which can't have consisted of more than a tiny kitchen, living room and bedroom. There were twenty such bungalows in the cramped close; I guess they were the final resting place for all his Lordship's tenant farmers, totally spent after a life of hard labour cultivating the moors.

'Just hang on a minute, my Lord,' Eva said, as she disappeared through her front door. Two minutes later she returned with three margarine containers brimful with black-berries. 'Just a small present for bringing me home; a few blackberries for your good lady, my Lord, and your good lady, Vicar, and your good lady, Father Bert.'

'I don't have a good lady,' Father Bert replied, his voice a cross between wistful and terse, accepting the berries never-theless.

'No, just like Joseph Foord didn't have a good lady. Really, whatever the century, you men are all the same,' she laughed, as she waved us goodbye.

Father Bert kept a ponderous silence for the remainder of our journey. With a cheery wave, Lord Feversham dropped the pair of us off at Canons Garth. 'She's not my good lady, she's just a good friend,' was Father Bert's parting shot as he nipped back home for a cuppa before returning for Evening Prayer. I thought of the juicy roast beef Margaret served up for him day after day from generations of cattle, hefted to hills no doubt watered by Foord's races. Not to mention washing muddy surplices clean. Good friend indeed!

Chapter Twenty-one

I raced along the A170 with just a quarter of an hour to cycle the four miles to Ryedale School for another near-death experience, otherwise known as taking an assembly. Once again the speeding traffic lured me to detour via minor roads where the air was like wine compared to sulphurous exhaust fumes. It was becoming a familiar route; over the old level crossing at Harome Gates, then a fast pedal uphill, anticipating an uninterrupted view over to the rounded Wolds. But this time disaster struck, as a hare, disturbed by a combine harvesting a field to my left, bounded straight into my path. I braked sharply but there was no way I could avoid the animal, the size of a border terrier, and I braced myself for a collision. It's funny what runs through your mind in the milliseconds before a disaster; images of me being catapulted over the handlebars before slamming into the tarmac's unforgiving surface, images of the beautiful hare, her back broken by the impact, writhing in her death throes.

Incredibly, there was no collision. The hare effortlessly leapt over me, springing six feet into the air as if avoiding cycling vicars was part and parcel of her every day. She made a good landing on the grass verge before ducking under a wooden fence and streaking across a ploughed field. Within seconds she was just a dot on the horizon. Ever since my child-

Above Castlegate in Helmsley, its bank festooned with daffodils.
Below The little town of Helmsley, red roofs huddled round a
Norman church and ruined castle.

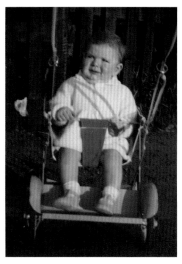

Above left Me aged eighteen months, not a happy bunny in my new pushchair. *Above right* Two years old, with my mum and dad in my grandparents' garden in Chesterfield. *Below* At the west end of York Minster in 1962, following my dad's ordination. What hats!

Above Playing the organ at St Giles',
Marfleet, 1963. The organist used to
rap my knuckles with a ruler when I
played the wrong note. *Right* Nativity
play at Bubwith Church, 1966. I'm the
one still standing. *Below* At the west
end of York Minster in 1982, following
my ordination, with Rachel, my father
and my brother Jonathan.

Left Rachel and Ruth at Surprise View, Helmsley, summer 1986.

Right Our wedding day at St Mark's Broomhill, Sheffield, Saturday 30 July 1983.

Below In Swaledale with Ruth, Hannah and two-week-old Clare.

Right All Saints' Church,
the view from the lychgate.

Left The wall painting depicting
St George slaying a red-scaled
dragon inside All Saints.

Below The market square in the
late Victorian period – little has
changed since.

Above Saints Ruth, Clare and Hannah in niches at Byland Abbey, where the monks decamped after Old Byland became too hot to handle.
Below Rievaulx Abbey with its magnificent and haunting high stone walls.

Above Looking for lost cricket balls at Canons Garth, autumn 1997.
Below A Christmassy Canons Garth, December 1997.

Above Duncombe Park, an awe-inspiring sight. *Below* An ice-train in
Duncombe Park, Christmas 1997, with Helmsley Castle in the background.

Above Looking for lost cricket balls at Canons Garth, autumn 1997.
Below A Christmassy Canons Garth, December 1997.

Above Duncombe Park, an awe-inspiring sight. *Below* An ice-train in Duncombe Park, Christmas 1997, with Helmsley Castle in the background.

hood days deep in the Vale of York, I have always paused in wonder at a hare's sheer speed. Now I added a hare's leap to my repertoire of things which didn't just flabbergast me, but came to my rescue.

'Swaledale sheep are t' best!' As I chained up my bike, Fraser was lecturing a small group of pupils of assorted sizes, huddled together outside the school entrance. He was sporting the same baggy woollen jumper, the same muddy corduroy trousers, the same ruffled wiry hair and the same air of nonchalance which I'd witnessed on my last visit.

'Why Swaledale, sir? My dad says Wenlseydales have a sweeter taste.'

'They don't have horns though. You need something to get hold of when you're sh—'

'Shagging them, sir?' one of the girls teased.

'Shearing them,' a totally unfazed Fraser continued. 'And the horns are good when it's lambing time too.'

'Oo, it proper brings tears to my eyes. I don't fancy giving birth at all, let alone a little bugger with horns attached!' the girl interrupted again.

'No, the horns aren't there at birth,' Fraser continued, refusing to be drawn. 'Those ewes having a particular difficult birth can get a bit skittish and take off. You'd never catch them again without the horns. And they're good sheep for rugged places like these moors. No fox is going to chance being butted by a Swaledale with a good pair of horns on her.'

'How much do they cost, sir?'

'Fifty quid seems to be the going rate. I've got half a dozen going spare at the moment so how about two hundred and fifty for t' lot?'

A promising deal was thwarted as the Head rushed out of

the main door. 'What are you lot doing hanging around out here? Go to your form rooms for registration this minute.' I didn't go to my form room, since I was getting slightly better at realizing the Head wasn't addressing me personally. Even so, I wasn't anywhere near as relaxed as Fraser, who clearly made blasé an art form. The youngsters rushed inside with Fraser ambling after them. 'Now, then,' he said as he passed by the Head, distinctly unruffled. In contrast, the Head looked as if he was going to burst a blood vessel.

My assembly was dead simple. Drawing on Galileo's swinging censer calculations in Pisa Cathedral (as you do), I had brought along a piece of string exactly one metre long, with a brass weight which I had pinched from Rachel's kitchen scales tied at one end. My limited experience with knots became all too clear, because as soon as I started swinging my improvised pendulum, the weight flew off, whistling past the Head's ear before clonking noisily down each of the steps. All 350 pupils started giggling. 'Be quiet,' barked the Head, giving me his infamous death stare. I jumped off the stage, retrieved the weight, and the deputy head came to my rescue, expertly securing it with a couple of half-hitches to prevent further incident. Spotting the lass who helped out at my last assembly lurking at the back of the hall, I called her up to act as timekeeper. She sauntered up to the stage, hips swaying, tucking in her blouse before the Head barked at her.

I swung the pendulum once again, asking the whole school to count to ten full swings out loud, a count-up rather than a count-down, 1,2,3 . . . 8,9,10.

'How long did that take?' I asked Tracy.

'I don't know,' she replied. 'The second hand on my watch is broken.'

Exasperated, I took off my own watch and passed it to her. 'Give me the nod when the second hand gets to twelve, and I'll start swinging.'

The second hand must just have passed twelve, meaning that we had to wait nearly sixty seconds before we could begin our count-up again. It seemed a very long minute, with me desperately trying to ad lib, telling the story of an eccentric Durham professor who only adjusted his pocket watch once a year. 'Professor, yesterday's lecture began seven hours late,' one student protested. 'On the contrary,' the professor replied, 'it began five hours early!' Cue laughter. Actually, the young German teacher laughed, but the rest of the school treated me to a stony silence.

At last the second hand reached twelve, and we began the count-up again, 1,2,3 . . . 8,9,10. 'How long was that?' I asked once again.

'Er, it got to the number four,' Tracy replied, nonplussed. I felt quite sorry for her, shamed in front of her smirking peers. I wondered whether the second hand really was missing on her watch, or whether she'd never quite mastered the intricacies of telling the time.

'That'll make it twenty seconds for ten swings, so how much per swing?' I asked, gently.

'Two seconds,' she answered, proving she wasn't that bad at maths after all. Deciding not to push my luck, I got the ever-helpful deputy head to do the rest of the equation, that the acceleration due to gravity was equal to four times pi squared, times the length of the pendulum, which was conveniently one metre, divided by the time of swing squared. I'd tipped him off beforehand.

'That will be four times twenty-two, divided by seven,

times twenty-two, divided by seven times one, divided by four which makes –' a short pause for dramatic effect – 'nine point eight seven,' he concluded, with the broadest of grins.

There was the hugest gasp as 350 unsuspecting pupils thought we had a Stephen Hawking in our midst. I had just raised that deputy's street cred sky high.

'It's about ten then,' I quickly added. 'For every second you fall, you go ten metres per second faster because of gravity. Ever since I was your age,' kids must get fed up by old gits going on about when they were their age, 'I've been totally amazed that simple stuff like a watch, a piece of string, a weight and a bit of maths puts you in touch with something as massive and universal as the invisible force due to gravity. I now spend my life wondering about how other simple stuff can put us in touch with the invisible force we call God.' Point made, leave it there, don't waffle on any more. If youngsters connect, they'll connect; if not, don't let your message die the death of a thousand qualifications.

The Head then harangued the pupils for using too many paper towels, a typical obsession in whatever school I ended up in. I whipped up my audience to a frenzy over eternal stuff; headteachers brought them down to earth with paper towels. Notwithstanding the pressure on the school budget brought about by excessive paper towel use, the Head invited me to stay for a cuppa. I guess my dog collar unnerved his secretary, because as she carried in our tray of tea to his office, she flung the door open with great force; it hit a filing cabinet and bounced back, knocking the tray from her hand and sending hot tea flying all over the place.

'You seem very enthusiastic, this morning, Diane,' the Head joked, rushing out and coming back with his arms full of paper towels, which he used to wipe down the splattered door and walls.

Once things had calmed down, we chatted happily. The main wall of his room was packed with row upon row of coloured cards, now splattered with specks of tea, each bearing a child's name.

'They're year nine GCSE options,' he explained. 'I like to keep track of every subject each child is doing, where they are, whenever, and follow them through year ten and year eleven.'

I reminded myself that years nine, ten and eleven were the third, fourth and fifth form in old money, just like I was always reminding myself that 17½p was 3s.6d and 500 grams were just over a 1lb.

'Goodness, that's so impressive. But do you mind if we take an example? For instance, what's my assembly volunteer, Tracy, doing at the moment?' I asked, testing the system. I had come across this sort of stuff before, brilliant in theory, but with no actual application when it came to the crunch.

'She's in maths at the moment, but you'll have realized she struggles a bit, borderline level three or level four. We've got the former head of PE to help her along. He's a no-nonsense sort of guy, no agonizing over why you do this or do that, he just tells them how to do it and gets on with it. He's had fantastic results with low achievers.'

I was so impressed. He talked for over an hour about the pupils, naming each one and describing what they were up to, what he thought they were capable of, what opportunities they had missed, who had let them down, who had enabled them to flourish. I had worked in over thirty schools and never come across care that was so meticulous, costly and time-consuming. John's Gospel talks about a good shepherd truly knowing his sheep; I realized I had the best of shepherds before me, the fiercest of exteriors but with the tenderest of hearts.

No hares crossed my path on my cycle ride back to Helmsley. But just before the Harome crossing I spotted a dead pheasant on the verge – recent roadkill. It was a male, its plumage a positive kaleidoscope of autumnal hues. I picked him up and clipped him to the back of my bike: he would make a tasty tea.

'I see you've been poaching, Vicar,' Bernard shouted across to me as I cycled into Helmsley. 'Don't bother plucking the wings, it'll take you ages and there's no' but a scrap of meat on them. Just nip them off at the breast with a pair o' pliers!'

Bernard was married to Enid, my doughty churchwarden who was typically sage and calm and very rooted in the area; she'd grown up in Rievaulx, playing with her sisters amidst the Abbey ruins as a little girl. She and Bernard had a cottage on the edge of the town – a smallholding where they kept a few sheep, along with chickens and ducks and the odd goat. Our three girls had stayed with them overnight when we'd moved in to Helmsley, and had slept the sleep of their lives on three ancient feather beds. They had woken early, because various women who also kept small flocks of sheep kept ringing Bernard for advice. Terms like 'blowfly strike', 'copper deficiency', 'liver fluke', 'pulpy kidney' and 'staggers' wafted up the stairs, making the girls think they had been transported to a parallel universe. I had come across quite a few like Bernard and Enid in my time at Aughton, and again at Monk Fryston; scratch farmers who eked out a living, and often a good living at that, from their smallholding. They also helped other farmers, or those trying their hand at farming, with trusted advice or just an extra pair of hands at harvest, and were paid in kind. Despite the lack of job security, their kitchen tables invariably groaned under the weight of cakes galore, and there was always some stew simmering in their Yorkshire range, exuding the most seductive aroma.

Arriving back to Canons Garth, I decided there was no time like the present, so began plucking the pheasant in our back yard. I competed with Rachel, who had washed all the sheets whilst I had been at school and was hanging them out to dry. In my enthusiasm, the odd feather strayed onto the odd wet sheet, but it was easy to pull off and hardly left a stain, so I couldn't understand why Rachel was making such a fuss. I'd cleared about a square inch of feathers from the breast when I paused.

'What's the matter?' Rachel asked, noticing the feather production factory had ground to a halt.

'I'm just amazed by how warm this bird is,' I said. 'It must be a couple of hours since it was knocked down, but its breast is still hot. In fact, it seems to be getting hotter rather than colder.'

'You'd be getting hotter rather than colder if some mad vicar started pulling all the hairs on your chest out!' Rachel laughed.

At that moment there was a huge squawk – the pheasant was very much alive. In my panic I threw the thing into the air, where it flew into white sheet after white sheet, leaving its calling card on each and every one – a pungent yellow-brown liquid dribbling down Rachel's pristine washing. Having completed its dirty-sheet protest, and having made itself considerably lighter in the process, it gained enough lift to clear the stone wall of the churchyard, and took refuge in the lower boughs of a convenient yew, still squawking loudly at me for inflicting such indignity upon it.

'Just look at my washing,' Rachel cried, 'I'll have to soak those sheets for ages to get those terrible stains out.'

'Oh, I'm really sorry, love. And I can't even offer you a delicious tea in compensation, since the bird seems to have truly flown.' I tried to look sympathetic, but then I began to laugh. To start with it was just the odd suppressed giggle, but in seconds it turned into snorts and pealing gales of laughter. 'I really am sorry,' I repeated, all too aware that Rachel was giving me the most thundery of looks. 'I'm just imagining what would have happened if – *ha ha ha* – I'd taken Bernard's advice and nipped the wings off with a pair of pliers first. We'd have been chasing – *ha ha ha* – the thing around the yard with it squawking and spurting jets of blood – *ha ha ha* – over everything!'

'Yes, and you'd have had the RSPCA on you like a ton of bricks,' Rachel said as she unpegged the filthy sheets and plonked them into my arms. 'You just go in and put these to soak in the sink, and consider yourself let off lightly, *very* lightly. And don't ever bring back a "dead" pheasant on my wash day again!' Then she too started laughing as we staggered into the house.

Chapter Twenty-two

This morning I had cycled up to Duncombe Park with details of the lesson Lady Polly was to read at the forthcoming Remembrance Day service. My second encounter with the uneven concrete roads laid by the 22nd Dragoons wasn't any better than the first. I was juddering like a pneumatic drill by the time I reached Lord Feversham's back door and rapped on the woodwork like a woodpecker on LSD.

I was shown into the kitchen, where his dome-headed Lordship sat on his large oak chair and Lady Feversham looked as elegant as ever – bustling around the Yorkshire range, once again stirring huge pans of bubbling, steaming soup. 'I thought we'd go for something from the Sermon on the Mount, "Blessed are the peacemakers, for they shall inherit the kingdom of heaven," that sort of thing,' I explained to Lady Polly.

'That'll be great. I do love a bit of irony,' Lady Polly replied, her eyes twinkling. 'A nice antidote to all that horrible jingoism that infects Helmsley at this time of year!'

'There speaks the president of the Women's British Legion!' Lord Feversham laughed, injecting his own brand of irony. 'For goodness' sake, sit down, David, you're shaking like a leaf. I know we lords can intimidate people, but I thought you'd have got used to me by now!'

'It's not you, it's your concrete roads! Haven't you ever thought of having them tarmaced?'

'Good heavens, no, they're a positive heirloom,' Lord Feversham replied.

'They didn't strike me as much of an heirloom when I was driving back from Morrisons with a load of delicate vegetables in the boot. By the time I reached the house they were so mashed up, all they were good for was this soup.' Lady Polly grimaced.

'Don't take on, it's not the beaches of Normandy, my dear. You should be thankful it's only your aubergines that took a bashing,' Lord Feversham chuckled. He went on to explain to me how the Dragoons, a flail tank regiment, were the first to hit Normandy's shore, clearing the minefields ahead of the infantry, at risk both from the mines and the heaviest enemy fire.

'Basically, they drove Sherman tanks with cutters attached to the front to take out the barbed-wire fences, and with something like a threshing machine attached to the back, to disturb and detonate the mines.' From the utensil rack, Lord Feversham grabbed a pair of scissors which he wielded in front of him with his left hand, and a whisk which he waved behind him with his right. It wasn't the best impression of a Sherman I had ever seen, despite him adding *phutt-phutt* noises as he staggered around the kitchen.

'For obvious reasons the tanks moved forward slowly, at little more than a mile an hour, dribbling a trail of chalk dust from a box attached to their side to mark out the track they had made safe for the soldiers following on foot.' He grabbed the bag of flour Lady Polly was using to thicken the soup, tucked it under his arm and squeezed it like a bagpipe's

bellows, leaving a line of flour on the stone flags as he continued. 'Because of all the muck and debris the threshing chains
threw up, the tanks couldn't shoot and flail at the same time,
so were sitting ducks for aggressive enemy fire, if a rogue
mine didn't blow 'em apart first. Boom, that's me done for!'
he exclaimed, collapsing back into his chair.

His voice softened. 'Their time in Helmsley must have been
like heaven compared to the hell that they found in Normandy. Within minutes of the D-Day landings' beginning,
most of the regiment had been destroyed, lads not much older
than our Patrick – not out of their teens, for pity's sake. So
few of them managed to return, but each D-Day and Remembrance Sunday the dwindling band of brothers come back to
Helmsley and we give them pride of place, their regimental
standard held high. So just make sure you put on a good show,
Vicar.'

I juddered back down the hill with Lord Feversham's clear
instructions ringing in my ears. That afternoon there was a
knock on the door. I couldn't believe my eyes, because there
on the step stood the world-famous actor Ian Carmichael. I
had long been a fan of his Boulting brothers films – including
I'm All Right Jack, in which he had co-starred with Peter
Sellers – as well as his major roles as Bertie Wooster in the TV
series of P.G. Woodhouse's *Jeeves* and Lord Peter Wimsey in
adaptations of Dorothy L. Sayers' detective novels. Throughout he portrayed the archetypal, perfectly mannered English
gent. Once I had recovered from the shock and said inane
things like 'Goodness me, you're Ian Carmichael!' I invited
him in. Over a cuppa in our kitchen he explained how he'd
served in Helmsley as a commissioned officer in the Dragoons, having been seconded from the Royal Armoured

Corps 'to lend the chaps a bit of a hand.' Like me he originated from Hull. 'I come from Hull, don't you know, somebody has to!' But he now lived at Egton; I envied him living in this beautiful hilltop village on the northern edge of the North York Moors, with stunning views over to Whitby's red-roofed town and ancient abbey perching on the cliffs, and the North Sea beyond. Since it was just twenty miles north of Helmsley, he often popped back for any Dragoon reunions.

He told me how, when they weren't practising flailing tanks in Helmsley, the Dragoons had helped the local voluntary firemen put out moorland fires caused by the dry heather spontaneously combusting and re-combusting in the legendary summers of that bygone age. Equipped with an endless supply of brooms, Ian was under strict orders to lead his crack squad to extinguish the flames once and for all. He made it sound like an episode from *Dad's Army*, with his men positively fanning the flames rather than extinguishing them, resulting in the voluntary fireman having to come to the troops' rescue when they were surrounded by a fierce ring of fire. Steering a course between Henry V and Captain Mainwaring, Ian had given his men the stiffest lecture: 'Now look here, chaps, if we can't lick these bally moorland fires, how the hell will we ever lick the Nazis?' The pep talk clearly did the trick, because by dusk every single ember had been extinguished, and Ian and his men, blackened with soot, had wearily returned to Duncombe Park – mission accomplished.

At dinner in the mess that night the Colonel invited Major Carmichael to step outside onto Duncombe Park's veranda, which overlooked the moors; the same privileged view which Rachel and I had enjoyed after our lunch with the Fevershams. 'So, Carmichael, you put out all the fires, did you?' was the Colonel's curt comment as both men surveyed the horizon, totally and utterly ablaze.

'But you know, Vicar,' Ian concluded, 'vexing though those moorland fires were, by night they were often mistaken by the Luftwaffe for Middlesbrough's string of steel furnaces which lit up the night sky twenty-five miles to the north, causing them to drop their bombs too soon. Not much harm done, after all.'

I recalled Eva's evacuees from Middlesbrough, holed up at East Moors, fearing that Teesside's blitz had followed them south. I guessed Major Carmichael wouldn't have been so relaxed about it had he been squeezed into the school house with all those children, screaming in terror.

He seemed to read my thoughts, because his 'Pip, pip, old Bean' facade suddenly gave way to a more serious tone. 'I'm sorry to bother you with this in your early days, David, but for a long time I've been feeling that my old regiment has been treated shabbily by the church.'

'Goodness, I'm so sorry,' I replied, absolutely appalled if these heroes hadn't been treated with the respect they deserved.

'Oh, don't worry, it's not your fault. But ever since the war, the Dragoons' battle standard has been hidden away in a shady corner beneath the church tower. I feel it deserves a more prominent position, worthy of the sacrifice that so many of my band of brothers made.' He told me how time and time again he'd tried to get the previous vicars to do something about it, but had been repeatedly fobbed off with claims that such a proposal would never get the approval of the Ecclesiastical Jurisdiction Measure; the cumbersome regulations which governed what could and couldn't be installed in

ancient church buildings. He himself had had a bad experience with the Measure – when his first wife died he had been
refused permission to put up a small plaque in her memory in
Egton Church.

I realize that rules are rules, but it seemed more than a bit
mean, turning down Egton's most famous son in his grief,
especially when church buildings were so often festooned with
all sorts of inappropriate memorials to slave traders, local
despots, absentee vicars and motley has-beens from previous
centuries. I felt so sorry for him that there and then I decided
to right the wrong by taking up a campaign to erect a proper
memorial to the Dragoons. Not wanting to do anything by
halves, I boldly proposed to move it to the sanctuary – centre
stage at Helmsley Church's east end. Since the expensive
Mouseman panelling around the sanctuary had been financed
by the surviving Dragoons in memory of their fallen comrades, it seemed a sensible move. But Ian Carmichael was not
optimistic.

'That's really very kind of you, old chap,' he said, 'but if
the powers-that-be couldn't give permission for the little
brass plaque in memory of my dearly departed wife, they're
hardly likely to let us fly a battle standard over the high altar!'

Personally, I felt that that was just where the standard of
these bravest of men should be, soldiers who had literally
given their lives for their friends. That night I contacted my
old boss, David Hope, the Archbishop of York. Despite being
the busiest of men in the most stressful of jobs, he made it
clear that he was always available for his clergy, 24/7. He
listened sympathetically, asked lots of questions and promised
to pursue our cause with the diocesan authorities.

'But you know what these legal wallahs are like, David.

Even with me behind you, I'd only give us an evens chance, if that. But I'll do my best, so leave it with me. Helmsley Church has been through a traumatic time recently what with your predecessor's shenanigans, so you all deserve a break.'

Chapter Twenty-three

Bound for a regular Friday appointment in Rievaulx, I cycled NNW out of Helmsley along the bottom of the steep-sided Beckdale, sneaking through Lord Feversham's pheasant pounds – the avian equivalent of a high-security prison. Reaching the end of the wire cages, I washed my bicycle in the ford over the eponymous beck, the mudguards clogged with droppings from the 30,000 frightened pheasants that roost here. Bernard, my churchwarden's husband and pheasant-plucking expert, had informed me that 29,000 are murdered annually, with 1000 spared to breed next year's kill.

'You see, Vicar,' Bernard went on, 'the keepers will tell you that pea-brained pheasants positively deserve to be shot – good for nowt else other than a quick death. So that entitles them to charge exorbitant prices for weekend shooting parties. City gents deck themselves out in plus-fours and pay thousands of pounds each to be bounced around in muddy Land Rovers. They skulk in lodges, scoff a lukewarm lunch of convenience food masquerading as Michelin star, and wash it down with swigs from hip flasks filled with Johnny Walker charged out at Glenfiddich prices.' Bernard shook his head in disbelief that these wizards of the financial world and kings of the stockmarket should be so gullible. 'Then beaters drive the pheasants into their path – they can hardly miss. But most of these Hooray Henries *do* miss. The few they do bag are taken home as trophies for suburban wives – then *they* don't know how to pluck and dress game, so the shot birds generally end up in the bin. And they claim it's the pheasants who are pea-brained!'

Bernard's tirade notwithstanding, Beckdale provided the loveliest of cycle rides. Most of the leaves in the wooded valley had fallen by then, forming a rich golden carpet on the valley bottom. Both the beck and path were ringed by the autumn sunlight, at last able to pierce through the bare branches of the trees. Once you rise out of the pheasant pound, the beck flows sparkling clear. The narrow path broadens to become a tarmac road so steep that the gutters aren't parallel to it, but have to cut across it at right angles; the only way to prevent a sudden downpour turning the road into a raging torrent. I huffed and puffed as I ascended, the pain in my legs like daggers sticking into my thigh muscles, my lungs burning with exertion. Just when I feared my strength was going to give out, just when everything around me became the dazzling bright that precedes a dead faint, I reached the top, entering another world. Here the dark forest gives way to bright green fields.

I cycled along, breathing heavily, my head turning to the right, drinking in the distant scene – mile after beautiful mile of purple-topped moors. There was a black-haired, barrel-shaped guy walking ahead of me behind a couple of dozen Friesians. He kept shouting at them, driving them on with a birch switch, cajoling them. Though he clearly knew each cow by name, that name was less than flattering.

'Don't you even think about it, Droopy Udders . . . Come away from that gate, Dribbly Bum . . . Leave that mistletoe alone, Big Tits.'

They remained oblivious to his direction, intent on having a leisurely stroll and pausing to chomp some tasty morsel lurking in the hedgerow, or trying their weight against a rickety gate to see if they could break through and romp around some forbidden field.

Still recovering from my near-vertical ascent, I couldn't summon up enough energy to overtake the man, let alone risk a collision should Droopy Udders take a surprising trajectory, so I cycled alongside him, doing my best to keep up.

'Gorgeous view,' I said.

'Ay, I never tire of it, though I look over it every day. That's t' farm where I work over yonder, you see,' he said, pointing to a smart stone farm house, surrounded by a cluster of ugly corrugated iron barns. 'Big Tits, leave Dribbly Bum alone,' he shouted when the former had become a bit frisky with the latter.

'So this is a dairy herd,' I said, stating the bleeding obvious. The Victorian philanthropist, Elizabeth Fry, was keen to show off her knowledge of things agricultural during a farm visit despite being urban to the core. 'What are those beasts over there?' she asked a stockman.

'They be heifers, ma'am.'

'Yes, yes, I know that, my good fellow. But are they male heifers or female heifers?'

The stockman must have given her the same sort of pitying look my cowhand gave me. 'Yes, this is a dairy herd. We milk 'em all, twice a day, never a holiday. They're good producers, but with milk prices so low my boss barely makes enough to scrape a living for us all. So he has t' diversify. Leave that buggering gate alone, Shitty Tail!'

'What else does he do, then?' I asked, once he'd headed off his errant bovine.

'He writes. He sets down his memoirs; life on a moorland farm. But he can't be doing with all these agents and publishers taking their cut, he's had enough of that with the Milk Marketing Board, so he's self-published.'

That reminded me of a chap in my Middlesbrough days who was always boasting he was a self-made man. Mm, no one else could have made such a bad job, I'd thought to myself.

'And he does all the marketing himself,' the man continued. 'T' farm's a bit quiet on an afternoon, so he and I often nip down to the market place with a 'oldall of his books, wait for a coach t' pull up, and sell them to tourists as they come off the bus. You've got to take every opportunity when you diversify. He never goes to a family funeral without taking a few copies of his book along, and touts his wares at the wake!'

He drove the cattle into a field and I cycled on my way, bemused by my cowman's tales of his entrepreneur boss with his once-in-a-death-time offers! I dropped down the steep wooded valley into Rievaulx, where the ancient Abbey still stands proud, despite the worst that Henry VIII tried to do to it. Everyone remembers seeing Rievaulx for the first time; a hidden place that comes upon you all of a sudden – an unexpected view, brim-filling the valley with tall limestone buildings and graceful arches and intricate vaulting so beautiful in countryside so beautiful that it just makes you want to cry.

The Abbey was built in the twelfth century, with the Cistercian monks who built it taking their precedent from Moses and the Red Sea by physically diverting the River Rye, which cuts through the valley floor. This gave them enough dry ground to squeeze in a massive church, kitchens, eating rooms, libraries, dormitories, meeting rooms and an infirmary. The surrounding area was gifted to the monks by the lord of the manor, who wanted to earn himself time off from purgatory for such good behaviour. Acre upon acre was worked by tenant farmers, labourers and shepherds, who all raised revenue for the Abbey. The monks, as well as providing them with employment, educated them and gave them medical and even hospital care, looking after their bodies as well as their souls. Rievaulx Abbey was a veritable industry, the largest in the North, and cared for locals from the cradle to the grave and beyond, enabling a barren area to flourish.

Then along came Henry VIII and his commissioners and despoiled the place, even tearing down the wooden roof timbers, setting fire to them, digging deep holes and burying the lead which had melted in the flames. This was no casual or gentle reformation, but total warfare from scorched earth to scorched roof timbers. And a whole welfare system which had benefitted the valley for centuries was wiped out at a stroke. It was as if a pit village had not only lost its mine, but everything else had gone too – from schooling to doctoring and all stops in between. It was a nuclear apocalypse, four hundred years before Rutherford split the atom.

Robert Aske, lord of the manor of tiny Aughton, where I'd lived as a boy, led a peaceful revolt against the monasteries' closure called the Pilgrimage of Grace. This had great success in the North, with the principal towns of York, Pontefract and Doncaster yielding to him without a single casualty. A very worried Henry sued for peace and the protesters disbanded, but then its ringleaders were arrested and tried for treason.

Robert Aske wasn't sentenced to be hung, drawn and quartered like the rest; instead he was condemned to be hung on chains on Micklegate Bar, and took ten days to die. Robert Aske was my local hero, not just because he provided little Aughton with a brief moment of fame, but because he stood up for faith against greedy kings. Since then I have always had a soft spot for monasteries and Roman Catholicism, and like David, my biblical namesake, the Goliaths of this world have never impressed me that much.

Robert Aske had gently tried to stem the tide, but had ended up being hanged for his trouble. Yet despite the shock and awe tactics visited on it by the Tudors, there was a deep soulfulness about Rievaulx that was indestructible. The stones remained; high walls and vaulted ceilings which even Henry VIII's merry men could not tear down, enabling faith to surge softly backwards through the intervening centuries. The last-but-one vicar had talked of feeling as if a spiritual steam engine was behind him whenever he visited Rievaulx. My indefatigable predecessor, Charles Gray, had tried his best to get the Abbey re-roofed, but couldn't raise the £30,000 to do the deed – a fortune in Victorian times. But at least he'd restored the slipper chapel – St Mary's – with its lethal stone tiles reminding everyone of their mortality.

The lead buried deep in the ground by Henry's commissioners had been rediscovered in the 1920s. It was put to good use; re-leading the Five Sisters Window in York Minster, which had been removed to safety during the Great War to prevent damage by Zeppelin raids. The commissioners had originally buried the lead because, with the onset of a very wet winter in 1539, any carts bearing such heavy cargo would have sunk to their axles on tracks which were little more than quagmires. They intended to return for their spoils the next spring, but for some reason they never came back. So it was nearly four hundred springs before the precious treasure was found and put to a far better use than sating Tudor greed.

Although the monks were driven out five hundred years ago, there is still a monastic presence at Rievaulx in that a couple of Anglican nuns occupy a cottage at the abbey's entrance, complete with their own tiny private chapel; a grasshopper overlooking an ecclesiastical giant. The two women were members of an order of nuns which I had first encountered way back in the autumn of 1962. My dad had taken a group from the church to stay at Wydale Hall, a retreat house staffed by nuns about twenty miles east of Helmsley, deep in the North York Moors. My mum went along, so I went along too. Though we had travelled fifty miles from Hull, fish still loomed and was served at every meal. The winter which followed was one of the severest for decades, and the van delivering fish to Wydale got stuck in the snow drifts and the delivery man froze to death in his cab. Despite the windfall of frozen fish, the nuns' fondness for the stuff understandably waned after that.

The retreat was a silent one, so I was baffled by all those adults not talking to each other, as if they had got into an almighty sulk after a terrible row – by no means an unusual occurrence in east Hull. One very young nun took pity on me. She hitched up her red-lined skirts and we scoured the woods together, hunting for conkers. Returning with our hoard, she used a skewer from the kitchen to drill a hole through their centre and threaded them with a piece of string. She then enlisted the other nuns to join a knockout conker competition which I won, although I think the other players were being extremely lenient. Over thirty years later, I mentioned the incident when preaching at the nuns' mother house in Whitby. An elderly nun sidled up to me afterwards and said, 'I was that nun!' She had never forgotten the copper-haired little boy from darkest Hull, and I had never forgotten her.

The retreat was my first visit to the deep countryside, and I was enthralled by the wildness of it all. By night I lay awake listening to the rasping cry of pheasants; I guess they were calling me home.

Since becoming vicar of Helmsley, each Friday lunchtime I'd cycled over and said a quiet Communion with the nuns. This day, as in previous weeks, we were joined by a small group of people who travel the length and breadth of Yorkshire to be there for a service which barely takes half an hour. All are women who have had their fair share of tragedy and are uncomfortable with conventional church. They feel safe coming to the sisters. As the only male present at the proceedings, I inevitably feel a bit self-conscious, and that day nervous old me accidentally knocked over a whole flagon of Communion wine. The whole congregation raised their eyebrows, as if to say, 'Hm, typical man!' The normally formal service then took a novel turn as they fussed around with dish cloths, tea towels and kitchen paper, trying to mop up the wine before it stained the carpet. Fortunately, the wine wasn't consecrated, otherwise the two nuns present, à la my college tutor's fantasies, would have had to consume the whole carpet.

Though in her nineties, one of the nuns at the Abbey, Sister Bridget Mary, thinks nothing of spending her annual fortnight's leave visiting her nephew and niece in Peru, scaling the Andes with them like a mountain goat and returning with the photos to prove it. As a girl she had attended the school in

Whitby run by the sisters, and then at eighteen had professed her life vows, just before the Second World War began. At the beginning of the First World War, just before Christmas 1914, a German destroyer had shelled Whitby, damaging the Abbey and several houses in the town, so in 1939 the seaside resort was more than a bit jumpy that history might repeat itself, and the sisters considered relocating their school inland.

But then, as the threat of Nazi invasion of the whole of Britain loomed in the spring of 1940, the nuns proposed a more drastic evacuation. It was Bridget Mary, by then a popular teacher at the school, who was assigned the task of single-handedly taking the girls by train to Liverpool and then sailing with them over an Atlantic criss-crossed by U-boats to the safe shores of Canada. The nuns, like most of the British populace, really believed that invasion was inevitable, and had felt that sending the girls to Canada would enable this bloom of British maidenhood to be preserved intact until the Nazis were vanquished and it was safe to return. Bridget Mary, truly an action-nun, often talked of the whole escapade in the same matter-of-fact way that teachers these days talk of a trip to Alton Towers.

Chapter Twenty-four

'If they don't live in Helmsley, they can't be buried in Helmsley, those are the rules, otherwise everybody the length and breadth of Yorkshire will want to be buried here,' the trustee concluded grimly.

The fiercely guarded parish cemetery lay in a sunny south-facing spot beneath Baxton's Hill, to the north of Helmsley on estate land. In fact, there was an inner cemetery with padlocked gates and high yew hedges, a cemetery within a cemetery to which only the Duncombe family had access and were laid to their final rest. The outer cemetery was available for lesser mortals. In Victorian times this was restricted to Anglicans or those who opted for a Church of England burial, with a less salubrious patch available for non-conformists, Roman Catholics or atheists, but in these more ecumenical times we were less fussy. Provided, it seemed, that they had lived in Helmsley immediately before their death.

'What about people who lived in Helmsley but who've been in hospital or a care home for a long time?' I asked the trustee.

'Well, strictly speaking, if they're on the electoral roll they can be buried here, if not they can't,' he persisted.

The thing was, all of a sudden I had not one but two people who didn't qualify to be buried here. The first was an eighty-six-year-old guy called Jim from Redcar, a grey sea-side town near Middlesbrough. Jim and his son, Chris, had called on me yesterday, out of the blue. I showed them into my study and brewed a cup of tea and listened. Jim looked so gaunt, and was in the last stages of lung cancer, with only weeks if not days to live.

'I was born in Helmsley, Vicar, and this has always been home for me,' Jim began, speaking in short spurts, catching his breath repeatedly. 'When I was a boy, come winter or summer, I'd stride up onto the moors, and it was always marvellous. My mum died when I was just a lad, but the moors seemed to ease the sadness. The grouse, the deer, the hares; wondrous things. I could just watch them for hours.'

'Yes,' I agreed, 'I try and cycle up to the top of Baxton's every day now, and it proves a tonic every single time.'

Jim took a sip of tea, caught his breath and continued. I had the sense he hadn't got long to tell his story. 'In our teens my brother and me learnt dry-stone walling. Repairing old walls, putting up new ones – it was the job which dreams were made of. Such views! And air like wine. And they actually paid us to be out on the moors!'

Then the Second World War dashed all that. Jim told me how he and his brother were conscripted as shipbuilders and were billeted in Middlesbrough, where they raced against time to convert trawlers into minesweepers. It was very urgent work, and the management turned a blind eye to health and safety.

'We'd only been working in the boatyard for a few months when there was this terrible explosion – they were arc-welding too close to a fuel tank, or something like that. My brother copped it, along with a dozen others. They hushed it up, not wanting to damage morale. There was a lot of hushing up things like that in the war; management getting away with shoddy practices.'

'Oh, I'm so very sorry, it must have been so hard,' I said, truly feeling for him facing a double bereavement; already grieving for his beloved moors in a town full of smoke and grime, then grieving for his brother and only friend.

There was a long pause. 'Ah well, the sorrow passed in time, like most things pass,' Jim said sagely. 'I met this wonderful lass called Nancy, and we fell in love and married, and she made life worth living again. We started off renting a back-to-back house in the centre of Middlesbrough. It was a rat-ridden hovel really, but you'll put up with anything when you're in love.'

After the war Jim had got a job in the steelworks, where the money was good. 'By this time Chris had come along, and we saved enough to move out to Redcar and buy a shiny new Ford Anglia,' Jim told me proudly. 'But I never forgot my old roots in Helmlsey, Vicar. I worked long hours, but whenever I had a half-day to spare, we drove the thirty miles over the moors to give us a taste of home.'

'Every single time he returns to Helmsley, it takes years off him,' Chris added poignantly. 'Even his accent changes from Teeside to Moors!'

'It's my heart's desire, sir, to be laid to rest here, to come home at the last,' Jim said, haltingly, every word costly, painful breath following painful breath. 'I realize you'll have your rules, but if it were at all possible, well, I would be in your debt for all eternity.'

'Leave it with me,' I'd assured them as I bade them goodbye.

Early the next morning I had had a call from Chris, inform-ing me that his dad had died during the night. 'It seemed like a great weight was lifted off him. He really liked you, believed you would fight his corner.' No pressure then.

No sooner had he rung off than the undertaker called. 'There's been a death in Helmsley,' he began; his usual grim, if unsurprising, icebreaker. Every undertaker I have ever dealt with has always sounded a bit miffed that death had come their way yet again, as if they'd really like to ring up the vicar and discuss Saturday's football results, or their wives' moods, or invite me out for a drink. Only once a year, just before Christmas, did they knock on my door when death wasn't on the agenda, presenting me with a bottle of Croft's, 'with the compliments of the season, Vicar, and thanks for all your help.' I'm not sure whether it was psychological, but the sherry always tasted of embalming fluid.

'Actually, it's not quite a death in Helmsley,' the undertaker continued, diverting from his usual patter. 'It's a bit compli-cated. It's a young lass, by the name of Sally, who's died of a drug overdose. She was just seventeen, had lived here, there and everywhere; with her dad, with her mum, in care. For a while her dad lived in Helmsley and she was so happy here, loved the place. In fact, in her short life, it seems Helmsley was the only place where she was truly happy, so they want to bring her back.'

'I'll look into the cemetery rules,' I promised. 'Leave it with me, I'll get back to you.'

Later in the day I'd had my discouraging conversation with the cemetery trustee, and so I didn't hold out much hope that either Jim or Sally could be buried at Baxton's. But in one of the damp attics in Canons Garth I had discovered a musty tome entitled *Helmsley Cemetery – A History*. Previously I had given this outstanding work of literature a wide berth, but now I poured over it, just to check whether the trustee was playing by the rules. It seemed the running of the cemetery was in the hands of three trustees; two who were elected, and the third being the Vicar of Helmsley, who served ex-officio, and whose decision, should any dispute arise, was final.

Even though I personally felt I was the most laid back, collaborative priest in history, Rachel often teased me that I had dictatorial tendencies. I had been unwise enough to share with her an episode from my childhood, during our Aughton days. There had been an election for head boy and head girl at our local primary school at Bubwith. By then I was the tallest and strongest boy in the class and was the monitor on the school bus, which meandered around the lanes driven by the near-blind Les. I made it clear to every child on that bus that they should either vote for me or else, and I won by a landslide – forty-nine votes out of ninety-six – with my nearest rival only achieving a mere dozen. I wasn't proud of the episode, and have felt ashamed and mortified that I shored up my vote with menaces. In my defence, I don't think I wanted to win to wield power or influence. It was just that I absolutely adored Mr Nixon, my head teacher, and simply wanted to work closely with him – in my infant mind believing that head boys and head teachers at least had heads in common. Ever since then, despite Rachel's teasing, I have shied away from taking advantage of my position.

Until now. I rang both cemetery trustees, intending to gently but firmly tell them I was overruling them, given the special circumstances. The one who had told me non-residents weren't allowed cut up a bit rough, suggesting that if I was going to exercise absolute power, then I could exercise absolute responsibility and cut the cemetery grass myself. The other trustee was Derek, the former postman I had encountered at the end of my day of prayer. Since he was profoundly deaf, his wife talked over the phone, writing down my every word for him and then relaying his reply.

'Oh, poor little soul,' she sobbed when I told her about the dead girl. 'Derek says, you go for it, David.'

So that made it a simple vote, two to one in favour, with me spared having to exercise absolute power – until the next time.

Jim's funeral turned out to be a very decent affair. He had never forgotten Helmsley and Helmsley had never forgotten him, because the church was full of locals with whom he had kept in contact, even if it was just the annual exchange of Christmas cards. They had all come to pay their last respects to this true son of Helmsley, who had bravely served in his own way during wartime. By the graveside, I threw the rich brown soil on his coffin, 'Earth to earth, ashes to ashes, dust to dust.' Chris, his son, was standing by my side. 'Thank you for letting him come home,' he softly said, tears running down his cheeks.

Sally's funeral was far more fraught. Her father and aunt had met with me in my study at Canons Garth, beside themselves. Life had clearly been difficult for them all, and they talked rather confusingly of betrayals, addictions, times when they were flush, times when they were strapped for cash. 'She could be a bit wild, and took some handling,' her dad explained. 'I realize I lost it sometimes, hit out at her, but she gave back as good as she got and used to hit me back. From time to time I just couldn't cope any more, and she had to be taken away into care. That really broke my heart.'

'Oh you did your best, you did your best,' Sally's aunt said, squeezing his hand. I guess every parent feels a sense of inadequacy, that they could have done so much more to cherish their children. Terry Wogan was always playing Abba's 'Slipping Through My Fingers' on his breakfast show, and it brought a lump to my throat every single time. I didn't judge this guy wringing his hands before me. There but for the grace of God, I thought.

Sally had collapsed in the back streets of Leeds and the post-mortem revealed that she had died of a heroin overdose, although her dad was convinced that the drug had been deliberately spiked. It was all a garbled tale of drug barons and of young girls being forced into prostitution, being beaten up or worse if they refused. He claimed that Sally had refused to kowtow and had been made an example of.

Whatever had actually happened, a young girl's life had been cruelly ended and Helmsley was to be her final resting place. The day of her funeral was the last Friday in October; market day. The dawn was angry red, ominous, and a thunderstorm was forecast. Alan, my churchwarden, had got up early and put out police cones by the church lychgate, to make sure the market traders kept their white vans clear for the funeral cortege. I stood by the lychgate in my robes, ready to receive the coffin, sheltering under the eaves from the gathering storm. Alan was by my side, his back ramrod straight, almost standing to attention. Gus was with him, straining at the leash. Father Bert had turned out too, standing with me in his robes, muttering in his Geordie accent, 'Po-oor lass, po-oor little lass.' I was very glad they were there, my right-hand men.

Clearly no expense had been spared: a highly polished

hearse and three limos drew up. The coffin was made from the finest oak and covered in flowers. Sally's dad, aunt and sundry relatives and friends gathered at the lychgate, along with five very rough-looking young lads, aiming to carry her coffin into church. Gus growled at them.

'What are you lot doing here?' Sally's dad suddenly shouted at them. 'You gave her the drugs that killed her.'

By this time the rain was pouring down, lightning flashing, thunder crashing.

'Leave it, let's go,' I said to Sally's dad.

The lads lifted the slim coffin onto their shoulders and shuffled into church, me and Father Bert leading them, Sally's dad, aunt and a collection of other folk walking behind. 'I am the resurrection and the life, he who believes in me shall never die,' I intoned as we walked through the church door.

The church was absolutely packed: family; local teenagers who had known Sally fleetingly during her time in Helmsley; teenagers from elsewhere who had been her friends or fellow addicts; heavily pierced and tattooed men who looked like thugs, no doubt suppliers and pimps here to see the end and give everyone the evil eye; others who I guessed were plain-clothed police officers with closely cropped hair, watching everyone, like cats stalking birds, waiting their moment. All too often, I had had funerals like this in Middlesbrough, but never for a moment expected one in Helmsley.

We sang 'All Things Bright and Beautiful' and 'Lord of the Dance' as the lights flashed on and off with each thunder crash: 'I danced on a Friday when the sky turned black / It's hard to dance with the devil on your back . . .' Sally's dad and aunt had wanted to say a few words: Earl Spencer had given a moving tribute to his sister, Princess Diana, at her funeral in

St Paul's, and they wanted to do the same for their Sally. But when it came to their moment they were sobbing uncontrollably, so I said a few words as the rain drummed on the church roof; how this was simply intolerable, such an utter waste of a young girl's life, how those who had supplied her with drugs had blood on their hands, how those who had bought and sold her had blood on their hands, how the weeping sky was a parable for God weeping over every child so cruelly lost. I was so angry.

We walked to the cemetery, the cortege bringing the market-day traffic to a halt. I wore the thick woollen cloak that a dear parishioner had made for me in my Middlesbrough days. It was guaranteed to keep out the pelting rain for about twenty minutes; enough time to bury the poor girl in the waterlogged cemetery, a pool of muddy water in the bottom of her grave. Father Bert stood beside me, in his thick black cloak, gently saying the time-honoured words in his beautifully softly spoken Geordie, 'The Lord gives, the Lord takes away. Blessed be the name of the Lord.'

Job done, we stood by the iron gates of the cemetery and shook everyone's hand, rainwater streaming down our faces. Local teenage girls and teenage boys, their eyes red with weeping; other teenagers, haggard with jaundiced tearless faces, tell-tale signs of addiction; thugs who refused to shake my hand, refused to look at me. Finally, Sally's dad and aunt, still utterly distraught, giving me a hug.

Then the undertaker stepped in. 'Seeing as you don't live locally, I've brought my invoice along. We did everything as you asked,' he said, holding out the bill. Probably not the best time to settle accounts. It certainly wasn't for him, because as soon as Sally's dad and aunt saw the envelope they legged it, running like Olympic sprinters through the torrential rain, the undertaker running after them, waving his bill, losing ground by the minute. Father Bert caught my eye and we both smiled at each other – the first smile that day.

Chapter Twenty-five

'Come on, bonnie lad, I think we deserve a spot of lunch,' Father Bert said as we stripped off our robes in the vestry following Sally's funeral. Though my trusty cloak had absorbed most of the downpour, a fair few drops of rain had got through, dampening my clothes, making me shiver. Rachel was out for the day doing a bit of supply teaching, so I gladly took up Bert's offer.

Of course, it wasn't him who was offering lunch, but Margaret. We drove up out of Helmsley through a driving rain which turned to thick fog on the moor tops, damp and chill. I was glad I was in Father Bert's warm jeep and not being drenched on my bike. We wound our way slowly, Bert peering through the windscreen, familiar landmarks obliterated. The swirling mist conferred an anonymity on well-known places, which popped up alarmingly, with no prior warning, no distant scene. Suddenly the high walls of Rievaulx Abbey loomed before us, so at least geographically we knew where we were. But the fog, aided by just a little imagination, transported me to different ages: the Abbey in its heyday, an industry of prayer and work, the valley thronging with bleating lambs; Henry VIII's cruel commissioners tearing the Abbey down, smoke and fire and cries of anguish, monks running for their lives, their livelihood gone with the stroke of Henry's pen; the Abbey's neglected ruins in the quiet 1950s, yet to be promulgated as a World Heritage Site; Helmsley's Vicar popping down to the school every Friday to cane the big boys who'd cheeked the nuns.

We left generations of ghostly voices behind us as we crawled up the hill to Old Byland and parked in Margaret's stack yard, the homing jeep knowing its way there despite the fog. Margaret bustled out of the back door to greet us.

'Just look at the pair of you,' she exclaimed, 'white as sheets. Come on in and get warm. I'll put a couple of chairs around the Aga.'

It was a re-run of my previous visit; Father Bert and Margaret teasing each other, plates piled high, thick slices of another roast leg of lamb, the fat crisp and sweet, done to a turn, followed by apple pie and steaming, creamy custard, followed by strawberry trifle domed with whipped Jersey cream.

'I've told you before, Margaret, we really should have fish on Fridays, and abstain from meat!' Fr Bert chided.

'Tush, fish wouldn't bring the colour back to your cheeks like a bit of juicy lamb. And anyway, the Lamb of God died on a Friday, so I always have lamb in His honour.'

It certainly did the trick. I felt thoroughly restored as we sat afterwards in Margaret's exquisitely furnished sitting room, a log fire roaring in the grate, finishing the meal off with a strong cup of tea and a stack of After Eight mints. My eyelids became heavier and heavier and I repeatedly had to stop myself drifting off. I thought of my friend Stephen, also a vicar, who had returned to work after a bad bout of mumps. Shortly after lunch one day he had gone to visit an old dear and settled himself down in her comfy armchair. The next thing he knew she was tapping his shoulder, 'Vicar, Vicar, I think it's time you were going to evensong.' It was 5.45, and he'd slept a full four hours, with his parishioner simply watching this man of God, slumbering in her midst.

Father Bert must have read my thoughts. 'David, if we stay here much longer we'll both be snoring the afternoon away. I need to go and see Edna, one of my former parishioners at Cold Kirby, who's been in hospital with pneumonia. You'll really like her, a very faithful soul, never eats anything but fish on a Friday!' He ducked as Margaret threw a cushion at him.

We drove along the ridge to Cold Kirby. A fierce west wind had cleared the fog and rain, meaning that we had fantastic views over the wooded valleys to our north and south. We pulled up outside a tiny terraced cottage, smack in the middle of this moorland village perched just above Sutton Bank. The hamlets surrounding Helmsley tended to have a very smart feel; their houses well-appointed. In sharp contrast, the houses in Cold Kirkby looked more than a bit battered and care-worn. The wind had had free rein, picking up speed over the long Vale of Mowbray then funnelling up Sutton Bank's five-hundred-foot cliff before blasting down Cold Kirkby's main (and only) street. I could see where the cold in Cold Kirby came from, and why Edna had succumbed to pneumonia.

'Brr, it's always like this, even in high summer,' Bert admitted, as we tumbled into Edna's cottage. The front door opened straight into a living room cluttered with dark oak furniture, with barely drawn heavy velvet curtains hanging at the draughty windows. Edna, a white-haired rotund lady, her face red and weathered, had been lying on the settee, but sprang up as soon as we entered.

'Father, it's so good to see you. I've been reet bad, but I'm on t'mend, thank God. Ee, it is lovely to see you. I were six weeks in hospital but t'new vicar never came once to see me. You were a saint, always popping in to check how we were!'

'I don't think I was. I was just partial to your scones,' Father Bert joked. 'Anyway, I've brought the new Vicar of Helmsley to see you, so put the kettle on.'

A few minutes later Edna bustled in with a tray of steaming tea and a generous plate of scones, spread liberally with butter and raspberry jam. The scones, though huge, were as light as a feather and fortunately slipped down a treat. Had they been heavier, I wouldn't have been able to face them after my massive lunch.

'Well, you haven't lost your touch, Edna,' Father Bert said, licking the jam off his fingers.

Edna's red face flushed even redder with pride. 'The jam's homemade, as always, freshly made yesterday with the last of my autumn raspberries.'

'Lovely,' Father Bert replied. 'Nothing better than your scones and jam as a chaser after one of Margaret's lunches.'

I was beginning to wonder whether Father Bert had spent his entire time as a parish priest wandering from farm to farm, sampling folk's cooking. 'Fortunately, David here does a lot of cycling, so will work off the pounds. Equally fortunately, I don't have to, because smoking this helps me to be naturally skinny!'

As he spoke, he packed tobacco into his pipe and lit up. Edna started coughing, violently. 'Ee, I'm so sorry, luv,' Bert apologized, putting his pipe out immediately, emptying its contents into his saucer, 'I'd forgotten about your pneumonia.'

'So you cycle then?' Edna asked me, once she had got her breath back. 'We all used to cycle when we were young. Every Wednesday night during wartime about a dozen of us would cycle down Sutton Bank to the flicks at Thirsk, eight miles there, eight miles back.'

'It would be an easy free-wheel down, but a reet hard pedal coming back, wouldn't it?' Father Bert asked.

'Well, we went t' chippie once the film had finished – with eight pence of cod and four pence of chips inside you, you could tackle anything! And we used to walk some of t' steeper bits.'

'That's cheating, Edna!'

'Not really. Most of us lasses paired off with a lad, so we didn't mind the chance to get our breath back and to get to know each other better.' Edna gave us a cheeky wink.

'Ay, I should think you would have needed a fair bit of mouth-to-mouth resuscitation climbing up Sutton Bank,' Father Bert laughed.

'I did need mouth-to-mouth resuscitation once, not when I were going up, but when I were coming down. I was at back of the pack, hurtling along at thirty miles an hour, when my brakes failed on one of them hairpin bends, and I ended up flying over the handlebars and landing in a gorse bush.'

'Good heavens, Edna, did you break anything?' Father Bert asked, real concern in his voice.

'Only my 'eart,' Edna replied, intriguingly. 'As I said, I was at back of the pack, but none of t' others, including the lad I was sweet on at the time, even noticed I was missing. They just carried on, got to Thirsk, watched the film, stuffed themselves with fish and chips and then sauntered home, without giving a thought about where I'd ended up.'

'So no one came to your rescue?'

'Fortunately, there was an air station at Sutton Bank's top, where the gliders fly from now. An American airman, on t' lookout for returning Lancasters, spotted me instead, and hurtled down hillside to my rescue. "Are you OK, Miss?" – he had this deep Southern drawl that would have made me weak at the knees if they'd not already been grazed and scraped on that wretched gorse. He were a real gent, walked me and my bike back up the hill, then he took me to the first aid post. After they'd patched me up, we walked arm in arm t' canteen and he treated me to a quarter-pound beef burger with lashings of salad and ketchup – it were a banquet compared to what we were used to on rationing, believe you me. "Only the best for Edna," he said t' chef, "she's had a terrible shock." They treated me like royalty. While all this was going on, he'd got the air station workshop to straighten my bike's buckled wheel and check it out. "Take it steady, miss," he shouted as he waved me on my way.'

'As you say, a real gent,' Father Bert agreed, helping himself to another scone. 'What happened to him?'

'Well, we went out on a few dates, the odd dance or two at the airbase, that sort of thing. The local lads used to jeer at me when I turned off at the top of the bank rather than go with them down to Thirsk. But then again, he'd picked me up when they'd left me. Some nights I'd just stand at the top of the bank, waiting for t' American bombers to return. I'd be straining my ears for sound of the engines. Then one night, a full moon – a bombers' moon – I waited and waited and waited, but he never came. I learned later that they'd taken a hit and had had to ditch in t' North Sea, only five miles from Scarborough. It seemed so cruel; they nearly made it home.'

She broke off, crying. Father Bert leant over and stroked her hand, soothing her. 'I know, Edna, I know, so many never came back. The very best.'

There was a long silence. Funny where talking about a simple thing like cycling can get you. After a few moments Edna dabbed her eyes, went into the kitchen and returned with a bucket. 'Come on you two, no point dwelling on the past, you can help me feed t' pigs.'

We followed her outside into a little garden, the wind whipping my hair across my face. I envied Father Bert's Brylcreem, because not a hair of his head was out of place. Most of the garden was taken up with a wooden pen which contained a huge sow lying on her side, suckling eight tiny pink piglets.

'Edna, that's an absolutely grand litter,' Father Bert said. 'Did you have any trouble with the birth?'

'No, it went grand, they just slid out one after one. I didn't even have to call the vet out.'

'Edna used to have a famous vet, didn't you?' Father Bert prompted.

'Alf White, otherwise known as James Herriot,' Edna replied. 'He were another gent, nothing ever too much trouble. He had small hands, a woman's hands, perfect for teasing the odd stubborn piglet out into the world.'

'I thought he practised in the Dales – Swaledale way,' I said.

'Oh no, that's just in t' books, he moved in his imagination thirty miles west, to protect his clients, you know. His actual surgery was in Thirsk, so he attended to us, day or night. He didn't come up on his bike, mind, but in a little battered Austin Seven, with dodgy brakes that frightened the hell out of him going back down Sutton Bank.'

'So did he carry on after he became famous?' I asked. I was a lifelong fan of James Herriot, and I felt I had found the Holy Grail.

'It didn't change him a bit. He used to type his books up on a little portable typewriter on his knee of an evening, whilst watching TV with his family – just a hobby really, once he'd finished his rounds. Even after he got famous, he were just the same Alf we'd always known and loved. When they made a film of his books he booked a coach and took us all t' cinema in Malton to watch it with him. He never seemed to appreciate that millions around the world hung on his every word. He were just a lovely, lovely man.'

'Well, you've come across some lovely men in your life, Edna, including me!' Father Bert joked. 'Now the sow and her little ones are fed, me and David had better be getting on. David fancies himself as a bit of writer, so who knows, he might be getting his portable Imperial out tonight and tapping out the story of James Herriot tapping out a story!'

Chapter Twenty-six

I leant my bike against a prickly holly hedge, and simply gazed at Helmlsey's castle, church and pan-tiled houses; all silhouetted against a starlit sky. With the nearest large town thirty miles away there was a spectacular array of stars, un-encumbered by urban light pollution. My eyes were tracing the distinctive shape of the Plough when a scraping noise brought me back down to earth. I found eighty-six-year-old Jack tottering about in the garden. 'I'm just putting the neigh-bour's bin out,' he explained, as if he were a helpful teenager. 'She's not too mobile these days!'

Jack was an old sailor who locals affectionately nicknamed Captain Birdseye – he sported the same white beard and cap, and his Yorkshire accent was tinged with the same 'shiver me timbers' drawl as in the infamous TV advert. His sea legs meant that on land he had a lumbering gait. Or it could have been the rum; whatever time of day I visited, early or late, he never failed to offer me a drink, and I never failed to decline. Had I succumbed to one of Jack's generous measures there would definitely have been no more visits whatsoever for me that day. Val, my very proper church secretary, had once accepted just one of Jack's tots, and had had to ring her hus-band to fetch her home afterwards because the room was spinning and her voice was slurred.

Ancient Mariner Jack's oft-repeated sea stories were epic, vivid and gripping. He'd bravely served in both the Merchant and Royal Navy in the Second World War. 'We left Scapa Flow in a devil of a rush,' he'd informed me during our first encounter, a few weeks before. 'Even things that were bolted down were washed overboard, with the paint on the ship's funnels being stripped off by the fierce seas. We were in danger of sinking.' And then he had suddenly switched from the icy waters of the North Sea to the tropics, where, prior to the war, Jack had been caught up in the 1937 Hong Kong Typhoon.

'As the typhoon got stronger, the ship's engine increased speed to full-on, just to keep us stationary. The big danger was if another ship drifted and hit us. Twenty-seven ships were sunk in harbour, one landed up on the mountainside, another in the middle of a football field.'

As we entered his little bungalow this night, I noticed once again the silver-framed photo of the ship stranded on the mountainside, given pride of place on the top of his well-stocked drinks cabinet. 'Are you sure you won't have a rum, Vicar? Go on, it'll ward off the chill!' Jack cajoled.

'I'd better not, Jack,' I replied, pointing to the photo. 'Look what happened after you gave the captain of that ship one of your tots!'

'Very droll, Vicar, very droll,' he chuckled.

Very soon after we had moved into Canons Garth, Val had asked if I could visit Jack, and his wife, Mary, who was very frail. Mary was the quiet one; white-haired, sitting in her chair, painfully thin in contrast to barrel-shaped Jack, hardly moving at all whilst her husband never stayed still, rummaging around, looking for this memento, that memento from his

sailor days. She had the sweetest of smiles, and listened attentively to his stories – which she must have heard scores of
times before – looking amazed, as if she was hearing them for
the first time, and laughing at his oft-repeated little jokes. She
listened attentively to me, too. I realized she hadn't got long
for this world, so each week I had taken her Holy Communion, reading her the Gospel from the previous Sunday's
service. She gave the impression of treasuring every word,
unlike Jack, who fidgeted throughout, a faraway look in his
eyes. On just one occasion did he calm down, when I read of
Jesus quietening the storm on the lake and reassuring the terrified trawlermen with his 'Hush, be still.' Despite his love of
alcohol, the wine on offer never tempted Jack to receive Communion. 'Not for me, thank you, Vicar,' he used to say, after
I had communicated Mary.

Following the war, Jack had settled down in Helmsley and
turned his hand to farming. For a while it seemed he had put
the sea behind him, but Val had confided in me that as Jack
had grown older, the sailor mannerisms, fuelled by all the tots
of rum, had returned and were given an even greater empha-
sis than when he was actually serving in the Navy. He and
Mary used to be the honorary caretakers of St Mary's, the tiny
Roman Catholic church adjacent to their little cottage which
overlooked the beck as it flowed down from the moors into
the northern tip of Helmsley. They kept the keys, letting in
the young priests from nearby Ampleforth Abbey who came
to say Mass. One priest, Basil Hume, used to come and have
a cup of tea with them around the hearth afterwards.

'He was a lovely fella,' was Jack's verdict. 'Never too busy
to have a chat, always loved my tales of the Hong Kong
Typhoon.'

Sadly, Mary had died the week before this latest visit, and I had written to Basil Hume – by then Cardinal Basil Hume, Archbishop of Westminster – telling him how Jack and Mary mentioned him almost as much as the legendary Hong Kong Typhoon. The Cardinal replied by return in a hand-written letter, remembering the good old days and their kindness. I handed Jack that letter, and as he read it tears welled up in his eyes and ran down his cheeks. He then refolded it, carefully put it back in its envelope and propped it beside his fabled picture of the ship beached on the mountainside, the most hallowed spot in his home. 'I always told you he was a lovely fella,' Jack said.

After Mary's death, everyone had rallied around Jack. He was so very grateful to the girls at the Co-op – Jack had got them sussed to a tee. He had only to appear at the shop door and myriad assistants would run around fetching things off the shelves for him, suggesting a bargain, a tasty titbit. He was their Jack and they loved him.

He seemed invincible. In 1946, when Jack the war hero was returning home to Helmsley, his car had careered off the road and flipped onto its roof. But Jack walked out unscathed. The man who had survived all the seven seas could throw at him wasn't to be finished off by a traffic accident. But though he seemed unstoppable, Jack had certainly had his fair share of tragedy. From his ship, the HMS *Echo*, he saw his brother drowned with nearly 1500 other sailors when the HMS *Hood* was torpedoed. We talked about that yet again on my visit, with Jack having to dab the tears from his eyes.

'It frightens me, Vicar, all this sabre rattling. We had it with Maggie in the Falklands and the Gulf, and now Blair's making noises about intervening in the Balkans, of all places. Why don't they ever learn, war only produces widows and orphans and broken hearts? I don't want to see a single one of our brave lads die in yet another war.'

Had Jack been Leader of the Opposition, then all wars would have been off.

'I know you preach forgiveness, but I find it hard to forgive those who got us into that mess,' he confided in me. 'Not the German sailors, or soldiers or airmen, they were just obeying orders, like us, defending what they thought was right; their country, their families. Some of them were brutes, but so were some of our lads. But in the main they fought a fair scrap, albeit to the death. It's the politicians I can't forgive, signing young men's lives away, signing innocent children's lives away. I know Jesus said "Father, forgive them", but I can't, I bloody well can't.'

'I'm not sure whether he did forgive them, really,' I admitted. 'He asked God to forgive them rather than doing the forgiveness himself. Maybe sometimes we've simply got to hand over the job of forgiving when it proves too hard for us.'

'Do you know, I've never thought of it like that,' Jack replied, looking pensive. 'Maybe I'll just give it a go. But it's so very hard, even half a century on.' He went on to confide in me how, when they had saved just three sailors from the 1500, he had hoped against hope that one of them would be his brother. 'Please, God, let it be Harry,' he had prayed and prayed, hanging on a 1 in 500 chance. It was beginning to dawn on me why Jack had always refused his Communion; all his prayer was, sadly, to no avail.

'One thousand, four hundred and ninety-seven died then, didn't they? Such a terrible waste, Jack,' I sympathized.

'On thousand, four hundred and ninety-eight,' Jack

corrected me. 'My brother Harold's fiancée took her own life. She just couldn't face living without him. It was just so tragic, Vicar.'

Here he was: a jovial man surrounded by tragedy, losing his brother, and now his beloved Mary. And yet his cheeriness and the twinkle in his eye survived. Some people suffer very little loss, but have a miserable mindset. I recalled how, when I was a boy living in Aughton way back in 1966, my dad had once run the church garden party of which dreams are made. The sun shone, the stalls sold out and nobody fell out over the price of the cream teas. But as my weary but proud dad was clearing away that day, some miserable git came up to him and said, 'That's all very well, Vicar, but what would you have done if it had rained?'

I'd been frustrated myself, during our Monk Fryston days, at one person who was always finding fault with our church. I had joked that at our next garden party we were going to have a most-miserable-person-in-Monk-Fryston competition. True to form, the most-miserable-person-in-Monk-Fryston had then promptly complained about having a most-miserable-person-in-Monk-Fryston competition, which somewhat proved my point. The tragedy was that this person had had very little to be miserable about that I could see, whereas Jack did, and yet there was still a tremendous sense of fun and joy there.

I'd not heard about Harold's fiancée's untimely death until that night – perhaps the memory had been prompted by Jack having lost the love of his life. But immediately after telling me, Jack pressed a twenty-pound note into my hand for the collection, something he had done every single time I had visited his home.

'That's very generous of you, Jack,' I said.

'Not at all,' he replied. 'Every little helps, as the old lady said when she weed into the sea!' A very old joke, which sounded as funny as new when Jack told it.

Chapter Twenty-seven

It's Monday morning. The girls have all left after a flurry of
Weetabix, hastily made packed lunches and last-minute pack-
ing of their school bags, with a fingertip search of Canons
Garth for Ruth's missing French homework. Rachel's gone
too, a last-minute call to cover for a history teacher who's
gone down with a strange bug – probably a phobia for teaching Year Nine Set Six, the educational equivalent of Alcatraz.

I am alone, with only the house for company. The ancient
beams creak and occasionally crack like gunfire. The radia-
tors knock loudly, struggling to keep this ancient vicarage
warm on this chill, windy November morning. Whatever the
weather, there is always a ten-degree centigrade temperature
gradient between Canons Garth and the outside; I guess that's
true for most homes, except that with ours the temperature
rises as you go out. The tiny panes of the leaded windows
rattle as a squall blows in from the east, a torrent of dirty
water breaks through and gathers in a puddle on the narrow
window sill, before running down the wall onto the threadbare carpet. The smell of damp is thick, gets into my clothes,
gets into my books. Over the weekend one of the attic bedrooms which we'd decorated and designed as an art room for
Hannah turned black with mould overnight. I put on a lint
mask and cleaned the lethal stuff off the sloping ceilings and

walls before repainting the whole. Sometimes it seems to me that I've spent a lifetime dealing with dank vicarages and their fifty shades of fungi.

I looked at the blank computer screen in front of me. Every Monday morning without fail, for sixteen years in ministry, I have sat down at my desk to write next Sunday's sermon. To begin with I had written them out longhand, and then progressed to a portable Imperial typewriter, manufactured in my dad's former parish in Marfleet, Hull, then onto an Amstrad computer screen whose green type burned into your brain. When Ruth was little, she used to sit devotedly beside me at my desk whilst her mum was busy with all the Monday washing; I once left her in my study as I answered a phone call, only to find she had inserted an unusual if entertaining line in next Sunday's sermon about her favourite book, *Spot the Dog*.

Every new sermon I tried to write took me back to the first time I preached when, at the tender age of just fifteen, I found myself having to deliver the sermon on Advent Sunday.

There's a joke about an elderly peer having a nightmare that he was making a speech in the House of Lords, only to wake up and find that he was. I knew how he felt, because speaking in public was a nightmare for me. I used to watch my dad preaching and think, Never ever in my wildest dreams could I do that. And there I was, on 29 November 1970, doing just that.

I spent hours beforehand learning my sermon off by heart, and I remember it to this day.

'Advent means coming in three ways,' I boldly began. A couple of teenage girls in the youth club who were more worldly wise than me tittered; fortunately, I was a bit of an innocent and was blissfully unaware of any double entendre. Most church congregations have had some sort of Sixties bypass anyway, avoid kissing and hugging at all times, and demurely sing stuff like 'Behold the bridegroom cries "I come!"' and 'Jesus, put your tongue inside my mouth, I can come no other way', without realizing the innuendo.

'Number one, Advent means Christ coming at the first Christmas at Bethlehem, when a baby's cry pierced our dark night, broke history in two, and announced God was in town,' I blurted out, as if nobody had ever thought of that before. But the congregation nodded encouragingly, as if the Nativity was a complete surprise to them, and they'd been wondering for ages why all the shops in Scarborough were strung with fairy lights and filled with plastic tat at this time of the year.

'Number two, Advent means Christ coming into our lives now, repeatedly calling us, never giving up on us,' I stammered.

'Alleluia!' one lad shouted out. He was a Methodist and prone to enthusiasm, and didn't really fit in. Several members of the congregation glared at him. Apparently, when Methodism came into being in the eighteenth century, one new adherent kept punctuating a staid church service with countless alleluias. 'Will the person who keeps shouting out "Alleluia!" kindly remember that this is the house of God,' came the frosty rebuke from the celebrant.

'Finally, Advent means Christ coming at our end, when we will stand alone before him and his dread throne, surprised to find it none other than a mercy seat. Amen,' I concluded, nearly tumbling down the pulpit steps in relief that I had got through it all.

As sermons go, it went, and went very quickly. In fact, for

some of the more elderly members of the congregation, their bottoms had hardly touched down on the pews before they had to spring up for the next hymn, accompanied by my friend, Simon, on guitar. Phew! I thought. That's over and done with, I'll never ever have to do that again.

Except I found myself doing it, Sunday after Sunday, writing every Monday after Monday for ever and ever, Amen.

Actually, even though I'd managed to come up with a few ideas this morning, it was a miracle I was able to write any sermon at all. Just before we fell asleep last night, Rachel had told me about a conversation she had had earlier that day with an elderly lady in the church porch, immediately following the main Sunday service. It seemed the old lady didn't twig that Rachel was my wife.

'I don't hold with that new vicar having all those girls in the sanctuary,' she had complained. 'It should be men and boys only around the altar.'

'How did you respond?' I asked. The girls concerned were our three daughters, who I'd conscripted to help with all the dance moves and portable-stove-around-the-altar shenanigans. I'd thought they'd looked rather fetching, robed in white albs, moving graciously, always in the right place at the right time, with absolutely none of the self-ostentation which is often the hallmark of people fussing around in the sanctuary. Not to mention the fact that the girls lowered the average age of the ancient choir and other hangers-on around the altar by about five decades.

Anyway, the girls had come to my rescue, because the rest of the serving team – other than Derek – had buggered off as soon as I was appointed, because they didn't approve of me approving of women priests. I'd come across this behaviour many times before; people who'd chuck the toys out of their pram unless they got their own way. Serving teams, choirs, flower ladies, bellringers, groups who conveniently forget that they are supposed to be on the Lord's side and instead pursue power for its own sake. It's all a bit pathetic, really.

'Oh, I was short and sweet,' Rachel replied. 'Or rather, short and tart. I said, "Oo, what a pity, if only I had known I would have only given birth to boys!" Then I flounced off before she could think of a reply. But judging by the way her jaw dropped, I guess she wouldn't have been able to say anything whatsoever for a few minutes.'

It took me ages to get off to sleep, and I was still seething as I hammered at the keys writing my sermon. My first meeting with the Church Council was that evening, which is a bit like a team of school governors – there to enable the Head and the school to flourish, as well as being critical friends. Once I'd put my more-angry-than-usual sermon to bed, I read through the minutes of the previous meeting, held during the vacancy. Item three leapt off the page at me, and made me see red ten times more:

3. That this Council resolves that under no circumstances should children be involved with worship.

The motion had been carried unanimously. Here we were, living in the oldest, dampest vicarage in captivity, with ceilings falling down about our ears. Our clothes and my books reeked of damp, and were frequently peppered with mould spots. Little Clare was missing her friends at Bishopthorpe and finding it hard to settle into her new school. True enough, Helmsley was an enchanted place, surrounded by gorgeous countryside, but I was beginning to fear this paradise had more than a few gorgons.

I took myself off for a furious cycle ride up Baxton's Hill, battling against the wind and the rain to work off my adrenalin. I reminded myself that the church folk here had had a rough time; one vicar dying, the next vicar going off the rails, with all sorts of grief swirling around. Grief often makes people or institutions close down, pull up the drawbridge, keep out all intruders, especially noisy children who'll disturb your calm.

I recalled an unhappy period during my first year at Cambridge. My parents had moved from a parish in west Hull because it hadn't really worked for them. It could be that the countryside around Aughton and Scarborough had actually eaten into their soul as it had into mine, making them unhappy in a city. Or it could be the particular church was in a process of transition. The vicar before my dad had rebuilt it after the previous building had had to be demolished because of subsidence, caused by being too close to the Humber. He had taken on the diocesan authorities, who didn't want to rebuild, organized all the massive fundraising, and won. Then he left, and my dad came along, and though he inherited a new and shining church building, fit for purpose, the church folk seemed fatigued by all their efforts. Tired people can get a bit cross, and everyone kept falling out with each other, one argument fuelling another. I guess one or two powerful women missed all the thrill of fundraising and weren't too keen on the spiritual side, which was my dad's strongest suit. Powerful women trying to bully him triggered memories from his boyhood, which fuelled the fires even more. I tried to help things by serving on the Church Council but I fear I made it worse, in that I inevitably leapt to my dad's defence when the arguments got personal, and people understandably didn't like being taken on by this upstart of a Cambridge boy.

So my parents moved on to calmer climes, and I learnt an important lesson for my future ministry about managing conflict, or not managing it. All that was swirling around as I plotted how to handle my entrenched Church Council. And whenever I felt sorry for myself being hard done-by as a priest, I reminded myself of the story of St Teresa of Avila. On a very long, wet, cold and tiring winter pilgrimage, the final straw was when her horse threw her into the muddiest, smelliest of ditches. As the visionary Teresa scrambled out, feeling totally wretched, she heard a voice from heaven, 'Don't worry Teresa, this is how I treat my friends.'

'Then I'm not at all surprised, Lord, you have so few!' came her acerbic reply.

Just before 7.30 p.m., a dozen stalwarts hobbled into our damp dining room, wrapping their thick woollen coats around them to keep out the November chill; coats which must have taken the fashion world by storm way back in the 1930s. We began with a prayer, and then I read them this extract from St Mark's Gospel, from the Bible that had been presented to me at my ordination as a priest in York Minster in 1982:

People were bringing little children to Jesus for him to place his hands on them, but the disciples rebuked them. When Jesus saw this, he was indignant. He said to them, 'Let the little children come to me, and do not hinder them, for the kingdom of God belongs to such as these. Truly I tell you, anyone who will not receive the kingdom of God like a little child will never enter it.' And he took the children in his arms, placed his hands on them and blessed them.

Val, the secretary, then read the minutes from the previous meeting. 'Any matters arising?' I asked.

'I have,' one curmudgeonly bloke growled. 'You've spelt my name with a *ph* again, and I've told you time after time it's spelt with a *v*. Will you never learn?'

'I'm so sorry, Steven,' Val apologized. 'I'll make sure we spell it correctly in the future.'

'That's what you said last time, and the time before that, it's not good enough.'

Val looked very tearful, and my heart went out to her. 'Erm, where is Steven's name mentioned?' I asked, emphasising the *ven*.

'Oh, he proposed item three,' Val gently replied.

'Remind us what it says,' I asked.

'"That this Council resolves that under no circumstances should children be involved with worship",' Val read, her eyes downcast.

'Well, never mind the peculiar spelling of Ste*ven*'s name, it seems to me that we need to look at the whole of that item again, because it directly contradicts Jesus in the reading we've just heard. We're a Church Council, and being faithful to Jesus is non-negotiable, otherwise we're a contradiction in terms. Since we're changing a *ph* to a *v*, I also propose that we omit the words *under no circumstances should* and add the word *always* after *children*.'

It took them a few moments to get their heads around that. Steven was the first to object: 'Hang on a minute, children should be taken out of worship to stop them disturbing us. They can do crayoning and stuff in the Church Room.'

The Church Room was even damper than Canons Garth, which was quite an achievement.

'If we're going down the "taking out" road, there are a lot of other factions I would like to take out before I'd get to children,' I responded, slightly tongue in cheek. 'During the first hymn those miserable so-and-sos who will only worship in Tudor English can take themselves off to the draughty shed in the graveyard, do some crayoning-in and then come back during the last hymn and tell us what they've been up to.'

'I never thought I'd hear a vicar speak like that about faithful traditionalists,' Steven fumed. 'That's absolutely disgusting.'

'No more disgusting than talking about children like that. After all Jesus never said "Let the traditionalists come to me." But whatever, once you go down the separation route, excluding groups who disturb your calm, spoil your nice little set, then my experience is that you find Jesus himself waving at you from the very midst of the group you've shut out.'

'I'm not putting up with any more of this utter claptrap. I'm off,' Steven spluttered, banging our dining-room door as he made a noisy exit. Flakes of white paint fluttered down from our fragile ceiling, settling on our heads and giving us all a frosty look. Yet despite that the temperature of the room seemed to rise a few degrees and make for a warmer atmosphere – there was almost an audible sigh of relief as everyone took a breath and relaxed.

'He pushed all of us into supporting that motion,' Enid, my churchwarden explained. 'If we didn't back him he said he'd leave and take all his cronies with him. Good riddance, I say.'

'Hang on a minute,' Mary objected. 'I'm not at all happy at having girls in the sanctuary.' She was a lovely soul, deeply prayerful and caring. Her husband, a retired vicar, had died just before we moved in. In his time, he had been quite a fierce traditionalist, and like all good clergy wives, she remained loyal to her husband however strange his views. I've always told Rachel that when I die she should forget everything I ever said and just get a life.

'I understand, Mary,' I replied, determined to take the softly, softly approach. After all, a PM doesn't want too many members of his cabinet storming out. 'It's just that my hero, James Herriot, used to take his children on his rounds with him when they were little. I suppose the altar is my working environment, and I just like having my children with me. It can get a bit lonely up there sometimes!'

Mary gave me a silent smile. 'So, all those in favour of my revised motion, "This Church Council resolves that children should always be involved with worship."' Eleven hands went up, so that was that. 'But we're not really here to talk about what we're against, against children in worship, against girls in the sanctuary. We're really here to talk about what we are for,' I said, pressing home my advantage. 'I thought I'd give you five things to think about, they're what I feel any church worth its salt should be for.' I then rattled off my five points:

1. We should be producing excellent, moving, convert-ing worship, match-fit for 1997 rather than 1897, which will make anybody dropping in feel it's really good to be here.

2. We should be sensitive to our community's hurting points and stand alongside people who are going through their personal Good Friday.

3. We should be aiming to transform and heal those hurting points, moving people on from Good Friday to Easter Day.

4. We should be making disciples, encouraging people to fish for Christ.

5. As a church we should have a care for each other, and make sure we are a forgiving, loving and accepting community, so that when people say, 'See how these Christians love one another', they really mean it and aren't being ironic.

I let the words sink in for a moment, and found that everybody was nodding their heads in agreement; after all, I was only stating the obvious. 'Look, I'll get Val to print off copies of all these points, but I wonder if we can divide into small groups, with each group looking at one point and come up with suggestions how we can run with it?'

They readily agreed, and broke into their groups for the remainder of the meeting, huddling in various corners of Canons Garth. And whatever my family felt about living in Canons Garth, one advantage was that there were an awful lot of corners. They reconvened just before 9 p.m. to report back, with all of them concluding that they'd like more time and wanted to come back with major ideas at our next meeting. Which seemed fine. We concluded business by saying the Lord's Prayer, and then I sent them to prepare for government.

'How did it go?' Rachel asked me as they all departed, pouring me a pint of Guinness, my favourite tipple.

'It went just fine. We got rid of the out-of-work U-boat commander looking for a war, and after that it was peace in our time. It was really just a case of "love me, love my kids",' I joked, raising my glass to toast my lovely little family.

Chapter Twenty-eight

Just three weeks after Ian Carmichael's visit, an official-looking letter landed on my doormat. Against all expectations, permission to move the Dragoons' standard to a more prominent position at the east end of Helmsley Church was granted, with a full week to spare before Remembrance Sunday. God bless Archbishop David Hope, who'd obviously pulled a few strings as well as pulling all the stops out – he'd truly lived up to his surname. I think we should only appoint people archbishops if they have a catchy surname. As a boy I was always fascinated by Makarios, the very militant Greek Orthodox Archbishop of Cyprus. Makarios is Greek for 'happy'. Imagine Archbishop Hope meeting Archbishop Happy. But what would happen if they encountered the head of the Roman Catholic Church in the Philippines, Cardinal Sin?

Ian Carmichael was so thrilled when I rang and told him the good news, that the very next day he drove over and helped me and the ever trusty Derek install the standard in its new position, holding the stepladders as I screwed the mount into the wall. Our labours coincided with a coach trip from Liverpool, who were seeking shelter in the church on this rainy November day. Eventually one elderly liver bird, ignoring the vicar on the top of the ladder, asked the man below,

'Excuse me, I hope you don't mind uz askin', but are you Ian Carmichael, luv?'

'I am indeed,' Ian replied, Lord Peter Wimsey to a tee.

'I'm proud to meet you; you've given uz such pleasure,' said the lady, shaking him warmly by the hand. Our DIY then had to be abandoned as a queue of Boxing Day sale proportions developed down the church, all eager to shake the hand of the man himself.

Ian gallantly brushed the drops of rain off the shoulders of one admirer. 'We don't want you catching your death,' he said. She coloured up; he had not just made her day, but her life.

'What yur doing here then? I didn't know you worked for the church,' she asked.

'I'm just helping my good friend the Vicar hang the standard of the regiment I served in in the war, the twenty-second Dragoons,' Ian explained. 'We were amongst the first to land on the beaches at Normandy.'

'Oo, you brave things. Did you get injured?' the woman asked, chattering on as if the actor were a long-lost friend.

'Afraid I lost the tip of this finger, when we had to close the hatch of my tank in a bit of a hurry. Those bloody Nazis were throwing everything they'd got at us,' he replied.

'Oh, you poor, poor luv,' the woman oozed, caressing his hand with her hand, as if the star of her dreams' missing finger-tip could be restored by sheer willpower.

'Goodness me, it was nothing compared to what my dear comrades took. They whipped me back to Blighty and did the neatest job, stitching my finger up.' Ian drew closer to the woman, treating her as his confidante, his voice dropping to little more than a whisper. 'Do you know, the Mess Sergeant

233

visited me in hospital. "I'll be a bit slow at pulling a trigger with only part of a finger," I joked. "Guess it will be mean I won't be rejoining the lads!"

'"No, sir," he replied. "We've taken so many losses you'll have to rejoin them. But if you have trouble firing the trigger, I guess it will mean that you won't ever be coming back home!" Very droll, these Mess Sergeants! But I did rejoin the lads, and I did get back home, so there we are.'

The woman laughed raucously. 'Thank God you did, sir. My sister bought me the box set of your Lord Peter Wimsey videos last Christmas, and we've been watchin' and re-watchin' them ever since. A real treat – I can't imagine anybody pullin' off the role like you do!'

'Oh, I say, how tremendously kind of you,' Ian replied, giving her a beaming smile. 'Well, better return to my duties and help the Vicar. But it's been a pleasure meeting you, don't you know. Thank you so much for dropping in!'

I sensed it wasn't so much Ian Carmichael who played Bertie Wooster and Lord Peter Wimsey, but rather Bertie Wooster and Lord Peter Wimsey who played Ian Carmichael. The very best of men.

On Remembrance Sunday, the very best of men and women lined the High Street, their freshly polished medals catching the morning sunlight. The two minutes' silence focused on the war memorial in the churchyard, some four feet above the street below, meaning everyone in the street had their eyes raised heavenwards whilst I read the list of the fallen. The list was too long, far too long: the heart of this community had been torn out, twice, within three decades. It is amazing, absolutely bloody amazing, that this community, that any community, survived. I thought of villages in medieval times that had been wiped out by the Black Death or the Great Plague, of the monasteries and their communities wiped out by Tudor caprice. Two world wars should have finished us, yet here we were, in the words of that great father of the Church, Elton John, still standing after all this time. And not just standing, but standing proud.

During the long silence I looked around, looking at the scouts and guides and cubs and brownies, standing to attention, shivering, their uniforms too thin for this cold November day. Each face white as a sheet, eyes staring vacantly ahead, wondering what on earth all this was about. Behind the youngsters, the older folk lined up, the crowd three or four deep. As I looked at them I thought of the stories that had been shared with me over the past few weeks. I looked at Lees, who had served with Monty in the North Africa campaign which turned the course of the war. He had been captured and recaptured after making not one but two escapes as a POW in Italy. The Nazis sentenced this troublesome prisoner to hard labour deep in a coal mine in Poland, and then forced him on the Long March as they fled the invading Russians. He and many others marched ten miles a day for two months, surviving typhoid, the poorest rations and night temperatures of minus thirty degrees Celsius. I'd have spent the rest of my life recovering from all that. He didn't. He taught: a head at primary and secondary level; a chair of Governors until he was 75; coached the handicapped to play football; taught in the Sunday School. Wow! Before the war both his young wife and unborn child had died when an old appendix scar burst during labour, yet there was not an ounce of bitterness about him. One dusk I had bumped in to him breezing through the churchyard, returning from his daily ten-mile walk. A few youths were larking about outside the church, low-level stuff, the odd can of lager, the odd hand-rolled cigarette, the odd catcall.

'These young people, how do we get them from outside the church to inside the church?' Lees asked me, his eighty-five-year-old-eyes bright and alert.

'I'm not sure,' I admitted. 'To be honest, I'm more interested in getting those inside to come outside and join in the fun!'

Lees had laughed.

I looked at Rosie, a spritely eighty-three-year-old grandmother. The eldest of a large family, she'd skived off school to care for her siblings. She'd married in 1936, given birth to a daughter, and then her husband had been whisked off to serve in the Far East. He had been captured, beaten, starved, and then with other POWs had been packed like sardines into a prison ship in the Java Sea, where he died when it was torpedoed by the Americans. The Japanese had scattered these prison ships amongst their fleet, either as decoys or hoping the enemy wouldn't fire on their own. Early in the 1950s, Rosie had got married again, but to a violent, angry man, who brought home a taste of war every day.

I looked at Rob, who as a boy had gone on the ill-fated rail excursion to Scarborough which had been strafed by a Messerschimdt as it steamed into Helmsley. Some Canadian soldiers on the train had thrown him to the floor, protecting his body from stray bullets by flinging themselves down on top of him. He'd had a strange life, working at Lord Feversham's sawmill and drinking heavily. But then he'd become addicted to the moors rather than alcohol, forever wandering over them with a succession of faithful terriers. He lived just across the road from us, simply, in the tiny terraced house his parents had owned; one cold tap, no television, no oven, no inside loo. It was adjacent to the Feversham Arms, and the plush hotel had its sights on his little house, though some improvement was certainly needed.

I looked at Frances, whose brother had flown Spitfires in the Battle of Britain. Their parents had been farmers in Bilsdale, and she'd grown up with a life-long interest in botany, shooting rare flowers with her SLR camera and posting off films daily to be developed by return. She'd ended up as head of a local primary school, treating naughty boys as fiercely as her brother had treated Messerschmitts; just one look from her and the biggest bully turned into a quivering wreck. Apparently, her former pupils often wrote her letters of appreciation, expressing how her firm but fair discipline had set them up for adult life. The letters were returned, any lapses of spelling or grammar corrected with red ink; very occasionally a well-written letter escaped her censure, and the writer was rewarded with a box of chocolates.

I looked at Len, who lived in one of the tiny ex-estate workers' bungalows near Eva, with a bizarre electronic croaking frog serving as his doorbell. Like Lees, he had fought at El Alamein. He too was captured, and became a POW in Italy and Germany in 1942, enduring forced labour on the railways. As the war drew to its close, he was liberated after his POW camp was bombed by the Americans, and he made his way to the Allied lines, dodging the SS thugs still at large. After the war he'd worked at nearby Flamingo Land, caring for the animals he had seen roaming free during his time in North Africa. Then he'd had a brief time in Liverpool, dealing with benefit fraudsters who'd accused him of acting like the Gestapo, before returning to Helmsley to do this and that. Beside him today stood his wife; restless, eyes vacant, wasting away with Alzheimer's.

I looked at Harry, ancient of days, in a wheelchair and cosseted in a thick, warm rug. He was an old soldier, but his heart's desire was for peace. He was only nine when his dad had died in the trenches, fighting alongside the ill-fated Lord Feversham. He was fiercely loyal to the Duncombe family, and had worked on the estate as Lord Feversham's horseman, organizing the local hunt and lending a hand with forestry. During the Second World War he had signed up with Lord Feversham's Yorkshire Hussars and had been shipped off to South Africa and the Holy Land. After the war he had stayed on as the scattered Jewish people returned to their homeland, and had tried to keep the peace in those fraught, troubled times in Jerusalem. Now he spent most of his days sitting in his doorway in Bondgate, hailing passers-by and greeting me as I cycled to and fro, his equally ancient wife fussing around him, making sure his rug was tucked in.

I looked at George, behind Harry, holding his wheelchair. Like Harry, he'd served in the Yorkshire Hussars, and they were comrades in arms. In peacetime he had worked at Ampleforth Abbey as a coalman – stoking the boilers and the little tank engine which shunted the boys' luggage. A widower, he lived in another one of the tiny ex-estate worker bungalows, next door to Len. His garden overlooked Helmsley Primary School playing field, and he idled away his daylight hours chatting over the fence to the children, regaling them with tales of his time as a Desert Rat.

I looked at Neville, like me a Hull boy, who in his youth had thought nothing of cycling the sixty miles to Helmsley and back. Formerly a manager at Yorkshire Penny Bank, he looked a bit like Captain Mainwaring of *Dad's Army* fame, and acted like him – barking orders at his sweet wife as if she were that 'stupid boy', Pike. During the war he served in the Far East as captain of a crack corps of Gurkhas: he made it sound like *It Ain't Half Hot, Mum*. After the war Captain Neville returned to Hull, where he was forced to serve as a mere junior in the bank before working his way up to be manager.

Despite his bluff exterior, he had a soft heart. The Hull connections made me warm to him, so I'd visited him often in my early months in Helmsley. He showed the greatest sympathy for our girls trying to settle into their new schools, and always sent me back home with gifts of sweets. He was just as concerned about Rachel setting up home in an impossible vicarage. When I had no one else I could really talk to, I trusted him, and poured out my hopes and fears for ministry in Helmsley. He always listened attentively, asked the right questions, gave sage advice. I suspect he saw my congregation as a band of unruly Gurkhas with me as their hapless captain.

Seeing Hull-boy Neville standing there in the silence made my own memories of Hull come flooding back. I recalled my old school, Flinton Grove Primary, perched above the black murky waters of the Hull Drain – a glamorous spot. Hull, and most of the South Riding towards the North Sea, is reclaimed land at or below sea level. The land is kept dry by a system of water channels and floodgates, which are closed when the tide comes in and opened when the tide goes out. The Drain next to the school was strictly out of bounds. Even so, every so often a trawlerman's child with sea-lust in their genes would climb over the railings, wander too close and fall in. The ever-vigilant school caretaker would pull them out with a hook on a long pole, which he normally used for opening the high windows in the school canteen. He would then drag the child, spluttering black water, to the headmistress's study, where the severest caning would ensure that he was completely resuscitated.

On my first day at the school all the kids had ganged up around me, chanting, 'Your dad's a vicar, na, na, na, na, na!' I was quite a serious child and I replied, 'He's not a vicar, he's just been ordained a deacon and he's the Assistant Curate of Marfleet.' This grasp of complicated ecclesiastical titles completely flummoxed them, and I didn't have any trouble with them whatsoever after that – 'Don't mess with him, he'll start quoting complex ecclesiology at you!'

In the early 1960s the labour-intensive docks were booming, and brought full employment to east Hull. My memory might be faulty, but every day in assembly we sang the same hymn:

> *When lamps are lighted in the town,*
> *The boats sail out to sea;*
> *The fishers watch when night comes down,*
> *They work for you and me.*

> *The boats come in at early dawn*
> *When children wake in bed;*
> *Upon the beach the boats are drawn,*
> *And all the nets are spread.*

It was all a rather twee view of an industry which involved massive trawlers spending weeks far away, fishing in the icy waters around Iceland, and then returning to land their catch in the Hessle Road markets, giving Hull its distinct aroma. But fish was plentiful and very cheap; you could buy a whole halibut for ten shillings, around five or six pounds today. This was just as well, because my dad was only paid £33 per month, in arrears, once again depending on whether the churchwarden remembered to drop by with the cheque. We had a lot of callers to the vicarage, usually dockers' wives or sailors, often late into the night, asking for a tide-me-over loan of ten bob or even a pound, which they would bring back the next day. My dad always helped out but they never returned the cash, and so it was us who went hungry.

It's funny the memories that surface on Remembrance Sunday. As the two minutes' silence drew to a close, I forced myself to leave my Hull childhood behind and concentrate on the present. I looked at Ted Dzierzek, who just prior to 11 a.m. had waved his walking stick angrily at a car which had tried to drive through the crowd. I looked at Minnie. I looked at Father Bert standing beside me, his head frequently turning, his eyes darting, looking for enemy craft stealing on him from behind.

'At the going down of the sun, and in the morning, we will remember them,' I said slowly and loudly, drawing the churchyard Act of Remembrance to a close.

The bugler played The Last Post and we moved into church. Three elderly Dragoons staggered in, eyes moist, bearing their battle standard, carrying it to its new, proud place by the altar as we sang: 'Eternal Father strong to save, whose arm doth bind the restless wave ... O hear us when we cry to thee, for those in peril on the sea.' Lady Polly read exquisitely well: 'Blessed are the peacemakers, for they shall inherit the kingdom of heaven. Blessed are those who hunger and thirst to see righteousness prevail, for they shall be satisfied.' And so say all of us.

Chapter Twenty-nine

The remaining weeks in November gave me the only shot to plan for the year ahead, before December and the frantic countdown to Christmas overtook me. Just like a maths teacher's year is bound by exciting things like quadratic equations and trigonometry and calculus lurking on the horizon, each year a priest has to incorporate a statutory range of Bible readings within his Sunday services. The gory and sexually explicit bits of the Old Testament are mostly censored, which strikes me as a great shame. A bit of sex and violence would help spice up a dull Sunday service, and leaving them out can skew the Bible, making it seem puritanical and lifeless, when actually it is a bodice-ripping yarn.

I realize church is family entertainment, before the 9 p.m. watershed stuff, but even so, children have their own way of hearing things, with some amusing results. As a boy I had read the books of I and II Samuel, which describe the story of my namesake David, the shepherd boy who became king. At the time it seemed swashbuckling stuff, with David defeating Goliaths at every turn. But I realize now that David was a bit of a James Bond, with girls galore (as well as the odd boy) seduced along the way. There is one episode where David's adult son Absalom stages a coup, and drives his elderly father out of Jerusalem. Just to show he's in charge, he lines up all his father's many concubines on the palace roof, and has sex with them all, in full view of the admiring crowds in the city below. The thing is, when I read the story as a boy, I thought concubine was a sort of porcupine, and imagined that the palace roof, rather than being a flat roof-top garden, would be steeply pitched, like all the roofs I had ever known. My King James Version didn't mention sex, but euphemistically described Absalom as 'going into his father's concubines'. I was baffled by most of the Bible in those days, so assumed *into* was just another word for *after*. In the midst of the coup, David's porcupines had escaped and shinned up the roof, and Absalom had gamely chased after them, clinging on to the slippery tiles for dear life. I thought long and hard about how he would actually have got hold of the prickly porcupines. Peering for ages at the strangely garbed picture of a well-endowed Absalom in my illustrated Bible, I deduced that he had a pair of very large and thick oven gloves dangling from the centre of his belt, which would have helped no end with porcupine recovery. Be it porcupines or concubines, the outcome is the same. Absalom is so exhausted by his extramural activities, that David stages a comeback and fiercely routs his son.

Sadly, this episode wasn't included in the set Bible readings for the year ahead. I breezed through the possible readings, selecting story in preference to theory, poetry in preference to prose, short in preference to long, powerful point in preference to muddle. I then tried to allocate the readings to appropriate people, thespians for dramtic accounts, GPs for healing miracles etc. My best ever match-up was when a church cleaner had once read the opening chapter of Genesis and startled the congregation by reading 'God hoovered over the abyss' rather than 'God hovered over the abyss'. It all sounded rather exciting, imagining God like a stressed 1950s housewife, forever cleaning up.

At the end of the day, or rather the end of a lot of days, all I had to show was one side of A4 paper matching fifty-two readers with fifty-two readings on fifty-two Sundays. I don't like sitting at a desk for very long. Even darkening and damp November days beckoned, and I frequently stole out for a quick cycle up Beckdale or Baxton's Hill or through Duncombe Park, its tank roads carpeted with golden leaves. These were all familiar places to me now, and the strenuous climbs followed by a hurtling descent concentrated my mind, enabling me to return fresh and ready for another couple of hours' administration until I felt the call of the wild once more.

Visiting was a good distraction too, although from my first days in ministry in Middlesbrough, my Vicar had made it clear that visiting folk was the whole point of ministry, with everything else a distraction. Clearly he was a latter-day Vicar Gray, who used to kick his team of assistant curates out of the vicarage after lunch and not let them back in again until 10 p.m., with strict orders to get out and mingle with their flock. Fortunately, I enjoyed the mingling. I enjoy hearing people's stories, and many times their hard-won faith and the way they put it into practice shames mine.

As November moved rapidly towards December, one episode gave me pause for much pondering. It was a routine baptism visit in The Limes estate, the allegedly dodgy end of Helmsley. The baby was asleep upstairs in its cot and the baby's dad, as so often happens when the vicar calls, was out, so I sat in the kitchen and chatted to the baby's mum, a bright and breezy young woman, busy with her many tasks. As she dried up the dishes from their evening meal, I took down a few details to record in Helmsley Church's ancient baptism register. Standard stuff – the date of birth, the names to be given to the child, its surname and address, Mum and Dad's Christian names, the names of the godparents. 'I work under my maiden name, so you might as well put that in for the record,' the child's mum added. 'It's Stillborn.'

'Fine,' I replied. Stillborn sounded a bit like Wilbourne, so its deadly connections didn't really dawn on me. Until I asked the next question. 'We might as well put your profession down as well. What is it?'

'Oh, I'm a midwife,' she nonchalantly replied.

Usually I'm good at conversation, but I dried up, as all sorts of questions ran through my mind. What impact would it have on mothers in labour when they were told that Midwife Stillborn was going to take them through the stages? Why hadn't she used her married name, since it would have been far less distressing to have been faced by Midwife Davies? How was anyone ever given the surname Stillborn to start with? I knew that surnames arose in ancient times to describe someone's profession or personal characteristics, but titles like Barren or Eunuch or Stillborn tend, by definition, to be epithets which last just one generation.

'I use it deliberately, Vicar,' the baby's mum explained, reading my mind. 'I've just been through a birth, and all sorts of worries are swirling around about whether your child will survive, whether it will be OK, whether you'll survive. Some worries are rational, some irrational, but whatever, worries cause stress and raise the blood pressure, just at a time when you want to keep the blood pressure down. They all look a bit shocked when they hear my surname for the first time, but actually we've named the demon – it's out in the open and we talk about it. We talk about how only one in every two hundred births end in still-birth, which reassures them big-time, especially when I wire up the heart monitor and they can see from the screen that their baby is very much alive. "I may be called Stillborn," I tell them, "but I am for life not death. I'm staying with you throughout, and by the end we'll have a live, healthy baby."'

'Looking at what harms you to heal you,' I replied, moved by her sensitive rationale. I recalled another strange incident in the Scriptures which I'd puzzled over as a boy. When the Israelite slaves had escaped from Egypt and were making the long journey to the Promised Land, their camp was attacked by hundreds of snakes, and many Israelites were bitten and died. Moses' solution was to make a bronze snake and impale it on a stick. Whenever anyone was bitten, looking at the bronze effigy somehow enabled them to miraculously recover.

Apparently, quite a lot of deaths from snakebites are caused by panic and the accompanying adrenalin surge rather than by poison. I guess seeing the snake impaled calmed people, making them realise that the snakes were mortal and fallible rather than deadly and terrifying. Just as well that Moses had completed a Psychology and Chemistry degree at the University of Alexandria before the Exodus, and that the Israelites had included a portable smelting works in their baggage prior to their rush across the Red Sea, otherwise they might never have made it. But whatever, as I cycled home I realized that, had I stayed in tackling my rotas, I'd have missed my latter-day Moses, lurking in The Limes.

Chapter Thirty

'Lo, he comes with clouds descending,' trilled the evensong congregation. It sent a shiver down my spine, actually singing the famous Advent hymn, which was set to the tune 'Helmsley', in Helmsley Parish Church. There were a dozen or so in the congregation on this last day of November; mostly clergy widows or retired clergy in the twilight of life. They sat as far away from each other as they could possibly get, scattered throughout the chilly church, their breath condensing in billows of white steam as their shrill Yorkshire voices struggled to span the tune's three octaves. 'Thou shalt reign and thou alone,' ended the hymn, on a variety of discordant notes. I blessed the congregation from the ornate high altar, and then sped to the back of the church to wish them goodnight as they rushed back to their warm homes and hearths to defrost.

'See you in five minutes,' silver-haired Joan said, as she bustled away.

I took off my black woollen cassock, white linen surplice, black and white silk Cambridge degree hood and black silk scarf – robes obviously dating back to an age before colour was invented, I thought, as I put on my more cheery yellow cagoule and cycle clips. Rooting about in the tall wardrobe in the vestry, I then unearthed the baby Jesus amongst the other Christmas crib figures. The whole set of half-sized nativity figures including; Mary, Joseph, sundry angels, shepherds and wise men, daubed in the gaudiest of paints, must have been bought from the bargain basement of an ecclesiastical boutique way back in the 1960s. Baby Jesus, with a somewhat chipped golden halo around his head, stared at me with stark, dark pin-point pupils set in a pink and distinctly un-Semitic face, clearly none too pleased to be disturbed four weeks before his actual birth. Reverently, I wrapped him in a linen cloth, put him in the front basket of my bicycle, and pedalled off. My cycle lamp, precariously perched above Jesus's head, cut a bright line of white light through the chill mist swirling up from the River Rye.

I hadn't gone mad. My plan was to take Jesus to stay in a different house every night during December in a sort of Advent Calendar roadshow in the countdown to Christmas. I was acting out a physical reminder that Christ is invisibly present in every home and every life, sharing every joy and every sorrow.

I soon reached Joan and Alan's home in Castlegate; the terraced stone-built house I had visited in my early days in Helmsley. As always on this street of near-identical houses, I wondered briefly if I'd got the right door, because I didn't really want to drop off Jesus any old where. Although, thinking about it, leaving him on random doorsteps like an abandoned baby of yesteryear and seeing what happened did have its attractions. I supposed I could write a book of my adventures called *The Importance of Being Jesus* and give Lady Feversham a star line: 'A bicycle basket! You left Jesus in a bicycle basket?!'

Gus's incessant barking and crashing around behind the front door snapped me back to the present, confirming I had definitely got the right house. I gingerly carried in baby Jesus, stooping to avoid banging my head on the low beams as Joan desperately tried to hold the baying boxer back. Once again the most obnoxious sulphurous fumes engulfed us, forcing Joan to apologize as well as making it quite clear that it was Gus who was the culprit.

'Alan, you've been feeding this dog far too much raw steak again!'

Twice Gus leapt up at me, and the second time actually knocked Jesus out of my hands. Jesus somersaulted across the room like a rugby ball destined for a conversion. Fortunately, quick-witted Alan resurrected his skills as a winger, which had lain dormant for forty years, and caught Jesus in the nick of time. Otherwise the Lord of heaven and earth would have been smashed to smithereens on their stone fireplace, ending my parish-wide tour before it had even begun.

Joan had cleared the top of the bulky Mouseman sideboard and laid a starched white handkerchief in the middle, with a candle burning at each end. I placed baby Jesus in the centre and we stood in silence.

Joan stood in a sort of rapture, every ounce of her being radiating her thrill in hosting the baby Jesus for twenty-four hours. Alan was standing by her side, stooping slightly rather than his usual habit of standing to attention, tonight a quieter presence than his wife. Having a baby in their midst – albeit a pot one – stirred memories. After a few minutes of silence, Alan softly told me how, as a newly qualified GP working in Leeds, he had once visited a newborn baby; a miner's son.

'They were so very poor, Vicar,' Alan said, his eyes filling with tears. 'They had to resort to using a dirty coal sack to wrap up the little mite, with the family's tin bath doubling up as a cot.'

Having got into his stride with baby stories, he recalled his early days as a GP in Leicester, when he helped out with shifts at the local maternity hospital. There'd been a premature baby with the palest skin and the brightest red hair, whose life had hung in the balance at a time when premature care was so primitive. Alan fought through the night to try and save that baby's life, and then in the morning handed him over to the consultant. Alan's heavy caseload meant he didn't have any time to return to the hospital to check how things had gone. But seven years later, he had gone to a local garage to get his car serviced, and had noticed there a seven-year-old, with bright red hair and pale skin, helping in the garage workshop.

'Who does that lad belong to?' Alan had asked the red-haired mechanic.

'Oh, he's my son – Bobby,' the mechanic proudly explained. 'He was a prem baby, born two months before his time, and we thought we'd lost him. But this absolutely wonderful doctor stayed up through the entire night, willing him to survive.'

The garage mechanic went on to tell Alan how the next day his tiny son had rallied, positively thriving over the years to become the strapping lad before them now. 'We often talk about that doctor. With all that was going on that night, we never got his name, but we owe our son's life to him. And me and my wife's life, to be honest. I don't think we'd have pulled through if Bobby had died; our only child,' he had concluded, fondly ruffling his son's hair.

I looked down at the sideboard at baby Jesus, another little one whose infant life had been held in the balance. Alan's poignant tale triggered my own memories, back to the 1960s when my dad had been a priest in east Hull and chaplain to Hull Maternity Hospital; a Humberside version of *Call the Midwife*. One of his cases became family folklore. Late in November 1963, on a stormy night, dad was called out to baptize a premature baby; a farmer's daughter from South Holderness. She'd been born on the flagged farmhouse floor beside the wooden kitchen table, before mother and child were rushed to the maternity hospital in Hedon Road. But, two months premature and just two pounds in weight, the little baby was dying and wasn't expected to last the night, so my dad was summoned. He'd cycled out from our vicarage in the pouring rain to baptize her, lorry after lorry from the docks overtaking him, drenching him with spray. By the time he reached the hospital, he looked like he was the one who'd been baptized.

He'd christened the little girl, using a kidney dish as a font, with the matron and the ward sister looking on. My dad had held the tiny, tiny baby in one hand. 'I baptize you in the name of the Father and of the Son and of the Holy Spirit.' And as the water had run down her face, her tiny tongue came out and licked the drops.

'That child's not going to die – she's a survivor,' Matron had blurted out, taking the baptism liturgy in a somewhat novel direction. 'Sister, call Mr Stokes out,' she commanded.

'But, the consultant will be in bed by now, Matron. I don't want to disturb him without good reason,' the sister had stuttered.

'Call him out!' Matron had boomed, rising to her full height of four foot eleven inches – a measurement which curiously coincided with her girth. In full flight she would have put the fear of God into God. The consultant was duly awoken, examined the child and decided life was worth a shot. The little one was placed in a shoe box and cocooned in cotton wool, with the hospital janitor – quite the Heath Robinson – clamping a pygmy light bulb to the side of the box to keep her warm. As Alan had said, these were primitive times for premature care.

One year later, late in November 1964, there was a knock on our door. On the doorstep stood a ruddy-faced farmer and his ruddy-faced wife holding their ruddy-faced one-year-old daughter: a beautiful lass brought to life by baptism.

I said a simple prayer for Joan and Alan and their home, then left them to babysit Jesus until tomorrow, the cold night air scouring my face as I cycled back to Canons Garth. It suddenly struck me how this childless couple had never had a baby in the house until tonight, and yet they'd enabled hundreds of babies to flourish, truly their children. Not to mention a succession of sulphurous boxer dogs. It wasn't just the night air that sent a shiver down my spine, but the thought of Gus left alone with the baby Jesus for twenty-four hours. Would I come back tomorrow and find Christ in pieces?

Chapter Thirty-one

I carried the baby Jesus in my arms to the Quaker Meeting House. As we crossed the busy road by the market place, an angel decked in white clung to my left arm. Potiphar's servant, with eyelids painted gaudily as ancient Egyptians are wont to do, clung to my right arm. Their breath condensed in front of them like clouds of incense in the crisp night air. Strangely enough, it wasn't some weird nightmare, but was actually happening. I had picked Jesus up from his previous lodgings, mercifully unscathed by Gus, and he was to spend the next twenty-four hours in the company of Helmsley Primary School. They were staging *Joseph and the Amazing Technicolor Dreamcoat* at the Helmsley Arts Centre, formerly the Quaker Meeting House. Our daughter Hannah was cast as an angel, Clare as Potiphar's servant.

I deposited Jesus on a table in the foyer of the theatre – the lady taking tickets and selling programmes promised to keep a kindly eye on him. The angel and Potiphar's servant disappeared backstage and Rachel, Ruth and I took our seats on the front row of the packed auditorium, with Minnie and her Zimmer frame sitting immediately beside us. Despite the frosty December evening, it was incredibly hot and stuffy. The Meeting House was so very small. Judging by Joseph Foorde's experience in 1744, it was forever excluding people for what they had or hadn't done, so was unused to large crowds. It was also ablaze with light, which made you feel even hotter – perspiring under the spotlight in front of everyone's gaze. It was a very public place where it was impossible for a vicar to blend inconspicuously into the background. For her birthday treat in October, Rachel and I had brought Ruth to the Arts Centre to see *GoldenEye*, which had at last reached Helmsley just two years after its release. I realized that whenever James Bond started getting a bit intimate with his leading lady, every eye in the cinema was on me, gauging my reaction, rather than on the screen. It reminded me of the saintly Pope John XXIII who, in the early 1960s, was at a party in Rome where the young Sophia Loren made a spectacular entrance, wearing a very low-cut dress. Someone asked him what he thought of such lewdness. 'I feel very sorry for Miss Loren's new husband,' he replied with an enigmatic smile. He was pressed to explain himself. 'Well, with such a stunningly beautiful wife displaying her charms so liberally, when she entered the room all eyes should have been on her. Instead they were all on me!' As Pierce Brosnan slid the dress off his latest shapely conquest and everyone looked in my direction, I knew how the Pope must have felt.

Fortunately, all eyes were on the stage tonight, with its elaborate Egyptian backdrop featuring painted sphinxes and pyramids and a plethora of Mau – sacred Egyptian cats. 'Ee, those cats have reminded me of some funny goings-on, Vicar,' Minnie exclaimed, poking me in the ribs. I turned awkwardly towards her in my cramped seat as she continued, 'I was doing the ticketing at Ampleforth station during the Second World War with my friend Audrey,' she said. 'One day a very large woman alighted from the York train at eight thirty in t' morning – she'd come to be interviewed for cook's post at the Abbey. Only problem was, she'd brought all her cats with her – eighteen of them, each in a separate crate. For some reason she hadn't bought tickets for all these when she'd got on at York – I think there'd been a bombing raid the night before, so things were a bit chaotic. Although how they managed to miss eighteen cats . . .'

Minnie raized her eyebrows, exasperated that York's station's staff couldn't hold a candle to her team out here in the sticks. 'So we had to calculate all the excess fares, which she paid in halfpennies, threepences and sixpences; all the change she had on her. No one came down from t' college to meet her, so we had to ring them. Their coal man brought his coal truck and stuck the crates in the back of that, but he was back again with her and the cats for the next train – not surprisingly, she hadn't got the job!'

Minnie's reminiscences were brought to a halt as the show began. We had performed the songs at Archbishop Holgate's grammar school in York 'way back many centuries ago' in the late 1960s. But in the 1990s the show had had a massive revival, with Jason Donavan, Phillip Schofield and Donny Osmond playing the lead part, as well as Richard Attenborough starring as Jacob and Joan Collins as the alluring Mrs Potiphar. Sadly, Joan Collins hadn't been able to make it to Helmsley tonight. Instead, Sharon Dubbins – a precocious girl in Year Five – stood in as Potiphar's wife, mistress to our Clare, and, so the book of Genesis would have us believe, anyone else who was up for it. Though Helmsley Primary School hadn't quite come up with the star-studded cast of a world premiere, the kids really entered into the spirit of the show, catching the script's witty take on the Bible story and timing the wisecracks perfectly. They thoroughly enjoyed impersonating 1950s and 1960s pop stars, though they were the heart-throbs of their grandmothers' generation rather than theirs. The boy playing Pharaoh took a well-earned break from his extensive pyramid building programme and asset-stripping of neighbouring Mediterranean states to deliver a truly excellent Elvis, decked in one of the outrageous costumes the mega-star sported prior to his untimely demise, which would have kicked even Pharaoh's sartorial elegance into touch. He had Elvis to a tee – lips curling, hips gyrating, and a voice which would have made the women in the audience swoon, had they not already been feeling faint because of the intense heat.

He should have stolen the show, but he was upstaged by Laura, one of his female slaves. She was eight, in our Clare's class, and had Down's syndrome. Her parents had opted for mainstream education for her, with her inclusion benefitting the school as much as it benefitted her. In short, the little girl seemed unashamed of her own tenderness, and led her contemporaries to be tender too, when eight-year-olds are normally less confident about wearing their hearts on their sleeves. Clare came home from primary school with tales of Laura, almost on a daily basis. Once the head teacher was telling the children off during assembly for the usual things – excessive use of paper towels or sprinting in corridors – but was clearly losing it as his face reddened and his voice rose. Spontaneously, Laura leapt up from where she had been sitting cross-legged with her classmates in the middle of the hall. She ran towards the Head as fast as her little legs would carry her; sundry teachers and teaching assistants tried to block her path, but she dodged them like a rugby winger with a try firmly in her sights. She reached the ranting head and just flung her arms around his legs, wrapping herself around him, giving him the cuddle of his life. For seconds there was a shocked and heavy silence, but then the Head laughed and everyone laughed.

Tonight everyone laughed as Laura really gave her all to a Shawaddywaddy dance, continuing long after the other dancing slaves had exhausted themselves and in fact rising to a crescendo of jiving. Her timing was perfect: she put all she had into the dance, lock, stock and barrel. At first the audience's laughter was condescending, 'Oh, isn't this Down's syndrome girl a real card!' But as she continued, their focus shifted. Pharaoh and the rest of the cast became almost invisible as the audience only had eyes for Laura, realizing they were witnessing a unique and marvellous act of which no other child present was remotely capable.

It was a great show. Afterwards, the cast lined up in the foyer to await collection by their parents and receive accolades galore from the departing crowd. Laura was embarrassed, ran off and sought refuge behind the ticket seller's table. Then she noticed Jesus. 'A baby, oh a baby,' she cried, picking him up and cradling him in her arms. Embarrassed no longer, she walked up and down the foyer, rocking the baby Jesus, singing him a lullaby, making up the tune as she went along. 'Sleep, baby, sleep, little Laura's here!' The departing crowd were stunned by her performance for the second time that night. When everyone had eventually departed, I tried to prize Jesus off Laura, who resisted and got into a right strop, becoming near hysterical at the prospect of losing her baby.

The ever-patient and maternal deputy head managed to calm her down, making it clear that Laura would be Jesus's chief carer from the moment school began the next day. I caught Jesus's eye as the deputy took him away with her for the night. It had the same miffed look in it that Pharaoh had had an hour before, as both realized that they'd been upstaged big time: tonight the show was definitely Laura's and not theirs.

Chapter Thirty-two

Cycling through rain is never fun.

Waterproofs help, but your exposed face and hands take the brunt and become soiled with a fine suspension of mud and goodness-knows-what that has lain in wait on the tarmac until passing cars spray it up on you. Mercifully, it wasn't a long cycle ride this stormy night. I had picked Jesus up in the twilight, in a light drizzle before the rain had set in, and had taken him to evensong to join the faithful stalwarts who would brave a hurricane rather than miss church.

By the time evensong ended the storm was at its worst, rain beating against the stained-glass windows. 'Ee, Jesus is going to get a typical Yorkshire baptism tonight!' Alan joked, as we turned off the lights and locked up the dark church.

After cycling a short distance up the high street I perched my bike against a stone wall where the crumbling limestone flaked off onto the wet pavement, glistening under the street-lights. I tapped on the grimy window, the torrential rain pouring on my uncovered head. As I waited on the doorstep, I wrung out the drenched linen cloth in which baby Jesus was wrapped, beads of water running down his porcelain forehead. Eventually the door was opened, just the tiniest crack. 'Who is it?'

'It's David, Sister Lillian. I've come to bring the baby Jesus to stay.'

Lillian opened the door a few inches wider and I squeezed through for my first visit to Lillian's home. Despite being crippled by arthritis and finding every step painful, she was a faithful attender at the Wednesday morning Communion service in Helmsley Church. Though very devout, she cut an eccentric, gaunt figure, always decked in the same worn cardigan, blouse and skirt whose colours clashed with each other. I noticed that other members of the congregation gave her a wide berth, apart from Rachel, who enjoyed having a chat with her whilst I cleared away all the Communion vessels after everyone else had scarpered. I had offered to visit her in her home repeatedly, but she had always come up with some excuse. 'No that's not convenient, I'm afraid. I'm going to the hairdresser's.' I sensed she was fobbing me off, because looking at the state of her bedraggled hair, I doubted she had seen the inside of a hairdresser's for years.

Last Wednesday I had booked Jesus in for an overnight stay, and wouldn't take no for an answer. As I entered Sister Lillian's house, every step took me back half a century. Just a bare lightbulb hanging precariously down from a roughly plastered ceiling, the walls bare plaster with one sizzling electric socket powering an old wireless, a wonky standard lamp and a rusty electric fire, its bars not so much red-hot as cool pink.

The place was freezing. To say the least, Lillian's room was cluttered. In desperation I put Jesus down on the top of the radio, the only space available, and stuffed the damp linen cloth into my pocket like an embarrassed dad secreting his baby's saturated nappy. The wireless was permanently tuned to Radio Two, labelled as the Light Programme on the dial from a previous age. Cliff Richard was crooning 'Bachelor Boy'. Hard-of-hearing Lillian had set the volume so high that the walnut case of the wireless vibrated, jigging the baby Jesus about.

Lillian's dog, Rusty, which moulted more hair than all the hounds of the parish put together, seemed to jig to the music too, continually orbiting my legs like a sheepdog rounding up his solitary flock, condemning my suit trousers to be trimmed with dog-fur for the rest of the week.

Breathless after admitting me, Sister Lillian had to recover with her 'beer'; a sip of Dandelion and Burdock which I decanted into a drinking bottle for her. The viscous liquid bubbled over and made my fingers sticky – the afore-mentioned moist linen cloth came in handy as I used it like a flannel to freshen up my hands.

Lillian wore a worn woollen cardigan. I'm not sure what the original colour had been, but by now it was a sort of dirty beige with interesting psychedelic stains. Wisps of wool were unravelling around the neck, sleeves, pockets and waist. One pocket bulged. From it she extracted an individual apple pie, which she put on the sofa arm.

'If I lie down, I might squash it,' she explained. Then from the same pocket she produced some scraps of raw meat, which she pressed into my hands to feed the dog. 'Is there much sickness in the parish?' she asked, with genuine concern.

There will be, I thought, if we keep carrying on like this. Not wanting to infuse my multi-purpose linen cloth with sal-monella, I stole into the kitchen to wash my hands, only to be appalled by the primitive home comforts I found there, too.

There was one cold tap above a chipped Belfast sink and a battered cabinet or two piled high with chipped, unwashed crockery, food dried on it from goodness knows when. On one plate there was even a discoloured bit of Spam; there was me, thinking Spam had been eradicated in the 1960s, along with smallpox!

I rinsed my hands under the tap and shook them clean rather than dry them on the grubby towel that was draped over a chair. I returned to Lillian, who was suffering from an attack of burping, no doubt caused by the Dandelion and Burdock. Not wanting to embarrass her, I averted my eyes and scanned the room. On one damp wall, festooned with pictures in damaged frames, hung an MBE. 'Goodness, Lillian, is that yours?' I asked in surprise.

'Oh yes, Vicar, King George VI presented it to me, for nothing really. All I'd done was run a Church Army refreshment caravan for the troops in the last war.'

I realized the immensity of all she had done, as she told me how she had taken her caravan all over Britain and Europe, chasing the action. Lillian was there to cheer the troops during Operation Tiger, a practice for D-Day off Slapton Sands on the Devon coast.

'The local churches were fantastic,' she enthused. 'They produced buns galore for the troops, made with fresh eggs, not the miserable dried eggs we townies had to struggle with. Where they got the eggs from, I can't imagine. I guess they pinched them from local hen houses, and just hoped the farmer would think a fox or weasel had been abroad when he found the hen house bare!'

It all sounded immensely jolly. But then her face darkened and her eyes filled with tears. 'It all went terribly wrong,

Vicar.' I thought at first a farmer had twigged what was going on, and Lillian must have appeared before the local beak for receiving stolen eggs. But there was a chill in her voice which hinted at a greater tragedy.

'They were such lovely lads, Vicar, nowt but boys really – my age, barely out of their teens. Joking with me, teasing me, flirting with me, with a twinkle in their eyes. "What's a lovely lass like you doing, wasting herself being a Church Army sister?" they'd say, "Let me take you to the flicks and we'll have a whale of time in the two and threepences!" I can see them now, fooling around in the sea, kicking water at each other, leaping the waves then hanging around my caravan, begging a steaming cuppa to warm themselves up.

'Next day they were in the sea again, but no frolicking this time. They were face down in the water, we were dragging them out with hooks, body after body after body, drowned, if they hadn't been already dead when they hit the water.' She stopped and wept.

I lent her the linen cloth to dry her tears, and gently asked, 'What went wrong, Sister?'

'Oh, the Americans in the gunboats offshore had got confused, and thought the landing craft the lads were practising in were U-boats surfacing, and fired on them, blowing them to smithereens. Then the next day German E-boats got in on the action and blew the Americans to smithereens. Such a waste. Nobody's fault really – fortunes of war – but such lovely, lovely lads.'

On the radio Cliff crooned about being a bachelor boy until his dying day. But no longer did the baby Jesus seem to be doing a jig; in my imagination, as the wireless vibrated, he seemed to be sobbing, his whole body wracked with grief. The Devon coast was by no means the end of Lillian's brush with tragedy. It seems that she crossed the Channel after D-Day and dragged her Church Army caravan around all the major battles and skirmishes, finally ending up at Belsen, of all places.

'We were too late, Vicar; they were so thin, just skeletons wrapped in skin – dried-up, wrinkled skin. I felt so useless. I held a cup of sweet tea to the lips of one poor woman, but she couldn't manage even a sip. I broke a bun up to make it easier to eat, and tried to feed it to her crumb by crumb, but she was too far gone, they all were.' Lillian shook her head, consumed by sorrow and remorse. 'Our lads who liberated them didn't feel much like eating or drinking either,' she added. 'Such horror, such utter cruelty, such pointless waste of life. It made us all physically sick.'

I began to understand a little bit why, having witnessed such utter deprivation and desolation, possessions and home comforts now meant nothing to her. After the war she had ended up in this Dickensian hovel in Helmsley, driving her battered Morris Minor to the nearby market town of Thirsk, James Herriot's old haunt. She had worked there as a Church Army sister, assisting the vicar. Helmsley was too High Church for her, so she commuted along the A170 to work with a more middle-of-the road guy. Alan and Derek had told me how Lillian drove in the middle of the road, terrifying oncoming traffic as she sped down Sutton Bank's steep slope. She sounded like Les, the dodgy bus driver from my boyhood days. She had given up the car long since, but having observed her wandering along the pavement, veering from side to side,

I realized she clearly walked in the same way as she used to drive.

'Oh Lillian, I feel so sorry for all those victims of such a terrible war,' I commented, ineptly.

'My family were war victims,' Sister Lillian boldly declared, as if that qualified her to have a solidarity with all victims. 'Our house in Sunderland was shelled just before Christmas 1914, when German destroyers sneaked through the fog and strafed Scarborough, Bridlington, Whitby and Hartlepool – the whole set. Then the Luftwaffe bombed us again in 1940. My auntie was gassed, too,' she told me, a surprisingly proud ring to her tones.

'Gassed?' I exclaimed. 'I didn't think the UK mainland was subject to gas attacks.'

'Well, the bomb that hit our house in 1940 made a massive crater by our front door. My auntie, in a panic, ran out of the house and fell straight into it and knocked herself out. At the bottom of the hole was a ruptured gas pipe, which gassed her as she lay there. The ARPs found her and carried her on a stretcher to Sunderland Hospital. She came round after a day or two, though, and was none the worse for wear. Well, not too much worse,' she chuckled.

I laughed too. When the laughter eventually subsided, we talked shop a bit, as ministers do. 'What did you preach about today, Vicar?' she asked.

'John the Baptist,' I replied. 'An obvious Advent theme, Prepare Ye the Way of the Lord and all that.'

'Oo, John the Baptist, John the Baptist, now he was a very good man, a very good man,' she exclaimed, as if he was a personal acquaintance. 'Mind you,' she added after a moment's thought, 'not as good as Jesus!' as if the two lads had helped staff her Church Army canteen and been weighed up by her shrewd gaze. When I glanced at baby Jesus as I left, his eyes seemed to be twinkling.

Chapter Thirty-three

Though a very small town, Helmsley is a place of many shops – nearly a hundred – and in the run-up to Christmas there was an annual 'Best Shop Window' competition. As the new boy on the block, I was commandeered to co-judge the event with Lord Feversham. Like Dracula, we got to work just after dusk, with the bright lights of the shop windows being a wonderful antidote to the dank and damp December chill.

We scrutinized each shop window as intensely as an art dealer checking whether the painting before him is a Picasso or a fake. The analogy is appropriate, because there actually were two art shops; one with a gaudy landscape in the window priced at a modest £50,000.

'What a pity, I've forgotten my cheque book,' Lord Feversham joked. 'Have you got any spare change on you, Vicar?'

We duly cooed over pyramids of handmade chocolates; rolls of thick, lush fabric, hand-block printed; exquisite jewellery, diamonds sparkling in the Christmas lights; countrywear shops with windows crammed with plus-fours and tweeds and green wellingtons priced at £75. 'Don't worry, Vicar,' Lord Feversham reassured me, noting my look of concern. 'It's seventy-five pounds per pair, not for each boot!'

We paused before gunshop windows that sported an arsenal which could have swung things for the second Earl of Feversham and his beloved deerhound on the Western Front. We halted before furniture shops, one window crammed with second-hand Mouseman furniture, the English oak seasoned dark brown, the tables and sideboards with characteristic adzed tops. We really lingered before the toy shop of which dreams are made; becoming little boys again, eyes as big as saucers as we drooled over a model railway steaming its way around the shop. Apparently the layout was based on the former Ryedale Railway, complete with stations and signal boxes and tunnels and bridges and viaducts and rivers.

We smelt the coffee, the freshly made bread, the fish and chips, the pizzas, the Yorkshire curd tarts, the cheeses.

'I might give Lady Polly a buzz and tell her she'll just have to cancel dinner,' Lord Feversham blurted out. 'For once I've fed through my nose rather than paid through my nose!'

Lady Polly was obviously to the fore of his mind, in that he stared long and hard at a pretty yellow dress on a sylph-like model in Pennita's dress shop. 'That's just Polly's colour and style,' he concluded. 'Any more loose change you can lend me, Vicar?' The dress was priced at a modest £239.

For obvious reasons we didn't linger in front of the lingerie shop. 'Would somebody kindly explain to me what is the precise point of a thong?' Lord Feversham asked as we approached the safer climes of Helmsley Exotic Fruit.

'It's something to do with sandals,' I replied, thinking back to my encounter with Sister Lillian. 'John the Baptist didn't feel worthy to do up the thongs of Jesus's sandals.'

'Mm, don't play the innocent with me, Vicar,' Lord Feversham mocked. 'I think your predecessor would have come up with a more exciting definition!'

We moved on quickly to the bright lights of Claridge's,

where there was an eye-catching display of bespectacled Steiff teddy bears reading the latest bestsellers, burying their heads in *Harry Potter and the Philospher's Stone*, *Cold Mountain*, *The God of Small Things* and *Notes From a Small Island*.

'I do like Bill Bryson,' Lord Feversham declared to a bewildered rustic who was struggling past with a huge bag of animal feed over his shoulder. He had an unshaven face and a dirty old Mackintosh with binding twine serving as a belt, doing its best to keep out the December chill. 'Oh, you do, do you?' he rasped before shuffling on. I guess his literary tastes never strayed beyond the hallowed pages of *Farmers Weekly*.

We finally came to rest outside Nicholson's butchers and salivated over the lush hams, plump turkeys, sides of beef oozing blood, strings of sausages bursting out of their skin and huge, glossy pork pies. Ben the proprietor was hosting Jesus for the day, and had placed him in the centre of his packed shop window. Below him was the simple sign, JESUS, BORN IN A STABLE, BE THE GUEST AT OUR TABLE.

Throughout our very long walkabout, the shops' proud owners looked on expectantly; most had a look in their eye that spoke volumes, 'Just you dare not choose me!' I realized by the end of the night that I was set to make one friend and over fifty enemies. Why did I ever agree to do this?

Everyone gathered in the market square for the presentation to the winning window. Lord Feversham's gammy leg was causing him to wince as he scaled the steps of the memorial to his esteemed ancestor, William Duncombe, the second Baron Feversham. The memorial had been erected during Victorian times by the renowned architect Gilbert Scott, with a life-sized statue of William Duncombe walking tall beneath a stone canopy, Albert Memorial style. As the December rain drizzled down upon us, I rather envied his canopy.

Standing by the side of his stony ancestor, the present-day Lord Feversham announced the result, which was unanimous. Both Lord Feversham and I really, really enjoyed our food, so we awarded Nicholson's the first prize.

'A meat fest with a theological garnish,' Lord Feversham pronounced, 'feeding both body and soul. What could be better!'

The piqued crowd clearly didn't share his Lordship's enthusiasm, with caustic comments filling the cold night air. 'What an utter fix. I spent hours dressing my window. Ben just let his lad run amok for five minutes.'

'Any fool can scatter a few pork pies – I bet they bribed 'em with the promise of a free turkey!'

'You have to be a mason to get anywhere in this town.'

'You could have put Jesus in the middle of a dung heap, and that stupid new vicar would have awarded it first prize!'

There were mutterings and grumblings galore, detracting from the festive spirit of the season. Since the first prize was just a bottle of champagne, retailing in Tesco at £9.99, I couldn't see what all the fuss was about. They were losers in every sense of the word.

The next morning, I took Jesus into Ryedale School. I'd cycled there at breakneck pace, just to keep myself warm. There'd been a heavy frost overnight and white crystals clung to the hedgerows and tree boughs, with the blades of grass in the surrounding meadows bleached white and standing to attention. At assembly, I took my cue from Butcher Ben and talked about a baby's presence at sundry tables, changing perceptions. I tried to get the kids thinking about the difference

271

baby Jesus would make if he popped up at everyday tables in their homes, or at the Cabinet Table in 10 Downing Street, or at an operating table in a hospital, or whatever table wherever. Some wag had once quipped that having a baby in the home was the best example of minority rule he knew.

Whilst still on the stage, I handed over the ultimate baby to the Head, who bristled visibly. He assumed the air of CJ in *The Rise and Fall of Reginald Perrin*, giving me a I-didn't-get-to-where-I-am-today-by-cuddling-pot-Jesuses-in-front-of-three-hundred-and-fifty-teenagers look.

'Mr Howard, perhaps you would take – erm take – erm take *this* off me,' he croaked, holding the baby Jesus at arm's length, as if he'd just filled his nappy with a particularly pungent stool. 'Design and Technology are going to have custody of – of erm – of Jesus for the next twenty-four hours, so I expect you all to treat him with the respect he deserves.'

I'd chatted to Ben Howard, the D&T teacher (Woodwork and Metalwork in old money), on my previous visits to the school – a fantastic guy who was a practising Roman Catholic. Whilst, in my experience, Roman Catholics can be trusted with Jesus, I was less sure about the D&T classroom and how safe a fragile china doll would be with wood chips and shards of hot metal flying around all over the place.

Jesus wasn't the only special visitor that week. The school was hosting a series of activities on fire awareness and prevention, led by the local voluntary fire service. One of the governors, Nicky, was a voluntary firewoman, and had organized the programme. Affectionately known as Nee-Naw-Nicky, her arresting start to the week hadn't quite worked out as she had planned. Her big idea was to deck herself in her uniform, complete with respirator, oxygen cylinder and mask.

Wielding a fire-axe in her hand, she planned to force open the door to the year seven class awaiting her visit. As soon as she entered she would then dive down to the floor and wriggle along the length of the room like a snake, keeping herself as near to the floor as possible, as if the room were filled with acrid smoke.

Her preparation had been meticulous. Unfortunately, on the day her mask had fogged up, making it well nigh impossible for her to see clearly. Thoroughly disorientated, she crashed into the wrong classroom. Instead of entertaining excited year sevens who were fully prepared for her unconventional arrival, she burst into a year ten English class, who were doing a read-through of Shakespeare's *Julius Caesar*. I had studied the play in my third year at Archbishop Holgate's grammar school, and had learnt great chunks of it off by heart, which often came to my rescue in later life when I was lost for words. Though the play is action-packed with assassinations, set speeches and large-scale battles, I was virtually certain it did not include axe-wielding firewomen writhing across the stage. To say Nicky's entry was a shock would be an understatement. Two year ten girls were so traumatized they had to go to Miss Linley, the ever-sympathetic Head of Upper School, for counselling. At the other end of the scale, one year ten lad had found it so funny he wet himself laughing, gaining the nickname 'Pissy Pants', a name which most probably will haunt him for the rest of his days. Even the ever stoic Head had tears running down his cheeks as he told me the tale. Single-handedly, Nee-Naw-Nicky had created her own one-woman disaster zone.

Wanting to make a major impact can go so badly wrong. I was once demonstrating to an infant assembly how they used to write in times gone by. I had sharpened a feather to create my own quill pen, which I dipped into a bottle of registrar's indelible ink. For some reason, at that point the bottle assumed a life of its own, leapt out of my hands and liberally showered the reception class sitting agog on the front row. I can still see their spotted sweatshirts, spotted socks, their little spotted innocent faces, wide-eyed, thinking this was all part of my act. I can still see the face of the reception teacher, as her studied look of intense interest turned to one of abject horror. As tears of laughter ran down my own cheeks, I wasn't laughing at Nee-Naw-Nicky; I was laughing with her.

Early the next morning I cycled back to Ryedale School to retrieve Jesus. The class had been busy and had made him a beautiful crib, made out of pine wood and stained deep brown. One of the girls, whose parents ran a stud farm, had brought in some hay to give the crib a real manger feel. Despite my concerns, the D&T department had done him proud; I should have realized that a carpenter's workshop was hardly a novelty for Christ.

Chapter Thirty-four

The caravan was old-fashioned; wooden, horse-shoe shaped, with a tin chimney attached to the side emitting smoke with the pale blue hue of a wood fire. I'd spotted the caravan parked on the verge the day before, with a couple of lean-looking piebald horses tethered alongside. As I cycled towards it today I noticed a slender young woman, raven-haired, hanging out nappies on an improvized washing line between the caravan and hedge. 'Good morning,' I shouted.

'It is indeed, Father,' she responded in a broad Irish drawl. 'Top o' the morning to you!'

I pulled up and leant my bike against the hawthorn hedge, making the washing line wobble. I left Jesus in his newly acquired crib on guard in the basket and introduced myself to the woman. 'I'm David, the local parish priest. How are you doing?'

'Ach, I was doing OK until you came along and put me washing in danger. I don't want these nappies dropping off into the mud and have to wash the whole lot of 'em again!' She smiled, her blue eyes twinkling. 'But we're doing fine, thank you. I'm Julia, by the way. My man has got a bit o' work mending fences and dry-stone walls, my bairn's thriving in this fresh country air, and there's enough tinder for me to gather in yonder woods to fire the stove and keep us as warm as toast on these frosty nights.' She gave my cycle a hard stare. 'Can I ask you something?'

'Go ahead,' I replied.

'What on earth are you doing with the baby Jesus in your cycle basket?'

I laughed, explaining how I was taking him on tour during December, leaving him here and there.

'I think that's absolutely wonderful, Father,' she said, moving over to my bike to have a closer look. When she returned she had tears in her eyes. 'I'm sorry to get emotional, Father, but he's the spitting image of the baby Jesus we had in the Christmas crib in our church in Cork, when I was a lass. I used to be a server, and at the Christmas Day Mass, Father Pat, our parish priest, used to get me to carry him in and place him in the crib beneath the altar, as the congregation sang "Adeste Fideles". I don't think I've done anything else in my life where I felt so special, so honoured.'

She made me a cuppa, pouring steaming water from a copper kettle boiling on an ancient stove inside their dark, cluttered caravan. On the same stove was a bubbling stew pot, containing what looked like a couple of pheasants, definitely dead. There was a table, kitchen cabinet, sideboard, wardrobe and double bed which reminded me of Alan and Joan's Mouseman furniture, with the same bulky look, the same ancient feel.

'Ah, I see you're admiring our furniture. My man made those with bits of oak he scrounged when he used to work in the sawmill!'

She chatted on, sharing the memories of a happy childhood in Ireland, then falling in love with her man, their adventures on the road, various troubles they'd experienced with the locals; wherever they parked up people always 'persuaded' them to move on. As she chatted, her baby daughter mewled quietly in her bulky cot. 'Where are you taking him, then?' she finally asked, nodding her head in the direction of my cycle basket.

'Actually, we've got a spare day,' I admitted. 'Nothing until tomorrow morning when we're having a visit to Mr Hacket and Mr Angel, the local dentists.

'Go on, you're having me on,' she laughed. 'Mr Hacket, the dentist, of all things!'

'No really, I'm not,' I said, laughing with her. I'd spent so much of my life bracing myself in dentist's chairs that hitherto I'd never given much thought to their names. Thinking about the letters after their respective names, I realized Mr Hacket's qualifications majored in restoring teeth, Mr Angel's in anaesthetics.

'Well, fancy leaving our Lord at the dentists', poor little mite!' she continued. 'But I suppose, though, wherever there is pain, there is Christ.' I did a double take, because she'd just put into seven simple words the heart of my Gospel. The professors of Theology from my Cambridge days would have spent hours rabbiting on without ever coming up with anything near as good as that.

'Can I ask you a favour, Father?' she pleaded. 'If he's nowhere else to go today, can we keep him here? I promise you we'll look after him.'

It seemed like madness, leaving the most indispensible part of our Christmas crib with a here-today-gone-tomorrow traveller, but something about the encounter triggered memories from my boyhood in east Hull thirty-five years before. In September 1962, our Sunday tea had been interrupted by a loud knock on the front door. I followed my dad to the door and there on the step stood a tall gypsy, shabbily clothed, his face care-worn and peppered with black stubble. 'Please, sir,' he began. I vividly remember my dad going rigid, bracing himself for the usual request for money. But no such request was made. 'Please, sir, we'd like you to baptize our babies.' The gypsy pointed to the gate, where there was a crowd of similarly unkempt men and women, as well as an awful lot of children and crying babies: his tribe.

Although my dad was keen, since he was new to the job and a mere assistant, he had to ring up his boss for permission. The Vicar hummed and harred, since normally seven days' notice was required for any baptism. It was a strange rule; I'm not sure where it came from. 'Jesus presented himself at the River Jordan to be baptized by John,' the Gospel began. '"Lord of heaven and earth or no Lord of heaven and earth, you have to come back in a week's time," John the Baptist barked, "Seven days' notice is required!"'

My dad might have been new to the job, but he wasn't new to faith. 'We can't apply seven days' notice to them,' he objected. 'They'll probably have been moved on elsewhere by next week, and I'm not going to turn them away. Everybody else rejects them, looks down on them. I'm not having the church turn them away as well. I'm just not having it.'

Faced by the most rebellious of assistants, my dad's boss backed down and gave him permission to have his tea interrupted. 'Just make sure that they're gone by evensong, though,' he insisted.

My dad conscripted me to go along to church to help him. The gypsies' horseshoe-shaped caravans were parked up in a circle around the churchyard; tethered to them were thin horses and dogs, their ribcages visible. All the gypsies packed into church. I remember their faces; old before their time, yellow in the lamplight, their babies swaddled tightly in yards and yards of yellow cloth, with only their little red faces peeping out. I remember the stench of unwashed bodies. I also remember the reverent hush – you really could have heard the proverbial pin drop.

My dad explained the baptism service as he went along; simple stuff, like we need water for life, we need God for life. He took his time, baptizing nine babies in all, letting me pour the water from a large jug into the ancient, lead-lined stone font. We'd pre-warmed the water at home, so as I stood on my tiptoes and poured it into the font, clouds of steam billowed out.

When all was done, he gave his surprise congregation a tour of the church. They all paused beneath the stained-glass window at the east end. It was a nativity scene, depicting a young girl, her face yellow in the lamplight, holding her baby swaddled tightly in yard upon yard of yellow cloth, only his tiny face showing, its hue a similar red to the gypsy babies' faces. The tribe leader stared in silence at the scene, and then turned to my dad and said words I will remember until my dying day, 'We believe in Him, sir, we believe in Him.'

My dad turned to the gypsy and put his hand on his shoulder. 'He believes in you, sir, He believes in you.' After a long, poignant silence, they departed, harnessed their horses, climbed into their caravans and clattered down the lane. We cleared up the church so that it was spick and span for the Vicar's precious evensong, returned home and finished our tea.

Back on the Yorkshire roadside, I climbed down the caravan's steps and retrieved the baby Jesus, complete with crib and straw, from my cycle basket and took him inside to hand over to Julia. 'I can't think of anywhere better for him to stay for the next twenty-four hours,' I said, and meant every word.

Julia took him, holding him reverently, and placed him beside her baby's spacious cot. 'Thank you, Father, that means so much to me, so very much. Don't you worry, we'll take care of him.' I arranged to return early the next morning, and pedalled off home, with an empty basket but a full heart.

Chapter Thirty-five

For reasons which will become all too clear, I'd decided it was politic to leave my bike at home and to walk to an outlying farm, about a mile up in the moors. By the time I set out I could barely see the road in front of me. There were dark silhouettes all around, and high hedges and trees which loomed over me, creating a very spooky feel. Every minute or so a pheasant would make its shrill call, piercing the countryside quiet and making me jump out of my skin.

I was visiting a farmer who had tried to overtake a bike in his Land Rover when the cyclist had wobbled, fallen under his wheels and sadly died. It was not the farmer's fault, but Enid, my churchwarden, had told me he was deeply sorry and deeply despondent, and urged me to go and see him. Despite the lateness of the hour, I decided I could put my visit off no longer. I had no magic wand to make things better, I just wanted to be with them.

As I knocked on the farmhouse door, I felt the peeling paint flake off beneath my knuckles. In these situations you never quite know what to expect. His wife let me in, her manner quite cheery, considering. 'Oh, it's you, Vicar, come on in, it's so good of you to call. Josh's so down, so very down. We're cutting up a pig to take his mind off it!'

I walked into the kitchen and there was Josh, the farmer, a

large meat cleaver in his hand smashing it down and crunching bone and flesh, blood splattering everywhere.

'Ee, I'm right down, Vicar,' he said, as he laid into the pig's hind quarters. Apparently the pig had been killed further up the moor, and now they were sorting out the various joints and cuts of meat.

As he cut the thing up, his wife mopped up the blood with a tea-towel, which she then used to dry the blood-speckled cups on the draining board. 'You'll have a cuppa, Vicar?'

'OK then.' The kettle was already sizzling on the top of the coal-fired Yorkshire Range, oven and hob all contained in one polished, black-leadened mass of solid cast iron. I hadn't come across such ranges since my boyhood. My experience of them was that they only had two settings; out or nuclear. Ours had had the luxury of the thermometer dial on the black oven door. Something must have gone wrong with it because the needle used to spin around like the altimeter of an aircraft plummeting to the ground. I guess the actual temperature must have been close to 1000 degrees Fahrenheit; the roast beef was done to a turn in less than half an hour, the Yorkshire puddings rose instantly like skyscrapers and scraped the oven's ceiling. I have never eaten anything quite so delicious since.

Fortunately, the tea was a strong brew, and I turned a blind eye and a blind tongue to the little globules of pig's blood floating on the top. I listened and talked with them for a couple of hours, conversation accompanied by the rhythmic sound of the chopping, which was strangely soothing.

'Ee, I'm right down, Vicar,' Josh kept saying, his face strangely speckled with polka dots of pig's blood. 'You won't

'ave met Robbie yet, will you? He's the one who massacred t'
pig for us.'

I confirmed that indeed I had yet to encounter this porcine
butcher.

'He lives right up Bransdale, no electric, not much really.
Just a few cows, a few sheep. T' barns are still lit by oil light.
His farm 'ouse is bloody draughty, only heated by wood
stoves which belch thick blue smoke up into t' rafters.'

Josh's Yorkshire range suddenly belched out a puff of blue
smoke, as if in solidarity.

'I was up there one winter's night, it were that bad winter
in 1982 and we were having to dig Robbie's sheep out of deep
snow drifts – blizzards cut through you like steel knives, and
no sooner had you dug t' sheep out of a gully than the wind
blew more snow in and filled it again. Eventually, wit' 'elp of
some brilliant dogs, we got all t' sheep into t' barn, along with
'alf a dozen 'eifers who were already in t' stalls there. "Come
and have a bev with me to warm you sen up," Robbie said.
"We're not far off midnight, so when we've had a drink or
two we'll come back and I'll show you something."'

Warmed by a couple or six hot toddies prepared by Robbie's wife, the two men had returned to the barn. They had
stood outside in the billowing snow, peeping through a crack
in the door. Inside, bathed in yellow oil light, the sheep and
cattle stood in their stalls, munching hungrily at generous
amounts of hay stacked up in the mangers. 'So Robbie whis-
pers, "It's nearly midnight" checking his pocket watch. "You
just wait."' There was a moment's pause before Josh continued. 'I couldn't believe it, Vicar, at the midnight hour, one by
one every sheep and cow went down on their knees, every
single one.'

'So was it Christmas Eve, then?' I asked, mindful of some ancient folklore that stalled animals knelt at midnight every Christmas Eve, mirroring the action of the animals in the original stable who had knelt as Christ was born and laid in their manger. Thomas Hardy had written a famous poem about that particular folklore called 'The Oxen'.

'No, it wasn't, it were sixth January,' Josh replied, as if his point was obvious. Then seeing he wasn't carrying me with him, he explained further: 'Robbie's family 'ave lived up in Bransdale for generation after generation, and wouldn't 'ave anything to do with that new-fangled calendar that came in two hundred years or so since. So they reckon that t' real Christmas is ten days after time that rest of t' world keeps Christmas. And he proved it by showing me t' animals kneeling.'

Stirring at the back of my mind were my boyhood history lessons, with ten days being added to the date in September 1752 to bring us back into line with the seasons, as Britain adjusted from the Julian to the Gregorian calendar. Clearly this innovation had yet to reach some of the more remote parts of my moorland parish.

I came back from my visit with a massive joint of pork – certainly fresh. Rachel cooked it for our tea the next day: its gorgeous aroma filled Canons Garth and it proved absolutely delicious. If only we still had had the Yorkshire range of my boyhood, it would have been doubly so.

Chapter Thirty-six

Way back in 1966, Mr Nixon, head teacher of my primary school in Bubwith, had decided to stage a nativity play in church. Nothing unusual in that, except, using his considerable imagination, he trawled through the Scriptures to find parts for all ninety-six children on the school's roll. For instance, the prophet Isaiah, Mrs Isaiah, and their three children – Emmanuel, Shearjashub and Mahershalalhashbaz (catchy names) – all had a speaking part: 'Ee, come on, Mahershalalhashbaz, eat up your Passover lamb, it's good for you!' Eric Whitehead was cast as Isaiah and Judith Southgate as Mrs Isaiah, and for most of November and December these two children filled angst-ridden hours trying to get their tongues around the names of their offspring, let alone deliver the rest of their lines.

And those lines were considerable: Mr Nixon had written the play himself and it was the length of a Shakespearean epic, with copies for all produced by his Banda duplicator. Bandas, with their ghostly purple ink and sweet aroma – a cocktail of alcohol and wax – have long since been superseded by more sophisticated printing processes. But in 1960s Bubwith, they were nothing less than a revolution. Previously, any writing intended for general circulation around the village had been chiselled on the church wall or a gravestone. One such inscription on Aughton's squat church tower had always intrigued me: CHRISTOPHER ASKE, SON OF ROBERT, PRAY REMEMBER 1536. It seems that during the ill-fated Pilgrimage of Grace, the aforementioned Christopher had struck some deal with Henry VIII and sold out on his brother (another Robert, who bore the same Christian name as their father). Below the inscription was a crude carving of a newt – newts were known locally as askes. Below that was an even cruder carving, declaring a local lad's undying love for an extremely well-endowed local lass, circa 1928. I guess 1928 was the year rather than her chest measurement, although from the drawing's proportions it was a close-run thing.

I was cast as Joseph because I was tall. I was also a tongue-tied child who, like Jonathan Ross and Roy Jenkins, found it difficult to roll his rs. Mr Nixon clearly thought that throwing me in the deep end would bring me out of my shell. He couldn't decide on Mary, so we had two pretty dark-haired girls; one for one night's production, one for the next. Secretly I adored both, so Christmas came early for me that year.

Mr Nixon's mistake was to cast the naughtiest boy in the school as a shepherd. There he was, watching his flocks by night, high on the Banda fluid he had inhaled whilst doing a final frantic check of his lines. He was wearing his dad's over-sized dressing gown, with an M&S tea towel on his head – sartorial elegance sported by all Palestinian shepherds. He quickly became very bored with watching his cardboard cut-out sheep, even though Mr Nixon had festooned them with wisps of wool to give them an authentic feel. So he whiled away his time by making his over-long dressing gown cord into a lasso, trying to flip it over the head of the brass eagle on the lectern opposite him, which he no doubt imagined to be a bucking stallion.

At the third attempt he succeeded, effectively roping off the stage. This drove the angels, whose visit our very bored shepherd had long anticipated, to bypass him altogether and divert via the Christmas candle stand. One angel caught her cotton wool wings on a candle, and suddenly there really did appear a flaming angel before us all. The churchwarden, a quick-thinking farmer, suddenly found himself with a walk-on part, or rather a rush-on part, as the ninety-seventh cast member, bravely leaping up and putting out the angel with his bare, calloused hands and saving her life.

All this high – if unexpected – drama happened during the carol 'Away in a Manger'. Normally it has three verses, which I, with my low boredom threshold, find tedious enough. However, Margaret, the organist, who was to play such a major part in my first jaunt to Helmsley the following Easter, had just been to see the film *A Night to Remember* at the Odeon in York. She was very taken with the orchestra, who, spurred on by the *Titanic*'s second officer (played by the actor Kenneth More), bravely continued serenading the passengers as the *Titanic* sinks. So Margaret, having fortified herself with a couple of gins prior to the production, merrily played not three but twelve verses of 'Away in a Manger' whilst the flames were doused and order was returned.

My dad processed with great dignity in his robes from his stall towards the flaming angel, bowing to the altar as he went. By the time he got there the fire was definitely out. There's always the danger that fussy church protocol can make you miss an angel's flames . . .

'Do you remember that Christmas we had the great storm?'

Enid asked the motley company. I stopped musing about my boyhood and focused on the present. Along with me, Father Bert, Alan and the inevitable malodorous Gus, about a dozen heavily cardiganed souls had assembled in our chilly living room at Canons Garth, and we were supposed to be finalizing plans for Christmas services. They were a sub-committee, commissioned by the Church Council to address the first of my action points, that worship should be joyful, moving, inclusive and converting, fit for purpose for 1997 rather than 1897. But they kept straying from the subject in hand.

'Yes, that was the very same year we had the terrible break-in in the vestry on Christmas Eve. The thieves forced through the skylight and attempted to jemmy open the safe,' Anne, the plumber's wife added breathlessly, as if she were relaying the plot of *The Italian Job*. 'It had to be closed off for two weeks because they'd scattered glass and asparagus all over the place.'

'Glass and asparagus?' I asked, intrigued. I wondered if she was confusing things with a recent spate of vandalism at Helmsley's Walled Garden.

'Oh yes, the thieves tried to prise open the safe door and had scattered asparagus all over the place. Terribly bad for your lungs, asparagus is,' Anne informed me.

The penny dropped. 'Ah, asbestos,' I said.

'Yes, that's what I said, asparagus!' she reiterated, giving me a fierce look. Father Bert chuckled.

It was ever thus. In Christmas 1974, just before the Midnight Mass, a few parishioners from the rougher side of our west Hull parish dropped in; rather sad and lonely people who had no one else to spend Christmas Eve with. My mum proved a bit of a Mrs Malaprop, proudly telling everyone that

I was going to Jesus to be an exhibitionist – I had just gained an Exhibition (a sort of scholarship) to read Natural Sciences at Jesus College, Cambridge. After briefly consoling with my mother over the impending if surprising death of her son, the conversation then turned to religious art, which I guess seemed an appropriate topic for a vicarage on the eve of Jesus's birth. However, their limited knowledge of the subject became all too obvious as the conversation ground to a halt with some awkward silences. Then someone mentioned Leonardo da Vinci's *The Last Supper*, which nicely got things going again, as various west Hull stalwarts were hailed as the spitting image of one disciple or other. 'They're all fishermen, after all,' some old dear concluded, with no qualms whatsoever about shifting the action two millennia, from the dazzling shores of Galilee to the muddy banks of the Humber.

'I've got a painting exactly like da Vinci's *Last Supper*,' another old dear piped up, 'only it's with ballet dancers!'

My gathering tonight in Helmsley danced around one subject after another, distraction after distraction. I had been chairing meetings like this for nearly twenty years, and I always felt like a collie trying to round up a flock of spooked sheep, who persistently scatter themselves to the four corners of a very large moor. My flock tonight suddenly became maudlin and reminisced about the old vicar's final Christmas in Helmsley. He was bed-bound with only days to live, but had written a heartfelt message to be read out by his church-warden at all the Christmas services. It began, 'My friends, after thirty-seven years as your vicar, this is my last Christmas with you.' The churchwarden had kept breaking down as he read, hardly able to contain his grief. The regular members of the small congregation, devoted to their vicar, were similarly afflicted. But I guess most of those gathered were either locals who only tended to go to church at Christmas or visitors staying in the town's numerous hotels. Eager for a burst of carol singing and general bonhomie, they probably wondered what the heck was going on.

'It was the most miserable carol service I ever went to,' Father Bert concluded. 'More like a death-knell rather than 'Ding Dong Merrily on High'. *Bong . . . Bong . . .*' he slowly intoned.

'Well, let's make sure we put on a joyful show this Christmas,' I said, attempting to get a grip of proceedings.

'Church shouldn't be about joy or putting on a show,' an elderly spinster contradicted me. 'It should be about convicting people of their sins, especially when they don't come for the rest of the year.'

Gus growled, bared his teeth, and strained at his leash in the woman's direction. Her distinctly dour take made me think of a story about an archbishop of York in Victorian times. Around Christmas he liked to sneak out of Bishopthorpe Palace incognito, drive his carriage out into the country and blend inconspicuously into a village church congregation to join in with their carol service. Apparently on one such occasion he was standing at the back, belting out carol after carol, when a local stalwart standing next to him sharply elbowed him in the ribs, 'Will you shur up, mister, you're spoiling t' show!'

'Well, people *do* come at Christmas,' I retaliated. 'So let's make sure what we put on makes them want to stay rather than puts them off. I'm afraid I just don't do misery, so that's the end of it.'

Father Bert winked conspiratorially at me, as if to say, 'Go for it, bonnie lad.' Though my distinctly unbiddable flock kept mumbling and muttering, I finally got them to agree on my modest programme of additional Christmas services. These included a carol service for Ryedale School, which I'd already booked anyway, to be led by their outstanding brass band. Then I'd proposed a simple service for children on Christmas Eve around the crib, followed by a carol service for the town. I didn't have the nerve to be as adventurous as my former head teacher, but I thought we could maybe introduce a tableau or two during the familiar Christmas lessons, with a young couple with a newborn baby quietly walking down the aisle during one carol, shepherds and kings walking in during other carols, and Lord Feversham playing his customary, chilling role by reading Herod's lines.

'Why can't we just have a Mass or two like we did when the old vicar was here?' my splenetic spinster complained. 'He said a lovely Mass, did Father Senior. He wouldn't have held with all this entertainment and brass bands cluttering up the aisles.'

'We'll have all the traditional stuff as well,' I reassured her. 'I just want to put on one or two other things that will make people feel drawn in rather than cast out.'

There were a few more grumbles and mumbles, as well as one or two brave souls who came on side – I wasn't entirely sure whether this was because Gus was growling fiercely at them, or whether they were naturally sympathetic. Whatever, the meeting eventually came to an end. I shooed my cardiganed committee members out of the door having spent too long in the chilly porch, reuniting several shapeless woollen coats with their shapeless owners.

I snuggled down with Rachel in front of the TV, my eyelids

heavy. *Crimewatch* was just coming to a close, as Nick Ross ended with his catchphrase, 'Don't have nightmares, do sleep well!' I duly drifted off and dreamed of naughty shepherds dragging lassoed brass eagles, and flaming angels, slithering on asparagus and howling with pain, piercing their bare feet on shards of broken glass. An elderly spinster tried to shoo the angels away, shrieking, 'We don't want any of your joy here', until my old friend the dragon sprung from his wall and vaporized her with darts of fire. Dream on!

Chapter Thirty-seven

The night before the meeting, I'd taken the baby Jesus to stay in Duncombe Park, cycling up to the dark house in a fierce snow storm. I knocked on the small door by the side of the steps. The woman-what-does eventually let me in, and deposited me and Jesus in a chilly ante-room. 'I'll see if his Lordship is free,' she said, as she limped down the dark passageway.

Don't worry, I thought, I'm only bringing Jesus to stay. Eventually his Lordship slowly descended. Whether it was the chronic pain in his leg or something else which was troubling him, he didn't seem at all chuffed to receive his Lord. And I wasn't that keen to leave Jesus there either, because by this time I'd become quite attached to him!

'So what do you think you're going to achieve, foisting this voodoo doll on everyone?' was Lord Feversham's abrupt introduction. He was clearly in one of his argumentative moods.

'Well,' I stammered, as he gave me the mean-eyed look that Henry VIII must have given to Anne Boleyn and her babe, contemplating whether the Lord High Executioner had a vacant slot next Tuesday teatime. 'I've no particular agenda. I just want people to host him and run with their imaginations, exploring the difference Christ's physical presence would make to their lives.'

'I've been thinking about that. I don't think people have the foggiest idea what a heck of difference he'd really make,' Lord Feversham grumbled. 'Just think of all those weirdos he hung around with, David – terrorists and quislings, tarts and perverts with every sort of filthy disease imaginable. Helmsley's house prices would plummet if that lot set up shop here. And think of all those miracles; enough bread to feed five thousand, 180 gallons of vintage wine at that wedding that ran dry at Cana, nets bursting they were so full of fish. Thomas the baker, the fish stall on the Friday market and all our hotels and pubs would go out of business at a stroke. It would be sheer anarchy if you really let Christ loose. As your patron, let me give you a piece of fatherly advice: far better to keep Christ confined to church and inoculate your congregation with a weekly dose of Christianity rather than let him ravage their lives!' he laughed.

I laughed too. It must be lonely being a lord, and I realized that from time to time he liked a sparring partner and the cut and thrust of debate; he liked someone to take him on rather than bleat 'Yes, my Lord, no, my Lord'. He was surrounded by enough sycophants.

'I'm not here to inoculate people against Christ, I'm here to encourage them to see Him as their constant friend, carrying them through their ups and downs,' I responded. My legs were starting to feel a bit wobbly. It could have been the effect of the uphill bike ride, or, more likely, that I was feeling a little bit like my boyhood hero, Robert Aske. The prospect of hanging in chains for ten days on York's Micklegate Bar would make anyone's legs turn to jelly.

'With them through life's ups and downs?!' Lord Feversham exploded. 'With them through life's ups and downs!

Come off it, David. As I boy I was fascinated to read about the Mesozoic era, when the dinosaurs ravaged the earth for one hundred and sixty-five million years – absolute killing machines stalking the world. Where was your Christ, who "carries everyone through their ups and downs", then? What the heck was your God of love doing for one hundred and sixty-five million years of carnage?'

'Waiting, I guess,' I replied, with little more than a whisper. 'Waiting for love's moment.'

'Waiting one hundred and sixty-five million years? Even the NHS wouldn't buy that, and they're the experts when it comes to waiting times! If I sat on a platform waiting one hundred and sixty-five days, let alone one hundred and sixty-five million years, I think I'd come to the conclusion that trains don't run on that line any more!' He chuckled at the brilliance of his own analogy. He was clearly enjoying this.

'I suppose love takes its time,' I replied, chuckling with him. 'But it will win, one day it will win. That's what I believe and if I didn't I wouldn't be doing this job. The era of the dinosaurs was a one hundred and sixty-five million-year Good Friday. A crucifixion that lasted one hundred and sixty-five million years. Horrendous. But all crucifixion is horrendous; if you're the one being crucified, the excruciating pain probably feels like it lasts one hundred and sixty-five million years. But that's not the end. Easter Day is the end – or rather the beginning.'

'So where was Easter Day for those poor souls in the death camps? Where was Easter Day for my great-great uncle, blown to smithereens on the Western Front like a million others?'

'I don't know, I just don't know,' I replied. 'Any crucifixion

295

is horrible, total pain, total darkness. I just believe light will come. Or rather that we're the light – we bring the light to a particular darkness.'

'You put up a good argument, David, I'll grant you that. It takes me back to my days as a barrister, all the thrill of the case for the prosecution versus the case for the defence.'

'I didn't know you'd been a barrister,' I said, realizing his former career explained a lot about his dogged nature and love of argument. Thinking about it, nearly all of our encounters had had a courtroom feel about them. After all, our very first meeting in the Purey Cust Hospital had culminated in the judge pronouncing sentence: 'Thou shalt be taken down and go unto Helmsley!'

'Well, that's a very long time ago,' he explained. 'I trained as a barrister after leaving Eton, but I only practised for a short while before publishing beckoned,' he chuckled, with a glint in his eye. Though his novel was out of print by then, I had heard on the grapevine that it was really rather racy with some steamy scenes shortlisted for the Bad Sex in Fiction Award. 'Anyway, be that as it may. It's a long time since a vicar stood up to me and gave as good as he got. But I still can't see the point of taking this voodoo doll on tour. The place for Christ is in church, not being hawked around here and there on a push bike!'

'Oh Peter, do stop teasing,' Lady Polly chided, making her usual graceful entry. 'You know you just can't lock Jesus up, any more than they could nail him to a cross or seal him in a tomb. He's always going to break out and run amok in the world. That's part of the fun.' Lady Polly was a very faithful Roman Catholic, but with a sharp take on her faith which gave any parish priest a run for his money. 'I've dug out Patrick's christening robe and I thought we could put the Christchild in that. We don't want the Lord of Lords to go down with a chill in these draughty haunts!' she said as she turned to me, her eyes twinkling merrily.

Peter looked pensively at the christening robe as memories of Patrick's birth stirred. The episode had clearly been immensely healing following the tragic death of his first wife – just one of a series of immensely healing episodes brought about by Lady Polly.

'You're right, Polly, a birth changes things. Patrick's birth was wondrous; you were wondrous. It must have been nearly midnight by the time I got back to Helmsley. I drove up to Duncombe Park and I just stood outside, staring at the night sky – so clear, so beautiful. It's just all so wondrous, I thought.'

I left Lord Feversham cooing over the Christchild, realizing, if I hadn't realized it before, that a baby is the ace of trumps and wins all arguments.

After the meeting with the sub-committee, I cycled back to the big house at dusk, snow falling snow on snow, and knocked on the back door once again. The woman-what-does answered more quickly than the night before and handed me the baby Jesus, roughly stripping him of Patrick's christening robe as she did so.

'There you are. We've done our bit with the voodoo doll, you can take him away now.' And with that the door was shut, as if I was a tradesman being dismissed.

I put Jesus into my bicycle basket and cycled down from the high moor at breakneck pace, the snowflakes swarming like dark moths around my cycle lamp. The uneven joins and the massive potholes in the Park's concrete roads once again made it a boneshaker of a ride. Despite the billowing snow, I took off my cagoule and wrapped it around Jesus; I didn't want his fine porcelain getting any more chipped as he jarred against my wire basket.

I sped through the wrought-iron gates out of the park and was straight into the town, instantly passing from one world to another. I leant my bike against the crumbling stone wall of a tiny terraced house and knocked gently on the place's only door; had I knocked any harder I'm sure my fist would have burst through the plywood panel. Such a thin door, such thin windows, such thin walls; it had all the hallmarks of an estate worker's cottage, offering scant protection against the worst of weathers.

The door was opened by John, a tall and ascetic man, who greeted me with a shy smile.

'My goodness, I thought it was the abominable snowman! Come on in, David. Sit around the fire and we'll see if we can defrost you.'

I was duly ushered into their small, cluttered living room, and a steaming mug of tea was pressed into my hand by Erica, John's wife − the black-haired and ivory-skinned young woman whom I'd first encountered at the church lychgate on Gift Day, with her ever-chuckling toddler; she of the blue eyes and blonde ringlets.

Isobel, the toddler, was still up, and immediately took baby Jesus off me, unpeeling him from my cagoule.

'Careful, Issy, don't drop him,' Erica warned.

Issy's three black-haired brothers fussed around her, like a wicket keeper and first and second slip ready for a catch. I'd brought along the little crib Ryedale school had made, which we put on the hearth before settling Jesus down for the night.

Issy disappeared upstairs and returned with her comfort blanket, which she wrapped around the babe.

'That's a first,' John said. 'She fights tooth and nail if ever her brothers tease her and try to take that off her.'

The three boys clearly adored their younger sister; playing with her, teasing her, she teasing them and wrapping them around her little finger. John and Erica cleared away the remnants of their tea on the table – homemade blackberry crumble, homemade shepherds pie – while frequently glancing at each other with fond smiles. When you encounter such a happy family as this, they make your day, ministering to you rather than you to them. As Erica had told me on Gift Day, John was a former monk. But even if she'd not tipped me off, I could have guessed that, just from the way he moved: graceful, never intrusive. The contents of their bookshelves also gave away his monastic past, in that they were packed with the office books used by monks and nuns when they join together in worship seven times a day, mostly singing the Psalms. I picked out one at random, which was well-thumbed and dust free; either Erica was an avid cleaner, or this was a book still in use.

Having found the love of his life, John had moved on from being a lab technician, and worked around and about; mending fences, repairing dry-stone walls, felling trees. In his spare time he was a voluntary fireman, like the bloke we had bought the organ from way back in 1967. Surly organ sellers notwithstanding, Helmsley's voluntary firecrew were an amazing bunch. When the siren sounded and their personal bleepers went off, they had four minutes to get to the station. These men and women, rushing from all quarters of Helmsley, donning their firefighter's trousers as they run towards the station, were utter lifesavers who spared little thought for their own safety as they cut motorists out of crushed cars or braved falling timbers to clear a house gutted by fire. More often than not, John's bleeper went off during our Sunday worship, with him invariably missing a big chunk of the service. I didn't mind in the least, because John was actually just where the church should be – at the heart of rescue.

Like Ian Carmichael before him, John and his buddies spent a significant amount of time trying to put out moorland fires. On one occasion the firecrew had been called out to the depth of the moors, seemingly on a false alarm, because there wasn't a glowing ember to be seen. Just in case, they decided to hang around for a while. It being a hot day, the firecrew had started snoozing in their stuffy cab, only to wake and find themselves surrounded by a circle of flame. On another occasion they had been called out to a moorland fire, but by the time they arrived only the embers remained. They kicked these around a bit to fan the flames and give them something to put out, only to find the fire really took hold, and they had to urgently call out engines from nearby stations to quell the inferno.

Tonight the only fire was in the hearth, blazing beside Jesus, snuggled down in Issy's comfort blanket. We gathered around and I said a little prayer for this lovely family. When I'd finished the eldest boy said to me, 'God kisses you with prayer, you know.' Now where had he got that from? I looked across at John and the penny dropped.

Chapter Thirty-eight

At 1.10 a.m., after celebrating the Midnight Mass, I made my way home through Helmsley's churchyard and simply paused – the first chance I'd had to stop for quite a few weeks. There was a force-ten gale blowing and the clouds in the night sky were scudding by, affording me just occasional glimpses of the moon and stars, but enough to make me wonder. Thus far my first Christmas at Helmsley had been fine. Ryedale School had packed the church to bursting for its carol service, with the haunting sound of the brass band giving a welcome element of pathos to the jauntiest carol. My splenetic spinster had moaned about the pools of spit left on the stone floor by the tuba and trombone players, but they didn't bother me. Rather they spoke to me of flesh and blood giving their all, exerting themselves to the limit.

My splenetic spinster didn't like my carol service either, because I got Julia – the Irish girl I had met in the caravan – to reprise the role she'd had as a girl in County Cork. Accompanied by her man, she had carried the Christchild into church as the choir struck up 'Once in Royal David's City'. 'How dare you bring in someone who's not one of us?' the spinster complained. I wasn't entirely sure whether she was referring to Christ or Julia.

Sister Lillian had read, 'Because there was no room for him

in the inn'. She had struggled to come to the carol service; inch by painful inch along the pavement and up the church path, inch by painful inch from her pew to the front, inch by painful inch climbing the wobbling steps to the brass eagle lectern. 'No room' seemed rather apt for her – her life spent giving room to those who had no room, ending up with not much of a room herself.

Other lines seemed strangely apt for their readers too. 'She gave birth to a son, her first-born,' Joan the midwife read, who had saved the day with countless births but sadly had no first-born of her own. 'Now in the same district, there were shepherds out in the fields, keeping watch through the night over the flock,' read Frank, who had spent many a night wandering the North York Moors looking for lost sheep. Sailor Jack, a man who had travelled from east to west, surviving Hong Kong typhoons and losing brothers en route, tottered up to the lectern and read, 'Wise men from the east travelled to Jerusalem, asking where is the child . . .' Lord Feversham narrowed his eyes and in his most sinister Richard III voice read, 'When you have found him, report back to me, so that I may go myself and pay him [*dramatic pause before injecting a sense of dark irony into his tone*] homage.'

A couple of hours before the town carol service we'd had the children's crib service, which I had introduced despite much opposition along the lines of 'What are you wasting your time doing that for? No one will come.' In fact, everyone came – the turn-out was brilliant, as parents and children from Helmsley and beyond had heard about the service and just wanted to spend forty-five minutes reminding themselves of the heart of Christmas. We had gathered around the crib for a few carols and prayers. Then, with the help of Ruth's Sooty puppet, I read them a very simple child's version of the Christmas story that I used to read to the girls when they were little. We had a treasure hunt – running around the church looking for baby Jesus, who was hiding behind the altar. The little girl who found him was presented with a Terry's Chocolate Orange by a very naughty Sooty, who pulled her pigtails and made her giggle uncontrollably. It was all terribly chaotic, hyped-up children out of control and running all over the show, high-pitched squeals frequently interrupting me, but at the same time I had the sense it was all just wonderful. Still I shuddered to think what my dyed-in-the-wool critics would make of it all. I returned to Canons Garth for a brief respite, feeling utterly drained, having played the buffoon for three-quarters of an hour. But my brief interlude at Canons Garth was interrupted by an earnest knocking on the front door. On the doorstep stood a young mother with a tiny baby in her arms, along with a huge box of chocolates.

'I just had to bring you these, Vicar, I was so grateful for that crib service,' she said, breathlessly.

'Goodness, but I was utterly rubbish,' I admitted.

'Well, you see, ever since Katie here was born, I felt my life was utterly rubbish – one chaos after another. When I came to church tonight, I felt at the end of my tether. Katie had been crying all day. I'd changed nappy after nappy, and still she stank. She wouldn't feed, even though I was literally aching to feed her. Then I saw you, trying to keep order, trying to keep things together, but losing it time and time again. And I suddenly thought: It's not just me, chaos is OK. I can't say how grateful I am.'

Her little speech concluded, she thrust the box of chocolates into my hand and disappeared into the night with her crying babe. It's a funny old world; had our crib service been more formal, she'd have felt totally out of it.

The Midnight Mass had been as magical as ever, with those staying in the Black Swan and Feversham Arms hotels for the Helmsley Christmas Experience filling the church. I could tell that they weren't from these parts because they laughed loudly at the jokes in my sermon, whereas the locals were more restrained. There were some Americans there who not only laughed but positively guffawed, which cheered me immensely. We started with the church in darkness and gradually undimmed the lights as the service progressed. Only there was a storm raging outside and the night sky had been lit up with the occasional flash of lightning, followed by loud crashes of thunder which caused the lights to dim when they shouldn't have. Not exactly the *son et lumière* I had planned. I thought of Sally's sad funeral; the last time a storm had hijacked our worship.

After Mass had ended, I crept back into Canons Garth. Rachel was still up, putting the finishing touches to the girls' Christmas stockings. For Christmas we'd bought them a full-size table-tennis table, which we had secretly installed in one of the empty bedrooms. When I was busy in church, Rachel had sneaked along the landing with four table-tennis bats wrapped in red and green Christmas ribbons, but had bumped into a sleepy Clare, tottering to the loo. Fortunately, she hadn't twigged what was going on and had assumed her mother routinely waved bats around in the middle of the night, marshalling the odd stray jumbo jet, or even the odder stray Santa, for a touchdown on our landing.

Father Bert had not been present at the Midnight Mass. 'These days I go to bed religiously at ten p.m., no exception to the rule, even for the birth of my Lord and Saviour,' he had starkly informed me following the carol service. To his credit he was there for the early service on Christmas Day morning at 8 a.m., keeping bleary-eyed me on track. The girls had got up at 6 a.m., and we had heralded the day with a knockout table-tennis competition, which, true to form, had knocked me out.

Father Bert was also present for the all-singing and all-dancing – well, at least all-singing along with the censer dance – 9.30 a.m. service. In a sort of Christmas morning stupor, I had got a bit over-enthusiastic with all the wafting of the incense during the offertory hymn, and – unbeknown to me – one of the tablets of red-hot charcoal in the portable stove had flown out and landed in the very full collection plate perched on the altar. As the service proceeded, I noticed flames billowing as the charcoal ignited five-pound notes, ten-pound notes, and even threatened to incinerate the customary fifty-pound note donated by his Lordship. Fortunately, Derek, my right-hand man, noticed too, and lifted the flaming collection plate with his bare hands before swiftly retreating to the church kitchen. Seconds later, my hallowed words over the bread and wine were accompanied by the sound of a tap running, together with much sizzling and loud laughter. The rest of the unusually large congregation, who normally and very wisely gave this sort of thing a wide berth, no doubt thought it was all part of the ceremony. 'Silent night, silent night. All is calm, all his bright,' they sang. Well actually, not that calm, although with a flaming collection plate exceedingly bright.

Whilst I battled through the gales on my bicycle, rising out of Helmsley towards Rievaulx, Father Bert stayed behind to clear up. Rachel told me later that he'd then pottered round to Canons Garth. She'd made him a cup of coffee and, while she got on with preparing lunch, he simply sat in our living room, watching, with the greatest glee, our girls opening their presents. I envied him that – never once in thirteen years since our Ruth had been born had I been there for them on Christmas morning. But then again, when I recalled they were always with me whereas Father Bert had no one, I didn't feel so envious after all, and didn't begrudge him his moment of fatherhood. Of course, it wasn't strictly true that Father Bert had no one, because he had Margaret. And once he had finished his coffee and the girls had opened their last present, he made his excuses and drove off to Old Byland. Given the feast Margaret served on a normal day, I couldn't imagine the banquet she'd serve on Christmas Day, perhaps it was of the swan stuffed with goose stuffed with duck stuffed with chicken stuffed with pheasant stuffed with quail variety no doubt served during the medieval glory days of Helmsley Castle. 'Stuffed' would truly be the operative word.

The gale was really blowing hard on the top of the moors, with gusts of 60 mph causing me and my bike to swerve from one side of the road to the other. I was grateful when I turned and sharply descended down Rievaulx Bank, because its high wooded sides shielded me against the worst of the wind. I parked my bike and walked into the little church, my ears ever alert for the sound of falling roof-tiles. Considering the miniscule village population, the church was really full, but those gathered had the air of a slightly sleazy Edwardian house party at which I was definitely not welcome. When I walked through the church door, I was sure I heard the sound of several bottles clinking as they were hurriedly hidden away; my congregation more like teenagers secreting illicit alcohol.

The cornet player had brought along a few of his friends from the Bilsdale Silver Band, and were knocking out Christmas numbers like 'Jingle Bells', 'Winter Wonderland' and 'Lonely this Christmas'. They looked quite miffed when they had to change their repertoire to more conventional Christmas carols. The two Rievaulx nuns were there in their grey habits, but like me they looked out of place – Maria von Trapps thrust onto the set of *Dirty Dancing*. I eventually got the congregation to knuckle down to a staid service of Holy Communion, but their responses were muted, and I felt they couldn't wait for me to finish so they could return to their alternative carousing. Such a shame when Jesus muscles in and spoils the Christmas show.

Chapter Thirty-nine

Good King Wenceslas looked out,
On the feast of Stephen.
When the snow lay round about,
Deep and crisp and even.

It was 9 a.m. on Boxing Day. Father Bert was serenading me on my doorstep in his Geordie tenor voice. 'I'll be just fine, Father, it's only a heavy frost,' I reassured him. 'I've only got a couple of home visits anyway; I did the rest on Christmas Eve morning.'

'You are not going out on your bike in this, and that's final,' he argued. 'I'm going to drive you around in my jeep. It's difficult enough to keep that on the road with all the patches of black ice lurking; I shudder to think what it's like on two wheels.'

Realizing that resistance was futile, I rushed upstairs and disturbed Rachel's well-deserved Boxing Day slumbers as I kissed her goodbye, before shouting goodbye to my pre-occupied daughters. 'Eighteen–nineteen!' they shouted back, already on their umpteenth table tennis game of the morning.

I climbed into the passenger seat of Father Bert's little red jeep, my robes case on my knee, and we slowly moved off, slipping and sliding on the ice. 'You see what I mean, David,' Father Bert pointed out. 'Absolutely treacherous!'

The conditions were indeed bad, but instead of focusing on the road ahead, Father Bert was, as ever, continually looking in his rear-view mirror. 'What on earth are you looking for, Father?' I said exasperatedly. 'We're probably the only ones out and about for a fifty-mile radius. All the other sensible souls are still tucked up in bed.'

'Ah, but you never know, David. Just when you think all is quiet, then they come!'

It was only 400 yards to our first stop, a bungalow belonging to an old guy called Norman who had ulcerated legs so couldn't get out and about. Formerly, he had been the manager of a railway hotel in Leicester, and his father had been a fireman on a steam engine, which explains why his home was festooned with pictures and models galore of steam engines. His bookshelves were packed with virtually every issue of Bradshaw's published since *Bradshaw's Railway Time Tables and Assistant to Railway Travelling* topped the charts way back in 1839. In theory, I was bringing Norman his Christmas Holy Communion, yet in practice it was actually me who was visiting a shrine and drinking deeply. I said the hallowed words of the service on automatic pilot, spending my time just looking from picture to picture and model to model, and adoring it all. I caught Father Bert out of the corner of my eye, snuggled down in an ex-GWR First Class armchair, looking as if he was in a little boy's heaven.

It was on Boxing Day in 1963 when, as a boy of eight, I played with my first railway set. My parents had bought it second-hand from a parishioner in east Hull, and had spruced it up a bit by buying a couple of Pullman carriages. It was an old-fashioned Hornby engine, which picked up the current from a live but temperamental third rail powered by a transformer the size and weight of a brick. The transformer was to come in handy in my teenage years, when I performed the miracle of changing salt water into Domestos.

I didn't get a chance to play with my new toy on Christmas Day because my dad and his fellow priest hogged it the whole afternoon, the pair of them arching over it throughout, resentful when dinner interrupted their Fat Controller fantasy. On Boxing Day, I sneaked beneath their scrum and changed the points, causing the whole train to derail. 'What do you think you are doing, interfering?' my dad shouted, and then he and his fellow priest smiled as it finally dawned on them who the railway set was really meant for.

My and Bert's next port of call was another little bungalow about half a mile away. A slow coming we had of it, with the jeep never exceeding 10 mph. 'How did lunch go yesterday, Father?' I asked, trying to distract him from excessive rear-view mirror gazing.

'Oh, Margaret had to scale things down, because she'd also invited her new vicar and his wife and they're vegetarians. She only cooked a turkey, a side of beef and a gammon joint. She usually boils up a bit of pheasant and grouse casserole, which nicely sets off the roast meat, but she decided to leave that out yesterday, in deference to her other guests. I was very disappointed.'

'What did she give the vegetarians, then?' I asked.

'She'd bought them a nut roast from Morrisons. I sampled a bit when she was serving things up, and I've never come across anything so tasteless in all my life. Yuk!'

'How did you get on with the new vicar and his good lady?'

'Well, they're all right, as vegetarians go. He's quite an academic, like you, but without your common touch.' I guessed that was some sort of compliment. 'He told me he was going to run a Lent course in the parish on Hinduism. I have to admit I'd never thought of doing that. Just what our local moorland stalwarts need, a bit of Hinduism!' he said, turning towards me with a wry smile.

We eventually arrived at Barbara's little bungalow. I had visited her every fortnight since our arrival in Helmsley. Twenty years earlier, rheumatoid arthritis had hit her hard. Her husband had walked out on her with the parting words, 'I can't abide living with a cripple.' When I first visited her, I'd been delayed on my rounds and she was quite cross.

'I can't be doing with Communion now, it's nearly dinner time,' she'd snapped.

Apparently her condition made her irascible and she fell out with numerous home-helps. But I decided to be gracious, came back later in the day and made sure I was always on time on subsequent visits. That's the thing about visiting the housebound; you think they have all the time in the world for you, but often they have only the narrowest of timeslots, with me being fitted in around the hairdresser, home-help, nurse, doctor, Rington's Teamen and sundry other callers. And the other thing about the housebound is that though they never get out, all the local news comes to them – they sift through all the gossip from this home-help or that nurse, and become a reliable source for every minute detail. From her still centre, Barbara had brought me up to speed with quite a few local issues which I had missed despite my gadding about here, there and everywhere.

By the time I came onto the scene in 1997, she spent

virtually all her days and nights confined to a special electronic chair, which massaged her muscles as well as launching her into her Zimmer frame for occasional trips to the loo or kitchen. During one of my visits the chair malfunctioned and catapulted her across the room, like the ejector seat in James Bond's Aston Martin. Fortunately, she missed me and landed on, or rather in, her settee – breach presentation. It took me ten minutes to extract her and settle her considerable weight back into her special, if temperamental, chair.

Beneath Barbara's brittle exterior there was a golden person, whose story had been gradually disclosed to me over my regular visits. She'd begun life at Whitby, one of three sisters whose father was at sea in every sense of the phrase. The three girls were brought up single-handedly on a pittance by their hard-pressed mother. They'd moved to York during the Second World War, fearful that the Germans might repeat the naval bombardment that had hit Whitby so hard in 1914. By then a teenager, Barbara had worked in the little Thornton's Chocolate Cabin in York's market place, managing the meagre wartime stock. Quite a few airmen from the local air force bases used to patronize the shop as well as patronizing Barbara, who became a northern Forces' Sweetheart.

'They were such lovely lads, Vicar, and I wanted to make sure they felt thoroughly loved before they went off to their possible deaths,' Barbara had informed me on my third visit, fixing me with a steely gaze which made it clear she had no time for the pickier aspects of the Church's doctrine on sexual ethics.

'There's only one doctrine, as far as I'm concerned,' I'd replied. Despite Barbara's sharp intake of breath, I'd continued, 'God is love. Everything else either follows from that, or it's not worth bothering with.'

I guess she was a sort of serial monogamist, with boyfriend after boyfriend failing to return from their latest bombing mission. On her mantelpiece was a charred ripcord, clearly a highly treasured possession. One boyfriend had managed to bail out of his shot-up Lancaster, only for his parachute to catch fire, causing him to plummet to the ground like a stone, dead on impact.

Despite her disability, Barbara was a skilled and practised needlewoman, turning her gnarled hand to anything from knitting to tapestry. She was fond of all sorts of music; classical, folk and pop. Often her CD player got jammed, and I had to sort it out before ending our Communion with 'I'll Walk with God' from *The Student Prince*, or even a bit of Elvis if I put the wrong disk in.

Considering she took no exercise whatsoever, she had a healthy appetite and really enjoyed her food. Her favourites coincided with mine, and we often compared the products of Helmsley's numerous pie shops. Her all-time favourite meal was battered scampi from her home town of Whitby, which she savoured annually when the local ambulance service took severely handicapped people on a seaside visit. Every time I popped into a supermarket I tried to find some battered scampi for her, but to no avail; she turned her nose up at the breadcrumbed variety.

She had a Christmas hamper bursting with goodies for me and my family, awaiting my Boxing Day visit. All a bit ironic, considering Boxing Day was her birthday, yet here she was giving me a gift. She told me how she had also given a Christmas hamper to her neighbour, Ken, who was a deaf mute. 'Ee,

he were right chuffed with it, Vicar.' Throughout my visit,
Father Bert sat on a chair in the corner, staring at a huge picture which dominated the wall opposite him. It featured a
Lancaster bomber, flying west over the Wash, a trail of black
smoke billowing out of one of its starboard engines: Barbara's
boys finally coming home. In the picture's top right-hand
corner, the rear gunner was in sharp focus, scanning the skies.

'You like my picture then, Father?' Barbara asked Bert as
our service concluded.

'I do, luv, I do. You see I was a tail-end Charlie.'

At that, the heavily disabled Barbara sprang from her chair
with a sort of superhuman strength. Father Bert stood up and
caught her, as Barbara simultaneously flung her arms around
him. 'God bless you, Father, God bless you for risking your
life, protecting our boys and us!' she cried, as Father Bert
blushed a deep red. The war may have finished over fifty years
earlier, but once the Forces' Sweetheart, always the Forces'
Sweetheart.

'Best not tell Margaret about that little episode,' Father Bert
said, as he drove me carefully back home. 'I don't want her
getting jealous!'

Chapter Forty

'A cold coming they had of it', the chilly start to Bishop Lancel of Andrewes' Christmas Sermon 1622, the inspiration for T. S. Eliot's famous poem, 'The Journey of the Magi'; the ultimate lament for hard journeys, harder arrivals and even harder returns. A cold coming I had of it too on 28 December, Holy Innocents' Day. The weather forecast had been dire: sub-zero temperatures, heavy snowfall and winds gusting in from the Arctic all conspiring against my Christmastide service at my tiny church at East Moors, five miles up the bleak North York Moors.

Canons Garth was chilly enough; when I drew the curtains at 7 a.m. there was frost on the *inside* of the ancient leaded windows. It reminded me of my boyhood in freezing vicarages. The only way to keep warm was to don three or four woollen sweaters – every so often a trunk arrived from the Poor Clergy Relief Fund and my dad and I fought over the gaudily coloured spoils. We weren't bothered about the sweaters' colour or whether they were in fashion; it was the thickness that won the day.

Before setting off, I had managed a game of table tennis with each of the girls (I'd beaten a fiercely competitive Clare, 21–18, eventually defeated Hannah 37–35 after deuce upon deuce, and lost to Ruth 19–21), which had warmed me up no end. I then made the lonely journey by bicycle along deserted lanes, with a chalice and paten, wine and bread and all other necessary ingredients for a Communion packed into my rucksack.

Usually cycling up 1:3 hills dispels the cold, but not today; the chill bitterness of the journey was unrelenting. The streams which normally tumbled down the hillsides had become ice and had crept across the road like mini-glaciers. In the middle of the lane lay a rabbit, stiff as a board. Her body was perfect – she hadn't been hit by traffic or attacked by a bird of prey, so I guess the cold had simply got to her and her arteries had frozen solid. I stopped and moved her body to the verge, kicking the cold soil from a rock-like molehill to cover her with earth: it seemed a more tender funeral than being mashed by the wheels of a passing car.

Not that there were any passing cars. I dropped down Cow House Bank, rear and front brakes full on, putting my legs down throughout the descent so I had four points of contact with the slippery road: two feet and two wheels. The road was lined to left and right with pine trees, needles brittle with frost. My arboreal guard of honour gave a false sense of security, because immediately behind the trees on the right-hand side of the road was a thirty-foot sheer drop. As I grimly held on for dear life, I fleetingly wondered how long it would take to find me if I slid off the road and catapulted down the cliff. Would my no-show eventually spring the congregation into action? Would they gamely start a fingertip search of the chilly hillside, communicating with each other with whistles or a medley of Christmas carols, before finding their errant priest just before nightfall, snoozing in the bracken, showing the early stages of hypothermia?

Eva had told me of how, during the war, a pilot had bailed out of his ailing Spitfire and come safely to rest just by the ford beneath East Moors Church. He had crawled up to the red public telephone box and managed to reverse the charges to RAF Linton-on-Ouse, near York, to inform them of the sad loss of their Spitfire, but that he had had a safe landing and was ready to be picked up.

'Where are you?' the duty sergeant had asked.

'I'm next to a church which says "St Mary Magdalene, East Moors" on its notice board.'

'Where the hell's that?' the sergeant snapped.

Eventually they had established that it was a remote spot in the North York Moors, but it was a whole ten days before the RAF had any transport free to make the long journey to come and collect him. Eva's family had taken pity on him and let him kip on their sofa. He returned their kindness by lending a hand around the farm, relishing both the country fare and country air.

I relished the country air too, thick with the sharp scent of pine. By this time, I had reached the bottom of the hill, mercifully unscathed, so was able to stand down my imaginary search party. I skated over the ford – now rock-solid ice – and arrived at the little church so celebrated by John Betjeman's famous poem; still hiding in a thicket of rhododendron bushes, but covered in white frost rather than pink flowers. I set up for the service, wondering if anyone else was going to come.

The first person to arrive, at 9.55, was Yvonne, the woman who had kept me company with Lina at Sproxton Church way back in September. She explained that she had parked in the car park at the top of Cow House Bank and watched me descend. Since I survived the slippery slope, she had decided it was safe for her to follow in her four-by-four. 'I calculated your speed at twenty-one miles per hour,' she informed me, ever the mathematician. 'That's far too fast in conditions like this, especially when you repeatedly refuse to wear a cycle helmet,' she further informed me, ever the headmistress.

At 9.56 Father Bert shuffled in, accompanied by a spritely Margaret. 'We called round at Canons Garth to give you a lift, but you'd already set off. You must be mad cycling in weather like this,' he chided. 'The girls tried to get me to play a game of table tennis, but I told them Mass always comes first. Mind you, it was a close-run thing – I think Margaret rather fancied a quick rally!'

At 9.59 Lord and Lady Feversham walked in, hand in hand, with Eva following them half a pace behind like a lady-in-waiting. 'Thank you so much, my Lord, for coming to my rescue and giving me a lift in t' Land Rover. I was planning to follow t' old water race because Cow House Bank was proving a tad slippy. Then you showed up, like my knight in shining armour.'

'It was absolutely no trouble, Eva,' a rosy Lady Polly responded, squeezing her hand. 'It's always good to have another gal on board to even out the odds in Peter's male preserve!'

At 10 a.m. precisely, the old guy who I had encountered back in September clattered in, together with his long-suffering daughter and the same four springer spaniels straining at the leash, setting off the hounds in the nearby school house. 'Is that the new vicar? When's the service going to start?' he whined.

'I am the new vicar and the service starts right now,' I snapped. 'Our Father, who art in heaven . . .'

The congregation mumbled along with me, the spaniels whimpered, the hounds bayed. The Prayer Book I was using was a century old, with its set prayers including 'We beseech Thee to specially save and defend Victoria our Queen, that under her we may be godly and quietly governed.' In 1901, Vicar Gray had put a line through 'Victoria our Queen' and written 'Edward our King' in his meticulous copperplate down the narrow margin, and altered 'her' to 'him'. In 1910, Vicar Gray had put another line through 'Edward' in the now cramped margin and written 'George' above it. In 1936, Gray's successor had put a line through George and written 'stet' (Latin for 'let it stand') above the crossed-out Edward. Almost before the ink had dried, he had angrily crossed out 'stet' above the disgraced abdicator Edward, re-inserting it above George. Then in 1952, Canon Senior's predecessor had undertaken a major revision, squeezing 'Elizabeth our Queen' into the tightest of spaces, as well as putting a line through 'his' and letting the hyperactive 'stet' finally come to rest above the previously crossed-out 'her'. All in all, a very busy page.

We sang a hymn, unaccompanied, 'Unto Us a Boy is Born', including a terse verse which matched the day's chill:

> *Herod then with fear was filled:*
> *'A prince,' he said. 'In Jewry!'*
> *All the little boys he killed*
> *At Bethl'em in his fury.*

As we sang, our breath condensed before us, compensating for the lack of incense. When it came to sharing bread and wine with everyone, I lifted the tiny chalice to my mouth, causing me to flinch as the silver gave my lips a freezer burn. Even though I had filled the chalice almost to the brim during our improvized carol, no wine came out. In these polar temperatures, even the alcohol had turned to gel, so I cupped my hand around the frozen grail to thaw out the blood of Christ.

Given the freezing conditions, why didn't I cancel the service? One reason was that ever since that survivor from Ernest Shackleton's Antarctic Expedition had addressed our primary school, I had never been fazed by even the fiercest cold; in fact, I found it positively bracing. But the main reason for continuing was that on my first visit to Ryedale School I had promised a mother whose teenage son had tragically died on that day two years earlier that I would pray for him on his death-day. I could hardly let Marjorie down with a cheery report-back, 'So sorry, it was a bit icy, so we called it off.' So as we sang about all the babies massacred by a paranoid Herod, we also remembered all children taken before their time, including Mike.

On the cycle ride home I huffed and puffed up Cow House Bank. A deer scrambled down the hill and crossed the road in front of me, followed closely by her fawn. It seemed almost as if they nodded to me before they disappeared once again into the dark forest, making it a morning for lost children and found children.

Chapter Forty-one

Though the Arctic conditions continued, there was a long journey the next day which I could not put off. So, mid-morning, I gingerly drove up the steep and icy hill out of Helmsley towards Sproxton. Having safely made the ascent, I coasted past the church that a former Lord Feversham, in rare harmony with Victorian Vicar Gray, had moved from one hilltop to the next. Lina, the octogenarian I had met on my day of prayer, was out in the churchyard on her knees even in this sharp frost, dressed in just a skirt, blouse, a green and red Christmas cardigan and headscarf, hacking at the frozen soil with her trowel, planting bulbs in good time for spring. She was one of life's indestructibles. I smiled as I gave a wide berth to the church gates, and thought of her taking on the tank commander who had dislodged the stone ball; even a Sherman would be no match for Lina.

As my car skated down the steep hill into Ampleforth, I was certain that just touching the brake pedal would send me into a dangerous skid, so instead I tried to slow the car down by crunching into second gear, the engine whining fiercely in protest. After what seemed like 165 million years of having my heart in my mouth, at last I reached the safety of the flat, wide valley bottom. I circled the famous Roman Catholic abbey and school; the sprawling buildings and the trees which surrounded them covered in hoar frost, which glistened and twinkled in the weak December sunlight. There was a ghostly feel to the place, with Benedictine monks in black habits walking here and there in the spacious grounds, their hoods pulled up to keep their heads warm, their closely cropped hair affording them little protection. I laughed to myself as I remembered Minnie's tales of Ampleforth's version of the Hogwarts Express and the cook with eighteen cats of excess luggage.

The icy road wound around three sides of every frosty field, my car skidding on every bend. After what seemed an age, I made it to York. For about the last ten miles York's Minster had been enticing me. I had spotted it first as I drove through the quaint hill-top village of Brandsby, straining my eyes to focus on a tiny black rock shyly peeping on the horizon. But as York drew near, the Minster's three towers, magnificent nave and transepts came into sharp focus, their limestone gleaming in the midday sun.

Circling the Minster, I drove clockwise around York's ring road in the shadow of the ancient city wall, and headed down Bishopthorpe Road, driving past Terry's chocolate factory. Breathing in chocolate with every breath took me back thirty-five years to my first visit to Bishopthorpe, and my spat with the Vicar of Helmsley's son at the Archbishop's Boxing Day party for clergy children. But thirty-five years on, those parties were mercifully no more. This Christmastide I wasn't quite bound for the Archbishop's palace, but the crematorium next door, squatting precariously on the banks of the swollen River Ouse. In the early 1960s the Archbishop had proposed to sell off part of Bishopthorpe Palace's extensive grounds. York Council came up with a bid to build a crematorium and memorial gardens, which the Archbishop accepted, doubtless on the principle that the dead and bereaved would prove quieter neighbours than the noisy inhabitants of a Barrett housing estate.

Despite my precarious journey, I'd arrived half an hour early, so I wrapped my cloak around me, sat on a bench in the memorial gardens and munched the turkey sandwiches which Rachel had kindly packed up for me. As I overlooked Bishopthorpe Palace, whose ancient limestone and red brick goes back eight centuries, I pondered over past archbishops. Though there had been ninety-five in all, and all but one now dead, a handful had become familiar friends during my time there. There was Lancelot Blackburn, who prior to becoming archbishop in the eighteenth century had been chaplain to a pirate ship. I was never quite sure what the role entailed – 'Stop the raping and pillaging, lads, it's time for evensong!' His portrait in the chapel made him look like a real rake, more pirate than bishop.

As I savoured my turkey, I also recalled Richard Scrope, who backed the wrong horse – or rather the wrong king – in the Wars of the Roses, and found himself leading a protest against Henry IV for neglecting his subjects in the North East. Henry promised to accede to Scrope's demands provided he and his men lay down their arms, but then once they were disarmed promptly changed his mind and arrested them all for treason. Scrope was tried in the dining room of his own palace, condemned to death and was beheaded on York's Knavesmire. In these more enlightened times, archbishops are no longer beheaded on the Knavesmire, freeing it up to serve as York's racecourse.

Biting into an apple made me think of Adam being tempted by Eve, which in turn made me think of Edwin Sandys –

Archbishop of York in Elizabeth I's reign – who was stitched up a treat. He had a long-running dispute with a guy called Stapleton over ownership of land near Doncaster. In those days Doncaster wasn't the urban sprawl and industrial waste-land it is today, and lands around it were prized possessions. Stapleton invited Sandys to stay at his mansion to discuss the matter. But, no doubt taking his cue from the story of Poti-phar's wife in *Joseph and the Amazing Technicolor Dreamcoat*, Stapleton induced his own wife to visit the Archbishop in his bedchamber whilst their guest was sleeping. Stapleton then 'discovered' them both, and threatened to publish the scandal unless the Archbishop gave up his claim to the disputed land. But the po-faced Sandys refused to give in to blackmail, pro-tested his innocence and was finally exonerated by Royal Council.

Rachel had packed a miniature bottle of red wine for me, to ward off the day's chill. As I sipped it, I thought of William Fitzherbert, who'd been archbishop twice in the thirteenth century. In those tumultuous times he had been appointed once, then deposed by his enemies, then reinstated by the Pope. He was clearly a popular fellow, because on his return hundreds of clergy turned out from the diocese and formed a guard of honour along the bridge that crossed the River Ouse to welcome him home. Their considerable weight caused the wooden bridge to collapse, and they were hurled into the Ouse's icy waters. The fact that not a single cleric drowned or caught pneumonia was hailed as evidence of Fitzherbert's saintliness. Unfortunately, the archbishop's proven ability to ward off death did not apply to his own person, in that shortly after his return he was killed in York Minster by his arch-deacon, who added poison to the Communion wine when he was serving his lord and master at Mass. I know over the centuries church disputes have got pretty heated, often murderously so, but dispatching an archbishop by slipping a slug of deadly poison into the chalice strikes me as the meanest of crimes.

Having finished my lunch, I thought of Michael Ramsey, who'd crowned Elizabeth II. He'd been Bishop of Durham and then Archbishop of York in the 1950s, prior to going on to be Archbishop of Canterbury. He was a rotund, teddy bear of a man, with bushy eyebrows that seemed to have a life of their own. He was a deep thinker with an innate holiness about him, but he was also a tremendous fidget and wildly eccentric, and not given to the slick soundbites required by the 1960s media pack. Of all the many funny stories about him, my favourite was where he was lecturing to the Oxford Union, fidgeting throughout in his black Oxford gown. Halfway through his lecture he put his hand behind his back and extracted a wire coat hanger from the folds of his gown. He looked at the hanger with some surprise, before spouting out, 'Ah, that's much, much better!'

As I sauntered over to the chapel, the dour crematorium attendant was looking anxiously at the river – very anxiously.

'If it bursts its banks, the water will channel straight into the ovens, extinguishing the blowers as quickly as you and me snuff out a candle,' he said. 'The last time that happened in eighty-two there was a terrible mess, with ash and debris swirling down the Ouse. We managed to fish most of it out downstream at Cawood and never let on to the mourners.'

At the York Crematorium today there were no mourners, other than the funeral directors and me. The deceased man was elderly, with a dwindling circle of frail family and friends.

They had duly gathered in Helmsley Church for a service first thing that morning, but had wisely decided against following the coffin to York in such icy conditions.

That hoary preface to so many tedious funeral homilies, 'Although I never met the deceased', was not quite appropriate this time. As a priest and an adult I had certainly never encountered him. But I had as a child when, thirty years earlier, my parents came to Helmsley and bought their new church organ from him. In my early months in Helmsley I had chanced upon further details about the man I had last met as a child. In November, I was taking Communion to a chap called Alan, who was housebound after a severe stroke, and for some reason I mentioned our organ-buying exploits in 1967.

'That would be my brother, Ernest!' he had piped up.

Truly local lads, in their prime both Alan and Ernest had both served as voluntary firemen. Alan told me how in the long hot summers of the 1970s, the fires on the moors had had the same ferocity as bushfires in the Australian outback; they raged for weeks, with the blue plume visible from my old haunts in the Vale of York, thirty or so miles to the south. He and Ernest and the other firemen fought a desperate daily battle to try and contain things, coming home late every evening, reeking of smoke, their clothes and skin caked in greasy soot. Most people's memories of those seventies summers include languishing on a sun lounger on a singed lawn, sipping an ice-cold gin and tonic, accompanied by Abba singing 'Dancing Queen' on their Bush transistor radio. Alan and Ernest and their fellow firemen spent the whole summer in smog, beating back flaming heather.

Ernest had initially worked as a farmhand, followed by a

stint at Duncombe Park Sawmill. He then lent Alan a hand, building the council houses down Elmslac Road in the 1950s. Like the one which contained Ted Dzierzek and his large family, these excellent houses of solid stone were now worth a fortune on the second-home market. Having built about fifty houses with his brother, Ernest then found his dream job, driving the delivery lorry at Ampleforth Abbey, to-ing and fro-ing with loads from Ampleforth rail station, their contents no doubt checked out by the omnipresent Minnie. He had taught himself to play the piano and organ, and apparently was quite bereft when he sold his harmonium, his 'lucky charm', to us, and had to make do with an inferior electronic model. Like me he was an avid cyclist, lumbering up the hills on his old butcher's bike through all weathers, taking sundry housebound relatives food parcels when they were snowed in by the occasionally fierce North York Moors winter. In his declining months he had ended up paralysed in an old folks' home at Drax, south of Selby, in the shadow of the string of cooling towers that flank the River Ouse. His last wish was that his body be brought back to Helmsley for his funeral, prior to cremation.

All these details corrected the unfavourable impression he had made on us in 1967, humbling me that I could read somebody so wrongly. I decided there and then that my New Year's resolution for 1998 would be to strive to take the longer view of folk and not judge them by just one incident. I said the words of the cremation service on automatic pilot, my mind wandering as I thought on all the things he'd done over the three decades since we'd last met, which were the quintessence of the Helmsley I had encountered in my first few months as its vicar.

I thought too on all the things I'd done since we'd last met. The iconic places which had shaped me, like York, Scarborough, Hull, Cambridge, Middlesbrough, Pontefract, Bishopthorpe, the Yorkshire Dales and the North York Moors. The experiences which had shaped me, like studying Natural Sciences and Theology, working for Barclays, teaching Greek, being surprised by priesthood, being surprised by schools, playing Private Pike to two archbishops' Captain Mainwarings. Finding Rachel, the love of my life, in the distinctly unpromising soil of the most boring Lent course since the creation of the world, and then being blessed by three daughters, the epitome of life in all its fullness. Finally finding Helmsley. It was almost as if Ernest, the organ seller, had been keeping this paradise warm for me these last thirty years, but could now safely hand it over and rest in peace.

Returning to my old haunts at York should have felt like coming home. But in the midst of Ernest's cremation, I suddenly realized that rather than coming home, I was missing home; our new home in Helmsley. Slowly we were getting there with the house, making it more warm and cosy. Slowly I was getting there dragging the church into the twentieth century, spurred on by people with joy in their very souls whose life stories were golden, and who had overcome the greatest adversity, to which my grumbles were as nothing. To cap it all there was the countryside – mile upon mile of moorland unveiling a kaleidoscope of colours as the seasons changed, with deep valley upon deep valley surprising you with ruined abbeys slumbering by raging torrents. Such a feast – no wonder I couldn't wait to get back home.

'How much do you want for travel expenses?' the undertaker asked me as the service ended, bringing me and my musings back down to earth with a jolt.

'How about four to five pounds?' I replied, smiling. Understandably he didn't get the joke.